Wall Pilates BIBLE [7 BOOKS IN 1]

Transform Your Body in 28 Days with Power-Packed Exercises for Firm Abs, Arms & Glutes. Boost Your Flexibility with Beginner-Friendly Routines for Women and Seniors

Geneva Simonds

Contents

BOOK 1

Pilates Fundamentals

Introduction: A Brief History of Pilates

The Birth of Pilates

The origin story of Pilates is as intriguing as the exercise itself. This remarkable form of exercise, known to improve strength, flexibility, and overall well-being, is the brainchild of Joseph Hubertus Pilates, a man with an intense passion for physical fitness and an unyielding determination to overcome his physical shortcomings.

Joseph Pilates was born in Germany in 1883 to a Greek father and a German mother. As a frail child suffering from asthma, rickets, and rheumatic fever, he found himself driven by a strong desire to enhance his health and fortify his body. This led him on an extraordinary journey of exploring various forms of exercise, which ultimately resulted in the creation of the Pilates method.

His first foray into physical fitness began with studying body-building, yoga, martial arts, and even gymnastics. His father was a prize-winning gymnast, and his mother practiced naturopathy, both of which significantly influenced his early life and his approach to physical fitness. The blending of Western and Eastern influences became a key characteristic of his method.

During the First World War, Pilates was interned with other German nationals in Britain. It was during this time that his commitment to physical fitness turned into a mission to improve the health of others. He began devising exercise regimes for his fellow internees, focusing on strengthening the body and mind. His efforts proved successful, as many of his peers reportedly survived the 1918 influenza pandemic due to their good physical health.

His dedication to helping those around him didn't stop there. When he was transferred to another camp on the Isle of Man, he worked as a nurse-cum-trainer, helping bedridden patients regain their strength and mobility. It was here that he began experimenting with springs attached to hospital beds to create resistance. This invention was the precursor to the Pilates reformer machine we know today.

Post-war, Pilates returned to Germany, where he continued to refine his method, often working with dancers to help them improve their performance and recover from injuries. However, the political climate in Germany led him to emigrate to the United States in the mid-1920s.

Together with his wife, Clara, whom he met on the boat to America, Pilates established a fitness studio in New York City. Their studio was located in the same building as several dance studios, which helped Pilates become particularly popular among dancers. The Pilates method, with its focus on core strength, flexibility, balance, and mind-body connection, was a perfect match for the needs of dancers. It wasn't long before the method started gaining recognition and respect in the wider fitness community.

In the studio, Joseph and Clara worked hand in hand, developing a deeply personalized approach to training. They believed that everyone was unique, requiring individual attention to address their specific physical needs. This bespoke approach is still a foundational principle of Pilates, whether practiced on a mat, with a reformer, or against a wall.

Joseph Pilates continued teaching and refining his method until his death in 1967. His legacy, the Pilates method, has since travelled far and wide, crossing oceans and continents. Today, it's practiced by millions of people worldwide, helping them to improve their physical fitness, manage pain, recover from injuries, and enhance their mental well-being.

The birth of Pilates, as an exercise form, was a journey marked by personal struggle, relentless determination, and a quest for holistic health. Every twist, stretch, and deep breath we take in a Pilates class echoes the life's work of a man who believed in the power of physical fitness to transform lives. The evolution of Pilates, including the novel adaptation of wall Pilates, continues to resonate with his original vision – a testament to the strength and flexibility of not just our bodies, but also of his enduring method.

In recent years, the Pilates world has welcomed an innovative variant, Wall Pilates, which embodies the original principles of Joseph Pilates in a contemporary context. In essence, Wall Pilates takes the age-old method to the vertical plane, using the resistance of a wall to challenge and improve strength, flexibility, and balance. It's a creative evolution that ensures Pilates remains fresh, relevant, and effective in the 21st century.

Like Joseph Pilates, we are all on a journey, seeking health, strength, and balance in our lives. His story teaches us that through perseverance, innovation, and a deep understanding of the human body, we can overcome obstacles and reach our full potential. Whether we are practicing traditional Pilates or exploring its newer adaptations like Wall Pilates, we are part of the ongoing journey that began with Joseph Pilates more than a century ago.

So, as we press our hands against the wall, feeling the resistance and the strength within us, we don't just perform an exercise. We participate in a legacy, we share in a passion, and we continue a quest that started with a frail child's dream of health and strength. The birth of Pilates is not just a historical event, it's a living narrative that unfolds each time we unroll our mats or stand next to a wall, ready to transform our bodies and minds, one breath at a time.

Indeed, the story of Pilates is much more than the evolution of an exercise method. It is an enduring testament to the resilience of the human spirit, the power of innovation, and the profound connection between the body and mind. As we engage in Pilates, we not only contribute to our physical well-being but also become part of a rich and inspiring history.

From its humble beginnings in the determination of a frail child, to its worldwide popularity in the field of fitness, Pilates stands as a beacon of holistic health and well-being. Joseph Pilates' vision and legacy continue to inspire and guide us, reminding us of the power and potential within each of us. As we embark on our own Pilates journey, we take forward his quest for physical strength, mental clarity, and holistic health.

Thus, we can say that the birth of Pilates is a compelling tale of resilience, vision, and passion. It's about a man who defied his physical limitations to create a method that has stood the test of time and continues to improve the lives of millions. As we practice Pilates, in any of its forms, we carry forward Joseph Pilates' legacy, embracing his belief in the power of movement and the strength within each of us.

Pilates Evolution

The journey of Pilates, like the human body it seeks to strengthen and shape, is marked by resilience, transformation, and an unwavering commitment to progress. Its evolution is a testament to the timeless power of innovation and the enduring appeal of a methodology that prioritizes the interconnectedness of body and mind, strength and flexibility, exertion and relaxation.

Imagine, if you will, the story commencing in a small, unremarkable town in Germany. A sickly child named Joseph Pilates is continually battling asthma, rickets, and rheumatic fever. However, rather than accepting his physical condition, Joseph decides to challenge it. He studies anatomy books, observes animals in the wild, and immerses himself in physical disciplines like bodybuilding, yoga, boxing, and gymnastics. His body transforms, becoming the living embodiment of his belief that physical and mental health are intertwined.

Fast forward to World War I, when Joseph is interned in England. It's here that his approach to physical well-being begins to take form, as he helps fellow internees improve their health through resistance exercises. It's also here that he starts developing what would later become the Pilates equipment we know today, repurposing bed springs to create resistance devices for patients confined to their beds. Even in these challenging circumstances, Joseph's commitment to promoting physical health remained resolute.

After the war, Joseph returned to Germany, where his method, which he initially called 'Contrology', began attracting attention from dancers and performers. Yet, the political environment was changing, and he decided to emigrate to the United States in the 1920s. This move would prove to be pivotal in the evolution of Pilates.

Upon arriving in New York City, Joseph and his wife Clara opened a fitness studio, introducing his method to a new audience. The studio's proximity to several dance studios and Broadway theatres meant that many dancers became his clients. They found that his exercises helped them recover from injuries, enhance their performance, and prevent future injuries. Gradually, the Pilates method began to make its mark on the American fitness scene.

For the next few decades, Pilates grew steadily but remained somewhat of a niche practice, primarily among dancers and elite athletes. However, the late 20th century saw a fitness boom, and Pilates rode this wave, expanding its reach to the general public. People from all walks of life began to appreciate the benefits of the method, from improved posture to increased core strength, from enhanced flexibility to a sense of mental clarity. The Pilates method had arrived on the mainstream fitness stage.

As the new millennium dawned, Pilates continued to evolve and adapt, embracing new research in sports science and integrating modern understanding of body mechanics. The rise of the Internet and social media opened up new platforms for sharing and teaching Pilates, making it accessible to a global audience. The development of online classes and digital fitness platforms, in particular, has been transformative, allowing people to practice Pilates anytime, anywhere.

In recent years, a creative evolution of Pilates has taken shape in the form of Wall Pilates. This variant uses a wall for resistance, much like Joseph used bed springs in the internment camp. The wall provides support, yet challenges the body, enhancing strength, balance, and alignment. Wall Pilates has breathed new life into the method, proving that even after a century, Pilates continues to innovate and inspire.

Wall Pilates, much like its traditional counterpart, begins gently. As one delves deeper into the regimen, the role of the wall becomes more apparent. From helping extend the range of motion as a reformer machine would, to supporting challenging exercises like glute bridges, the wall becomes an integral part of the workout. The use of the wall in these exercises significantly intensifies the workout, leading to a more robust engagement of the targeted muscles.

As practitioners progress through their Wall Pilates journey, they often discover subtle asymmetries in their strength and flexibility. For instance, during single-leg glute bridges, it is not uncommon for one to notice a difference in strength between the two sides. The ability of Wall Pilates to spotlight these disparities is one of its strengths, as it enables practitioners to address these weaknesses head-on, thus helping to avoid potential injuries.

The wall serves another critical function in Wall Pilates – it aids in ensuring correct alignment. For those new to Pilates, maintaining the correct posture can be a challenge. The wall provides a reliable reference, enabling practitioners to better align their bodies during exercises, ensuring effective muscle engagement and reducing the risk of injury.

Even as the landscape of Pilates continues to evolve, the primary benefits remain consistent. Practitioners of Wall Pilates, like those of traditional Pilates, report increased flexibility, muscle strength, and muscle tone, alongside stress reduction and mental clarity. These benefits, coupled with the accessibility and cost-effectiveness of Wall Pilates, have contributed to its rapidly growing popularity.

The global pandemic of 2020 had a profound impact on the fitness industry, including Pilates. With studios shuttered and social distancing norms in place, practitioners turned to online classes and home-based workouts. This shift saw an increased demand for on-demand workout providers and a surge in the purchase of Pilates equipment for home use, including Reformers. As such, Wall Pilates, with its minimal equipment requirement, emerged as an attractive alternative.

With the easing of restrictions, we are witnessing a slow return to in-person classes. However, a significant number of practitioners continue to prefer home-based workouts, and Wall Pilates is poised to serve this growing demographic. The future of Pilates thus points to a hybrid practice – a combination of online and in-studio workouts. Wall Pilates, with its adaptability and accessibility, is well-positioned to be an essential part of this future.

CHAPTER 1

Understanding Pilates: Principles and Benefits

The Six Principles of Pilates

At the heart of the Pilates system, beyond the exercises and the equipment, lie six foundational principles. These principles, conceptualized by Joseph Pilates himself, define the essence of the practice and set it apart from other fitness modalities. They are concentration, control, centering, flow, precision, and breath. Each principle is unique, yet they are interwoven, collectively shaping the Pilates experience. As we embark on this exploration of the principles, let's remember that they are not isolated concepts, but parts of an integrated whole. Each one sheds light on the others, and together they illuminate the path to mastery in Wall Pilates.

Concentration, the first of these principles, is the cornerstone of the Pilates practice. It's the mental glue that holds everything together. Pilates is not just a physical workout; it's an exercise of the mind. Engaging fully with each movement requires a high degree of mental focus. When you concentrate, you become aware of your body, your muscles, and how they all connect. This awareness is crucial in Wall Pilates. The wall, as a prop, provides feedback that can guide your movements, but it's your focused mind that translates this feedback into actionable insights. You learn to listen to your body, understand its signals, and adjust your movements accordingly.

Control is the second principle. Pilates is not about doing as many repetitions as possible or moving as fast as you can. It's about moving with intention and control. Every movement in Pilates, whether you're performing a spine curl or a glute bridge against the wall, should be deliberate and controlled. This control stems from the mind-body connection you develop through concentration. It's about understanding your body's capabilities and boundaries and moving within them. In Wall Pilates, control becomes even more critical. The wall provides resistance, and controlling your movements against this resistance can intensify the workout and amplify its benefits.

The third principle, centering, refers to the concept of initiating all movements from the body's core or 'powerhouse,' which includes the abdomen, lower back, hips, and buttocks. The core is the body's center of gravity and the source of all movement. In Pilates, the focus on the core is relentless. Every exercise, every movement, is an opportunity to engage and strengthen the core. In Wall Pilates, exercises like the wall bridge demand intense core engagement. The wall, with its solid and unyielding presence, offers a unique challenge and an opportunity to work the core muscles deeply.

Flow, the fourth principle, brings grace and fluidity to the Pilates practice. Each movement should flow into the next, creating a seamless, rhythmic dance. Flow brings a sense of elegance to the exercises, but it's more than just aesthetics. It promotes efficiency, coordination, and muscular synergy. In Wall Pilates, the challenge is to maintain this flow against the static resistance of the wall. As you transition from one exercise to another, the wall serves as a constant, steady partner, providing a unique dynamic to your flowing movements.

Precision, the fifth principle, underscores the importance of doing each exercise with meticulous attention to detail. In Pilates, how you perform each exercise matters more than the number of repetitions. Precision ensures that each movement targets the intended muscles and delivers the maximum benefit. In Wall Pilates, precision takes on added importance. The wall provides constant feedback, and any deviation from the correct form or alignment becomes immediately apparent. This feedback loop helps refine your precision, making your practice more effective.

The final principle, breath, breathes life into the Pilates practice. Joseph Pilates once said, "Breathing is the first act of life, and the last." This statement encapsulates the significance he placed on proper breathing. In Pilates, the breath guides the movements, establishing their rhythm and pace. It's a powerful tool that not only oxygenates the muscles but also focuses the mind and helps connect with the body's inner rhythm. In Wall Pilates, as you press against the wall, stretch your limbs, or hold a challenging pose, the breath serves as a grounding force. It steadies you, sustains you, and reminds you of the inherent rhythm in each movement.

Now, as we delve deeper into Wall Pilates, these six principles become our compass. They guide us, shaping our movements, refining our practice, and deepening our understanding of this profound system. Concentration sharpens our mental focus, enhancing the mind-body connection. Control ensures that every movement is intentional and purposeful. Centering shifts our attention to the core, the powerhouse of the body. Flow brings elegance and efficiency to our movements. Precision demands meticulous attention to detail, while the breath infuses life into our practice, grounding us and guiding our movements.

In Wall Pilates, these principles acquire new dimensions. The wall, with its constant, unyielding presence, challenges us in unique ways. It tests our concentration, demands control, engages the core, disrupts our flow, refines our precision, and underscores the importance of the breath. But as we embrace these challenges, we also discover new strengths. We learn to listen to our body, understand its language, and respond with grace, power, and precision.

Let's remember that these principles are not just techniques or strategies. They are the essence of Pilates, the life force that flows through every movement, every breath, every moment of our practice. They embody Joseph Pilates' vision of physical fitness, a vision that transcends the physical and touches the mental and spiritual dimensions of our being.

By embracing these principles, we embrace Pilates in its purest form. We connect with its roots, honor its tradition, and participate in its evolution. And as we press against the wall, stretch our limbs, and breathe into our movements, we also press against our limits, stretch our possibilities, and breathe life into our potential. Through this journey, we don't just transform our bodies; we transform our perception of what our bodies can do, of what we can do. And in this transformation lies the true power of Pilates.

The Benefits of Pilates

In the world of fitness, Pilates stands as a beacon of holistic wellness. A practice that transcends mere physical exertion, it harnesses the power of the mind, the spirit, and the body in harmony. Its benefits are plentiful, and they extend far beyond the visible. Pilates, especially Wall Pilates, is a symphony of controlled movements and conscious breathing, each note resonating with a promise of better health, improved fitness, and a deeper connection with the self.

The first and perhaps most tangible benefit of Pilates is its capacity to develop a strong and stable core. Your core is the powerhouse of your body. It's the foundation upon which every movement is built. Pilates exercises are designed to strengthen this foundation, promoting better balance, improved posture, and enhanced physical performance. Wall Pilates, in particular, is excellent for core development. The wall provides resistance, which intensifies the engagement of your core muscles. As you press against the wall, your abdominals, obliques, and lower back muscles work in unison to maintain stability and control. Over time, this leads to a stronger, more resilient core.

Pilates is also renowned for its ability to improve flexibility. It encourages a fluid, full range of motion, gently stretching and lengthening the muscles. Regular practice can increase your flexibility, reduce muscle tension, and enhance your overall mobility. This increased flexibility can be particularly beneficial for runners, cyclists, and individuals involved in sports that put a lot of strain on the lower body. Wall Pilates, with its unique combination of dynamic and static stretches, can further enhance this benefit, leading to greater flexibility and improved performance.

Beyond physical fitness, Pilates offers an oasis of mental wellness. It cultivates mindfulness, encouraging you to stay present and focused during your workout. This focus on the present moment can help alleviate stress, reduce anxiety, and promote mental clarity. Many practitioners find their Pilates practice to be a form of moving meditation, a time to step away from the chaos of everyday life and find tranquility in movement and breath. Wall Pilates amplifies this effect. The physical contact with the wall provides a grounding sensation, helping you to stay present and focused during your practice.

Pilates is not just about strength and flexibility; it's also about control and precision. It emphasizes quality over quantity, teaching you to execute each movement with maximum efficiency and minimum strain. This aspect of Pilates can help improve your overall body awareness, leading to better posture, more graceful movements, and a reduced risk of injury. In Wall Pilates, the wall acts as a tangible reminder of alignment. It guides your movements, encouraging precision and control.

Pilates can also play a vital role in injury rehabilitation. Its low-impact exercises are gentle on the joints, making it an excellent choice for individuals recovering from injuries. The controlled, mindful nature of Pilates ensures that the body is not subjected to sudden, jerky movements, reducing the risk of re-injury. Wall Pilates can be particularly helpful in this regard. The wall provides support, allowing you to adjust the intensity of the exercises to your comfort level. It also aids balance, which can be beneficial for individuals recovering from injuries that affect their stability.

Lastly, Pilates fosters a deep sense of body positivity. It's a practice that celebrates what your body can do, rather than what it looks like. It teaches you to respect your body, to listen to its signals, and to respond with kindness and care. This can lead to improved body image, increased self-esteem, and a more positive attitude towards fitness andhealth. Wall Pilates furthers this sense of self-connection and body positivity. As you press against the wall, you engage in a tangible dialogue with your body, a dialogue that can deepen your understanding of your strength, your resilience, and your capacity for growth.

In summary, Pilates is more than just a workout; it's a pathway to improved physical and mental health, a journey of self-discovery, and a practice of self-love. Its benefits extend far beyond the mat or, in the case of Wall Pilates, the wall. It improves your strength, flexibility, and body awareness. It fosters mindfulness, reduces stress, and promotes mental clarity. It aids in injury rehabilitation and encourages a positive body image. But perhaps the most significant benefit of Pilates is its capacity to inspire change. It's a practice that, once embraced, can transform your body, your mind, and your approach to health and fitness. It's a testament to the power of mindful movement and the remarkable potential of the human body.

As you incorporate Pilates into your life, remember that it's a journey, not a destination. Each session is an opportunity to explore your capabilities, challenge your limits, and celebrate your progress. It's a chance to connect with your body, to listen to its wisdom, and to respond with care and respect. It's a moment to breathe, to move, and to find joy in the sheer act of being alive.

In the hustle and bustle of modern life, we often forget to pause and appreciate our bodies for the incredible machines that they are. Pilates, and especially Wall Pilates, offers us this much-needed pause. It invites us to step onto the mat or against the wall, to leave the world behind, and to embark on a journey of self-discovery. It's a journey that is as challenging as it is rewarding, as transformative as it is enlightening.

So, whether you're looking to improve your fitness, rehabilitate an injury, reduce stress, or simply connect with your body in a deeper, more meaningful way, consider Pilates. It's more than just a workout; it's a celebration of the human body, a testament to its strength, its resilience, and its remarkable capacity for change. And Wall Pilates, with its unique blend of strength, flexibility, and mindfulness, is an exciting variation of this practice, one that promises to challenge, inspire, and transform you in ways you never imagined.

Pilates, in essence, is a celebration of life. It's a practice that honors the body, nurtures the mind, and uplifts the spirit. And with each session, with each breath, with each movement, it brings us closer to the best version of ourselves. It's a journey of a thousand steps, a symphony of a thousand notes, and each step, each note, is a testament to our potential, our resilience, and our capacity for growth. Whether on the mat or against the wall, in the studio or at home, Pilates invites us to step into our power, to embrace our potential, and to celebrate the incredible journey that is life.

CHAPTER 2

Pilates Equipment: From Mat to Reformer

Understanding Pilates Equipment

Pilates is a symphony of movement and breath that invites us into a world of grace and strength. At the heart of this symphony, lies the instrument - the Pilates equipment. Let's take a walk through this world and get acquainted with these instruments that make the music of Pilates so enchanting.

Imagine walking into a Pilates studio for the first time. You're likely to feel like an explorer stepping into a treasure trove. The Pilates equipment, with its intriguing shapes and sizes, beckons you to embark on a journey of discovery. Amongst these treasures, the Reformer holds a special place. The Reformer is the backbone of Pilates equipment. A marvel of design, it offers a plethora of exercises that challenge and engage every muscle in your body. The carriage, springs, straps, and bars harmonize to create a versatile platform for strength, flexibility, and balance. The beauty of the Reformer is in its adaptability; it caters to the needs of beginners and seasoned practitioners alike. The gentle resistance of the springs is like a whisper, guiding your movements and correcting your alignment.

Now, let's talk about another gem - the Cadillac, also known as the Trapeze Table. Picture a four-poster bed adorned with springs, bars, and straps. The Cadillac is a playground for the imagination. It's here that you can truly explore the depth and breadth of Pilates. The Cadillac's trapeze and bars invite you to swing, stretch, and strengthen. It's a sanctuary for those recovering from injuries, as well as a canvas for Pilates artists seeking to paint new patterns of movement.

Next, the Wunda Chair awaits. Think of it as a magic box that holds secrets to core strength and balance. It may look like a simple bench, but the Wunda Chair is an alchemist. The pedals and springs work in unison, pushing you to summon your inner strength. This seemingly unassuming piece of equipment is a testament to the adage that great things come in small packages. It's here that you'll find the essence of Pilates distilled into a series of movements that challenge even the most seasoned practitioners.

As we continue our journey through the Pilates studio, the Barrel catches our eye. With its elegant curves, the Barrel is reminiscent of a gentle wave. It's here that the spine finds its rhythm. The Barrel is like a friend that supports you as you arch and curl your way to a flexible, strong spine. The beauty of the Barrel lies in its simplicity. It's a piece of equipment that offers support and challenge in equal measure. It's a reminder that sometimes, going back to basics is the most advanced thing you can do.

Now, let's not forget the smaller, yet equally significant pieces of equipment that grace a Pilates studio. The Magic Circle, for instance, is a ring of resistance that challenges your inner and outer strength. It's like a wise sage, constantly reminding you of the strength that resides within. The resistance bands, or Therabands, are like the wind beneath your wings. They support you, guide you, and sometimes challenge you to fly higher.

Finally, let's talk about the wall, an often-overlooked piece of equipment. In Wall Pilates, the wall becomes your partner. It offers resistance, support, and feedback. It's a mirror reflecting your movements, a guide showing you the path, and a friend walking beside you. The beauty of the wall lies in its accessibility; it's a piece of equipment that's available to everyone, everywhere.

As we step out of the Pilates studio, let's take a moment to reflect on the journey we've just undertaken. The Pilates equipment is more than just machines; they are instruments that create the music of movement. The Reformer, Cadillac, Wunda Chair, Barrel, Magic Circle, and even the humble wall – they all play their part in this symphony. They are the tools that help us sculpt our bodies into works of art and our movements into poetry.

The Pilates equipment whispers to us in the language of resistance and support. It invites us to explore the depth of our strength and the breadth of our flexibility. It challenges us to find balance in asymmetry and grace in strength. Each piece of equipment is an invitation to embark on a journey - a journey that's as much about discovering our physical capabilities as it is about connecting with our inner selves.

As you move through your Pilates practice, allow the equipment to become an extension of your body. Feel the springs and straps as an integral part of your movements. Let the resistance guide you, let the support elevate you. Embrace the versatility and adaptability of the Reformer as you sculpt your muscles and carve your movements with precision. Allow the Cadillac to expand your imagination and the Wunda Chair to challenge your core. Let the curves of the Barrel be the waves that your spine rides on towards flexibility. Allow the Magic Circle to be the sage that reveals the wisdom of inner strength. And let the wall be your anchor, grounding you and reflecting your movements.

Pilates is more than a form of exercise; it's a dance of the soul. A dance that's choreographed by the breath and performed on the stage of Pilates equipment. It's a dance that speaks of the stories etched in our muscles and the dreams woven in our movements. The Pilates equipment is our partner in this dance. It's the wind that carries us, the earth that grounds us, and the fire that transforms us.

Through the Pilates equipment, we not only sculpt our bodies but also craft the very essence of our being. In this sacred space, each spring, strap, and bar is a thread in the tapestry of our soul. In the embrace of the Pilates equipment, let's find our strength, let's spread our wings, and let's dance to the song of the soul.

Mat vs. Reformer Pilates

As an expert trainer in Wall Pilates, I understand that stepping into the world of Pilates can sometimes feel like stepping into a new language. Mat and Reformer Pilates are two such terms that seem to have a veil of mystery shrouding them. As we journey together through this chapter, let's lift that veil and dive into the beautiful and fascinating world of Mat and Reformer Pilates.

The first touch of Pilates for many is often the welcoming, unpretentious mat. Mat Pilates is the classic variant where you use, quite simply, just a mat. It's like a warm, friendly handshake inviting you into the world of Pilates. It's where many of us start our Pilates journey, drawn by its simplicity and accessibility. With Mat Pilates, there's a sense of comfort knowing you can practice anywhere – in the quiet corner of your home, in a sunny park, or even while traveling. It's Pilates unbound, Pilates for the free spirit.

Mat Pilates, at its heart, is about mastering control and precision with just your body weight and gravity. It's the art of listening to your body and understanding its needs and abilities. The mat is not merely a surface; it's a silent guide, quietly encouraging you to connect with your body. Every twist, stretch, and curl on the mat is a dialogue between your body and your soul. It's a gentle whisper that echoes the strength of your core, the flexibility of your spine, and the fluidity of your movements.

Meanwhile, in the Pilates studio, the Reformer waits. The Reformer – a Pilates machine with a sliding carriage rigged with springs, bars, and straps – can seem daunting at first. It is the ocean where the mat is a lake. It's Pilates in three dimensions. When you engage with the Reformer, it's like a dance between the body and the machine. The Reformer guides you, challenges you, and supports you. It's not just a piece of equipment; it's a partner in your journey towards strength and flexibility.

The Reformer offers a dynamic, full-bodied experience that truly elevates your Pilates practice. The adjustable springs provide tailored resistance, challenging your body across different planes of movement and encouraging the development of long, lean muscles. The straps and the bar, meanwhile, provide support and stability, enabling a wider range of exercises. With the Reformer, every push, pull, and stretch is amplified. Your body is not just moving; it's conversing with the tension and resistance.

Mat and Reformer Pilates might seem like two different languages, but they're two dialects of the same beautiful language of movement. They are two paths to the same destination – a stronger, more flexible, more connected you. While the mat offers simplicity and freedom, the Reformer offers depth and dynamism. One is not better than the other; they're just different. And it's this beautiful difference that makes Pilates such a versatile and enriching practice.

Imagine your Pilates journey as a river. Mat Pilates is like the river at its source – pure, simple, and serene. As you practice and progress, this river of movement gains strength and momentum. And then you encounter the Reformer – a waterfall on your Pilates journey. It's powerful, dynamic, and transformative. As you engage with the Reformer, you plunge into this waterfall, emerging stronger and more flexible.

In this journey of Pilates, it's not about Mat versus Reformer. It's about understanding and embracing the unique gifts that both bring to your practice. It's about the joy of movement, the strength of the core, and the song of the body. Whether you're flowing through a sequence on the mat or dancing with the Reformer, the essence of Pilates remains the same – it's a celebration of the body's potential and a journey towards a healthier, happier you.

Some say that Mat Pilates is the foundation upon which the house of Pilates is built, while the Reformer is the intricate architecture that makes the house uniquely beautiful. Both are essential in their own way. The mat teaches us the fundamental principles of Pilates – control, precision, centering, concentration, breath, and flow. It's Pilates in its most distilled form. On the other hand, the Reformer builds upon these principles and adds depth, variety, and intensity. It's Pilates in its most expressive form.

Embracing both Mat and Reformer Pilates is like listening to a symphony. The mat is the melody – simple, soulful, and comforting. The Reformer is the harmony – complex, dynamic, and exhilarating. When you tune into both, you can hear the beautiful symphony of Pilates. You can feel the rhythm of your body, the melody of your movements, and the harmony of your strength and flexibility.

As we continue this journey together, remember, there's no rush, no finish line. The beauty of Pilates lies in the journey itself. Whether it's on the mat or the Reformer, every breath you take, every move you make, is a step towards a healthier, happier, and more harmonious you. It's about finding joy in the movement, strength in the stillness, and harmony in the balance.

Embrace the mat for its simplicity and freedom. Embrace the Reformer for its depth and dynamism. Both are your partners on this journey. They're your guides, your mentors, your companions. Listen to them, learn from them, grow with them. Let them inspire you, challenge you, and transform you. Remember, in the world of Pilates, there are no strangers, only friends you haven't met yet.

In the end, the choice between Mat and Reformer Pilates isn't about choosing one over the other. It's about choosing yourself – your needs, your goals, your journey. So, whether you're rolling like a ball on your mat or gliding like a swan on your Reformer, remember, you're not just practicing Pilates, you're practicing self-love, self-care, and self-discovery. And that, my dear friend, is the true essence of Pilates. It's not just a workout; it's a lifestyle, a philosophy, a celebration of the body's extraordinary potential.

As we close this chapter, I hope you carry forward this understanding of Mat and Reformer Pilates. May it guide you in your practice, inspire you in your journey, and empower you in your life. Remember, Pilates isn't something you do; it's something you live. So, live it with passion, practice it with joy, and embrace it with love. After all, the true beauty of Pilates lies not in the exercises we do but in the person we become while doing them.

CHAPTER 3

Core Principles of Pilates

Alignment

As we embark on this exploration of Wall Pilates, we enter a world where the wall isn't just a barrier or boundary, but a partner and guide in our journey towards better health, strength, and flexibility. The wall, in its simplicity and solidity, becomes our mirror, our measure, and our mentor. Let's dive into the core principles of Pilates alignment, specifically in the context of Wall Pilates.

To truly appreciate Wall Pilates, we must understand that the wall serves as a constant, stable, and unchanging point of reference for alignment. It offers immediate feedback, helping us correct and perfect our posture. It's an unwavering teacher that guides us in mastering the art of proper alignment, a crucial element in Pilates.

Pilates, in its essence, is a dance between control and freedom, power and grace, strength and flexibility. And at the heart of this dance lies alignment – the fine balance that brings our body, mind, and spirit into a harmonious whole. Alignment in Pilates is not just about straightening our back or balancing our weight, it's about aligning our body's natural symmetry with the force of gravity. It's about creating an inner architecture of strength, balance, and stability that supports our body in every move we make.

When practicing Wall Pilates, it's essential to cultivate an intimate awareness of our body's alignment with the wall. This awareness starts from the ground up, quite literally. Our feet, often overlooked, are the first point of contact with the ground and our primary connection with the earth. As we press our feet against the wall, we should aim for an evenly distributed weight across all corners of our feet. This creates a firm and stable foundation that anchors our body and aids in maintaining balance throughout our practice.

Moving upwards, our focus shifts to our knees and hips. As we perform exercises like the wall sit or single-leg glute bridge, we need to ensure that our knees are aligned over our ankles, and our hips are squared off towards the wall. Misalignment here can put undue stress on our joints and ligaments, leading to discomfort or even injury. The wall helps us maintain this alignment, offering a tangible reference point that guides our movement.

Our spine is the central axis of our body, a magnificent structure that protects our nervous system and supports our body weight. In Pilates, a neutral spine – that is, a spine that maintains its natural curvature – is of paramount importance. While pressing our lower back into the wall during exercises like the spine curl or wall roll-down, we learn to preserve this neutral spine even when our body is in motion.

Our shoulders, often the bearers of stress and tension, require special attention. As we press our arms or shoulders against the wall in exercises like the wall push-up or shoulder opener, we strive to keep our shoulders relaxed and away from our ears. This encourages an open chest, facilitating deep, expansive breaths that nourish our body with oxygen.

Lastly, we come to our head, the crowning glory of our body. While performing Wall Pilates, our aim is to keep our head in a neutral position, with our gaze directed forwards and our neck long and relaxed. The wall, with its unwavering presence, reminds us to keep our head aligned with the rest of our body, completing our body's beautiful architecture of alignment.

The beauty of Wall Pilates is that it allows us to not just see, but feel this architecture. It helps us discover and correct imbalances, reinforcing proper alignment and promoting efficient movement. As we align our body against the wall, we are not just aligning bones and muscles, but also aligning our body's energy and intention. This alignment permeates beyond our physical body, affecting our mental and emotional states, bringing theminto harmony with our physical self. It fosters a sense of inner balance and peace, leaving us feeling centered, grounded, and whole.

In the practice of Wall Pilates, the wall acts as an external extension of our internal awareness. It helps us bring to light the subtle shifts and changes in our body's alignment, enabling us to address them promptly and effectively. Every exercise becomes an opportunity to deepen our understanding of our body's alignment, to refine our movements, and to create a seamless synergy between our body, mind, and spirit.

But it's not just about the exercises. It's about taking these principles of alignment and integrating them into our daily lives. It's about standing tall, walking straight, and moving with grace and efficiency. It's about embodying these principles in our actions, our posture, our gait, and our demeanor. When we do this, we carry the essence of Wall Pilates with us, wherever we go, whatever we do.

In conclusion, Wall Pilates is more than a workout, it's a way of life. It's a journey of self-discovery, of finding our center, our balance, our strength. It's about creating harmony within ourselves and between ourselves and our environment. It's about learning to move with power, grace, and ease. It's about becoming more attuned to our bodies, more aware of our alignment, and more mindful of our movements. And ultimately, it's about living a healthier, happier, and more fulfilling life.

To those who are new to Wall Pilates, I encourage you to embrace the wall, for it is a friend, a guide, and a mentor. To those who are already on this journey, I commend you for your dedication and invite you to delve deeper, to explore further, to challenge yourselves more. For in the world of Wall Pilates, the learning never ends, the journey never ceases, and the rewards are boundless.

As we continue to practice and learn, we should remember that everybody is unique and each of us may experience Wall Pilates differently. But regardless of our individual experiences, the core principles of Pilates alignment remain the same. They are the backbone of our practice, the beacon guiding us towards improved health, strength, flexibility, and well-being.

Breathing

Breathing is an essential process that sustains life by delivering oxygen to the body and removing carbon dioxide. It is an automatic function that is generally not under conscious control. However, by intentionally controlling our breath, we can influence our physical and mental states. In the context of exercise, wellness practices, and daily life, breathing is a fundamental component that should not be overlooked.

Types of Breathing

There are two primary types of breathing: diaphragmatic breathing (or abdominal breathing) and chest breathing. Diaphragmatic breathing involves the diaphragm, a dome-shaped muscle at the base of the lungs. When you breathe in, the diaphragm contracts and moves downward, allowing the lungs to expand and fill with air. Chest breathing, on the other hand, involves the intercostal muscles and results in the chest expanding outward.

Diaphragmatic breathing is generally considered to be more efficient and beneficial for health, as it allows for deeper breaths and better oxygen exchange. Chest breathing can sometimes be shallower and is often associated with stress and anxiety.

Breathing in Pilates and Other Wellness Practices

In Pilates, breathing is an essential component of the practice. Joseph Pilates, the founder of Pilates, believed that deep and conscious breathing was integral to cleansing the body and mind. He emphasized using the breath to help engage core muscles and to facilitate movements.

In Pilates, lateral or ribcage breathing is often taught. This involves inhaling deeply through the nose, allowing the ribcage to expand out to the sides, while keeping the abdominal muscles engaged. Exhaling is usually done through the mouth, with a focus on fully expelling the air and engaging the core muscles.

Yoga is another discipline where breathing plays a central role. Pranayama, the practice of breath control in yoga, consists of various techniques designed to improve mental clarity, physical health, and spiritual well-being.

Benefits of Controlled Breathing

Controlled breathing can have a range of benefits, including:

- **Stress Reduction:** Slow, deep breathing can activate the parasympathetic nervous system, which helps to calm the body and reduce stress.
- **Improved Focus and Mental Clarity:** Controlled breathing can help to clear the mind and improve concentration and focus.
- **Increased Energy Levels:** By optimizing oxygen intake, controlled breathing can help to increase energy levels.
- **Pain Management:** Deep breathing can be used as a technique for managing pain.

- **Improved Physical Performance:** In physical activities and sports, efficient breathing can improve endurance and performance.
- **Lower Blood Pressure:** Regular practice of deep breathing can contribute to lower blood pressure.

Breathing Techniques

There are various breathing techniques that one can practice. Some popular ones include:

- **Box Breathing:** Inhale for four seconds, hold the breath for four seconds, exhale for four seconds, and then hold the breath again for four seconds.
- **4-7-8 Breathing:** Inhale for four seconds, hold the breath for seven seconds, and exhale for eight seconds.
- **Alternate Nostril Breathing:** A yogic technique where you alternate breathing through one nostril at a time.

In conclusion, breathing is not just a biological function but also a powerful tool that can be harnessed for better physical and mental health. Whether through Pilates, yoga, or other practices, learning to control and optimize your breathing can have far-reaching benefits.

Centering

Centering is a foundational principle in Pilates that refers to the concept of maintaining physical balance and stability through a strong and engaged core. In the context of Wall Pilates, centering takes on an even more significant role because of the unique challenges and opportunities provided by the wall as a prop.

The principle of centering in Pilates is rooted in the belief that all movement should originate from the center of the body, often referred to as the "powerhouse". The powerhouse includes the muscles of the abdomen, lower back, hips, and buttocks. By focusing on this central region, you can strengthen these muscles and create a stable base for all types of movements.

In Wall Pilates, the wall serves as a feedback mechanism, providing instant input on your alignment and stability. When your back is against the wall, you can immediately feel if your spine is aligned or if you're leaning to one side or the other. This feedback allows you to make immediate corrections, enhancing the centering aspect of your practice.

As you practice Wall Pilates, you'll likely find that the wall helps you engage your core muscles more deeply. Exercises like wall squats and wall planks, for instance, require a significant amount of core activation to maintain stability and proper form. As you become more adept at using the wall in your Pilates practice, you'll likely notice a significant improvement in your overall core strength and stability.

But centering in Pilates isn't just about physical alignment and core strength. It's also about mental focus and intention. As you perform each exercise, you're encouraged to remain fully present, focusing your attention on the muscles you're engaging and the movements you're making. This mindful approach not only improves the effectiveness of your workouts, but it also promotes a sense of calm and relaxation.

Ultimately, centering in Wall Pilates is about achieving balance—both physically and mentally. By engaging your core, aligning your body, and focusing your mind, you can enhance your overall Pilates practice and enjoy the unique benefits that Wall Pilates has to offer.

Concentration

Concentration is one of the core principles of Pilates, and it plays a pivotal role in Wall Pilates as well. Concentration is all about bringing your full attention to each exercise, every movement, and the entire workout experience. This focus on mindfulness enhances your awareness of your body's strengths, weaknesses, and its alignment, leading to more effective and safer workouts.

When practicing Wall Pilates, the wall provides a constant point of reference that can help heighten your concentration. As you execute each movement, the wall offers immediate tactile feedback, helping you maintain your focus on the task at hand. Whether you are performing a wall-supported squat, bridge, or a simple stretch, the wall's presence can help you stay connected to your body and the exercise.

Concentration in Wall Pilates is not just about focusing on the physical movements. It's also about understanding and connecting with your body's response to each exercise. For instance, as you press your palms or your back against the wall, you need to pay attention to how your body feels and how it reacts. This might involve noticing the engagement of specific muscles, the alignment of your body, or the way your body weight shifts. By concentrating on these elements, you can ensure correct form and alignment, thereby maximizing the benefits of each exercise.

Moreover, concentration also plays a role in breath control, another key principle of Pilates. By focusing your attention on your breathing pattern as you perform each exercise, you can better synchronize your movements with your breath. This not only enhances the fluidity and efficiency of your movements but also deepens your sense of calm and relaxation.

In the context of Wall Pilates, the concept of concentration extends beyond the workout itself. By being fully present and engaged during your workout, you're also practicing mindfulness—an ability that can benefit many other areas of your life. With consistent practice, you'll likely find that the concentration you cultivate during your Wall Pilates workouts can help improve your focus and mindfulness in your day-to-day life.

Control

Control is another fundamental principle in Pilates, and it's of equal importance in Wall Pilates. The essence of control in Pilates, and consequently in Wall Pilates, lies in the idea that each movement should be intentional and deliberate. This is not about the speed or the number of repetitions, but rather about performing each movement with precision and a deep understanding of its purpose.

In Wall Pilates, control takes on a unique dimension because of the presence of the wall. The wall acts as a point of reference, a support system, and a tool for feedback, all of which can enhance your control over each movement. For instance, when performing a standing leg lift against the wall, your control is not just about lifting and lowering your leg. It's also about maintaining a firm contact with the wall, keeping your body aligned, and ensuring the stability of your standing leg. The wall, therefore, offers an external source of control, helping you stay connected with your movement.

Control in Wall Pilates is also closely linked to your body awareness. The more aware you are of your body's position, alignment, and movement, the greater control you can exert over your exercises. This awareness, when coupled with a focus on precision and intentionality, allows for a more effective and safer workout.

Furthermore, control in Wall Pilates extends to the management of your breath. Just as you control your physical movements, you also need to control your breathing pattern. The act of inhaling and exhaling in synchronization with your movements can help improve your control over each exercise. This intentional breath control not only enhances the rhythm and fluidity of your movements but also deepens your mind-body connection.

Lastly, it's worth noting that control in Wall Pilates is not about rigidness or stiffness. On the contrary, it's about finding a balance between strength and flexibility, between exertion and relaxation. It's about controlling your movements in a way that is fluid, graceful, and efficient.

In sum, control in Wall Pilates is about much more than simply executing an exercise. It's about developing a deeper understanding of your body, enhancing your body awareness, and cultivating a sense of harmony and balance in your movements. This focus on control can ultimately lead to a more mindful, effective, and fulfilling workout experience.

Precision

Precision is an integral principle of Pilates that holds equal prominence in Wall Pilates. The practice of precision involves executing each movement with the utmost accuracy, paying close attention to the finer details of alignment, technique, and execution. In Wall Pilates, precision takes on a new layer of significance due to the unique interaction with the wall.

The wall serves as a tangible guide that offers immediate feedback about your alignment and movement patterns. For instance, during a wall squat, the wall can help ensure that your back is straight, your hips are aligned with your knees, and your knees are aligned with your ankles. If you deviate from the correct alignment, the wall will provide instant feedback, prompting you to adjust and realign yourself. This immediate feedback mechanism fosters an enhanced sense of precision, allowing you to fine-tune your movements and improve your technique.

Precision in Wall Pilates is closely tied to the concepts of control and concentration. As you perform each exercise with control and maintain a focused mind, you are better equipped to execute movements with greater precision. Similarly, practicing precision reinforces your control and concentration, creating a virtuous cycle that elevates the quality of your Wall Pilates practice.

Wall Pilates also encourages precision through the use of your own body weight and resistance. Unlike traditional Pilates exercises that use a variety of equipment, Wall Pilates requires you to leverage your body weight against the resistance of the wall. This necessitates precision in positioning, movement, and engagement of the correct muscles.

However, precision in Wall Pilates is not about achieving perfection. Instead, it's about striving for continuous improvement and learning. It's about understanding that every small adjustment, every slight improvement in alignment, and every subtle enhancement in technique brings you closer to a more effective and efficient practice.

In essence, precision in Wall Pilates is a journey of exploration and refinement. It invites you to delve deeper into each exercise, pay attention to the details, and strive for improvement. As you embrace precision in your Wall Pilates practice, you will not only enhance the effectiveness of your workout but also develop a deeper connection with your body and movement.

Flow

Flow in Pilates, including Wall Pilates, is the smooth, continuous, and seamless transition from one movement or position to another. It is the harmonious rhythm that strings together individual exercises into a symphony of movements. This principle is closely linked to the essence of Pilates as a method that promotes the development of a healthy, balanced, and efficient body.

In Wall Pilates, the concept of flow takes on a unique significance because of the unique interaction with the wall. The wall is a constant companion throughout your workout, supporting you, challenging you, and guiding your movements. This interaction with the wall helps create a distinctive rhythm and flow in your workout.

When practicing Wall Pilates, your movements aren't isolated; instead, they're part of a bigger picture, a flow that connects one exercise to the next. For instance, you might transition from a wall squat into a wall bridge, or from a standing leg lift into a wall push-up. These transitions are not abrupt but are performed with a smooth, controlled flow.

The wall supports this flow by providing a stable, unchanging point of reference. You can use it to guide your transitions, maintaining contact with the wall as you move from one exercise to another. This can help to create a smoother, more fluid practice.

Flow in Wall Pilates also extends to your breath. Breath is the life force that fuels every movement, and coordinating your breath with your movements can help to create a rhythmic flow. When your breath and movements are synchronized, your Wall Pilates practice can become a moving meditation, each breath guiding your movements and each movement guiding your breath.

But flow is not just about the physical aspects of Wall Pilates. It's also about the mental and emotional flow that comes from a focused, mindful practice. As you concentrate on each movement, tuning into the sensations in your body, you may find that your mind quiets, your emotions balance, and you enter a state of flow where you're fully engaged in the present moment.

In essence, flow in Wall Pilates is about harmony - the harmony of breath and movement, mind and body, challenge and ease. It's about moving with grace, control, and precision, making each transition as important as the exercise itself. When you embrace the principle of flow in your Wall Pilates practice, you'll not only enhance the physical benefits of your workout but also promote a sense of calm, focus, and mindfulness.

CHAPTER 4

Basic Pilates Exercises

Wall Roll Down

The Wall Roll Down is a fundamental exercise in Wall Pilates that encourages spinal articulation and core engagement. Here is a step-by-step guide to perform this exercise:

Position: Start by standing tall with your back against the wall. Your feet should be hip-width apart and approximately six inches away from the wall. Your head, shoulders, and buttocks should touch the wall, and there should be a small space between your lower back and the wall. This is your starting position.

Roll Down: Begin by taking a deep breath in. As you exhale, tuck your chin into your chest and start to peel your spine off the wall one vertebra at a time, starting from your head. Let your arms hang loose and heavy as you continue to roll down, with your abdomen pulling in towards your spine. Go as far as you comfortably can while maintaining contact with the wall through your feet and hips. You should feel a stretch through your back and hamstrings.

Roll Up: Inhale deeply at the bottom of your roll down. As you exhale, start to rebuild your spine against the wall, one vertebra at a time. Think about stacking each vertebra on top of the one below it, starting from your lower back. Your head should be the last thing to come up.

Reset: Once you're standing tall again, adjust your posture if necessary to ensure your head, shoulders, and buttocks are against the wall and you have that small space in your lower back. You have now completed one repetition.

The Wall Roll Down is a great exercise for enhancing body awareness, as it encourages you to pay attention to the alignment and movement of each individual vertebra. It also promotes greater flexibility in the spine and can help relieve tension in the back and shoulders. Remember to pair your movements with your breath, exhaling as you roll down and inhaling as you roll up. As with all Pilates exercises, precision and control are more important than speed, so take your time to perform this exercise correctly.

Wall Push Up

The Wall Push Up is a great exercise in Wall Pilates. It primarily targets your upper body, including your chest, arms, and shoulders, while also engaging your core for stability. Here's a step-by-step guide to performing the Wall Push Up:

Positioning: Start by standing arm's length away from the wall. Your feet should be hip-width apart for balance. Place your hands on the wall at shoulder height, also shoulder-width apart. Your fingers should be spread wide for stability.

The Push Up: Keeping your body straight and your core engaged, slowly bend your elbows and lower your body towards the wall. Imagine a straight line running from your head through to your heels, and try to maintain this alignment throughout the movement. As you lower your body, your elbows should bend out to the sides.

Push Away: Once you've gone as far as you comfortably can without straining, push your body away from the wall by straightening your arms. Ensure the movement is controlled, and avoid locking your elbows at the top of the movement.

Repetition: This completes one Wall Push Up. Aim for a set of 10 to 15 repetitions, always focusing on maintaining your body alignment and controlling your movements.

The Wall Push Up can be adjusted to suit your fitness level. If you find the exercise too easy, try standing further away from the wall. If it's too challenging, move a little closer. Remember that Pilates is not about how many repetitions you can do, but rather about performing each one with precision and control. The Wall Push Up is a great way to build upper body strength while practicing these core Pilates principles.

Wall Squats

Wall Squats are an effective exercise in Wall Pilates that primarily target your lower body, specifically your quadriceps, glutes, and hamstrings. They also engage your core muscles, providing a full-body workout. Here's how you perform a Wall Squat:

Positioning: Begin by standing with your back against the wall. Your feet should be about hip-width apart and about two feet away from the wall. This distance can vary depending on your height and comfort, so adjust as necessary.

The Squat: Slide your back down the wall, bending your knees as you do so. Aim to lower yourself until your thighs are parallel to the floor, like you're sitting in an invisible chair. Keep your knees directly above your ankles and ensure they do not protrude past your toes. This alignment is critical to protect your knees from strain.

Hold and Rise: Hold this squat position for a few seconds, engaging your core and keeping your back flat against the wall. Then, slowly push through your heels to rise back up to your starting position.

Repetition: This completes one Wall Squat. Try to do a set of 10 to 15 repetitions, always focusing on maintaining proper form and control in your movements.

The Wall Squat is an adaptable exercise. If you want to make it more challenging, you can hold the squat position for longer periods or add a resistance band around your thighs to engage your muscles further. As with all Pilates exercises, remember the importance of control, precision, and breath. The Wall Squat is a great way to build lower body and core strength while practicing these core Pilates principles.

Standing Leg Lifts

Standing Leg Lifts are a fantastic exercise in Wall Pilates that focus on strengthening your glutes and hamstrings, while also challenging your balance and engaging your core. Here's how you perform a Standing Leg Lift:

Positioning: Stand with your back against the wall, feet hip-width apart. Extend your arms to the sides for balance if needed.

The Lift: Shift your weight to your right leg, keeping your right foot firmly planted on the floor. With your left foot flexed, slowly lift your left leg straight up in front of you. Aim to lift it as high as is comfortable, while keeping your back flat against the wall and your lifted leg straight.

Lowering Down: Lower your left leg back down, controlling the movement and maintaining your alignment.

Repetition: This completes one Standing Leg Lift. Perform a set of 10-15 lifts with the left leg, then switch to your right leg for the same number of repetitions.

The Standing Leg Lift is a great way to work on the precision and control that are core principles of Pilates. It's a more challenging exercise when done with proper form, but also quite rewarding. As always, remember to breathe naturally and maintain your alignment throughout the exercise. You may also find it helpful to focus on a spot on the wall or in the room to maintain your balance.

Wall Bridge

The Wall Bridge is a unique Wall Pilates exercise that focuses on strengthening the glutes, hamstrings, and core while also challenging your range of motion and control. Here's how you perform a Wall Bridge:

Starting Position: Lie on your back on a mat or comfortable surface with your feet flat against the wall and your knees bent at a 90-degree angle. Your feet should be hip-width apart. Place your arms down by your sides with your palms facing down for support.

The Lift: Engage your core and lift your hips off the floor, pressing your feet into the wall. You should aim to create a straight line from your knees to your shoulders. Try to lift your hips as high as you can while keeping your shoulders and head relaxed on the floor.

Lowering Down: Slowly and with control, lower your hips back down to the starting position. This completes one Wall Bridge.

Repetition: Perform a set of 10-15 Wall Bridges, focusing on maintaining control and alignment throughout the movement.

The Wall Bridge can be a challenging exercise, but it's also incredibly beneficial for developing strength, flexibility, and control. Just like with any Pilates exercise, it's important to focus on your form and breathe naturally throughout the movement. As you become more comfortable with the Wall Bridge, you can challenge yourself further by lifting one leg off the wall during the bridge. This variation will engage your core even more and increase the intensity of the exercise.

Wall Plank

The Wall Plank is a Pilates exercise that targets the core, specifically the abdominals and obliques, while also challenging the arms and shoulders. Here's how to perform a Wall Plank:

Starting Position: Stand facing a wall with your feet hip-width apart. Place your hands flat against the wall, shoulder-width apart, at about chest level. Walk your feet back until your body is in a diagonal line from your head to your heels. This is your starting position.

The Plank: Engage your core to stabilize your body. Keep your body in a straight line from your head to your heels, avoiding any sagging in your lower back or hiking up your hips. This position should resemble a standing version of a traditional floor plank.

Hold: Hold this position for 20-60 seconds, or as long as you can maintain good form. Remember to breathe normally throughout the exercise.

Release: When you're ready to release the plank, walk your feet toward the wall and stand upright.

Repetition: You can perform multiple sets of Wall Planks, allowing for a short rest in between.

The Wall Plank is a fantastic exercise for beginners or for those who find the traditional floor plank too challenging. It allows you to build core strength and stability in a more manageable way. As you get stronger, you can increase the difficulty by placing your hands lower on the wall or by moving your feet further back. As with all Pilates exercises, it's crucial to maintain proper alignment and form throughout the exercise to ensure its effectiveness and to prevent injury. Remember, quality over quantity is key in Pilates.

Wall Mountain Climbers

Wall Mountain Climbers are a dynamic exercise that targets the core, specifically the abdominals, while also engaging the arms, shoulders, and legs. Here's how to perform Wall Mountain Climbers:

Starting Position: Stand facing a wall with your feet hip-width apart. Place your hands flat against the wall, shoulder-width apart, at about chest level. Walk your feet back until your body is in a diagonal line from your head to your heels. This is your starting position, similar to the Wall Plank.

Mountain Climber: From this position, start by pulling your right knee towards your chest, keeping your foot flexed. Try to maintain your body position and avoid sagging your lower back or hiking up your hips.

Switch Legs: Quickly switch legs, extending your right leg back to the starting position while pulling your left knee towards your chest.

Repetition: Continue alternating legs for a set amount of time or for a certain number of repetitions. Remember to keep your core engaged and your body in a straight line throughout the exercise.

Rest: After completing your set, slowly walk your feet towards the wall and stand upright to rest before starting the next set.

Wall Mountain Climbers are a great way to add a cardio element to your Pilates workout while also strengthening your core. They can be modified to increase or decrease the difficulty level by changing the speed of the leg movements or the position of your hands on the wall. Remember, in Pilates, it's important to maintain control and precision during each movement, even when performing more dynamic exercises like Wall Mountain Climbers. It's not about how fast you can go, but how well you can maintain your form while moving.

Wall Angels

Wall Angels

Wall Angels are a simple but effective exercise for improving posture and working the muscles in your back and shoulders. Here's how to perform Wall Angels:

Starting Position: Stand with your back against a wall. Your feet should be about 2-3 feet from the wall and your knees slightly bent. The back of your head, your upper back, and your buttocks should be in contact with the wall.

Set Your Arms: Bend your elbows and raise your arms to the sides so that your hands are level with your shoulders. Your arms and the back of your hands should be touching the wall, forming a "W" shape. This is your starting position.

Move Your Arms: Slowly slide your arms up the wall, straightening them as much as you can while keeping your hands and arms in contact with the wall. Your body should now form a "Y" shape.

Return to Starting Position: Slowly lower your arms back down to the starting position, bending your elbows and returning to the "W" shape.

Repetition: Repeat this movement for a set number of repetitions.

Wall Angels are a great exercise for opening up the chest and shoulders, areas that can become tight from hunching over a computer or steering wheel. They also work the muscles in your upper back, which can help improve posture and reduce back pain. Remember to keep your movements slow and controlled, and pay attention to keeping your arms and back in contact with the wall. It's not about how many reps you can do, but the quality of each movement.

Remember, in Pilates and especially in Wall Pilates, the alignment of your body is very important. This exercise not only strengthens your muscles but also helps you become more aware of your body alignment. You'll notice if you're arching your back or if your arms are not in full contact with the wall, which indicates areas you need to work on.

With practice, Wall Angels can help improve your posture, reduce tension in your upper body, and enhance your overall Wall Pilates practice.

Wall Side Plank

The Wall Side Plank is a challenging exercise that targets your core, specifically the obliques, but also engages your shoulders and arms. Here's how you perform the Wall Side Plank:

Starting Position: Stand sideways to the wall with your feet stacked or staggered for stability. The side of your right foot should be on the floor and the side of your left foot should be resting against the wall.

Set Your Arm: Place your right hand on the floor directly under your shoulder, and extend your left arm along the wall above your head.

Lift Your Body: Engage your core and lift your hips off the floor, creating a straight line from your head to your feet. Your body should be leaning against the wall, but not relying on it for support. The wall is there as a guide to ensure your body stays in alignment.

Hold and Breathe: Hold this position for a few seconds while continuing to breathe deeply and steadily. Remember, the principle of breathing in Pilates is not just about inhaling and exhaling, but about fully engaging your diaphragm, pelvic floor, and deep core muscles.

Return to Starting Position: Slowly lower your hips back to the floor to return to your starting position.

Repetition: Repeat this movement for a set number of repetitions, then switch sides to ensure balanced strength and flexibility on both sides of your body.

The Wall Side Plank may be challenging at first, but with regular practice, you will see improvements in your core strength and balance. As with all Wall Pilates exercises, precision and control are essential. This means moving slowly and deliberately, and being aware of the alignment of your body. It's not about how high you can lift your hips, but about maintaining control and alignment throughout the movement.

The Wall Side Plank is a versatile exercise that can be modified to increase or decrease difficulty as needed. For a greater challenge, you can add a leg lift or a twist. For a less intense version, you can keep the bottom knee on the floor. Remember, the goal is not to push yourself to the point of strain, but to work within your limits and gradually increase your strength and stamina.

This exercise perfectly encapsulates the Pilates principles of centering, concentration, control, precision, and flow. You're centering by engaging your core, focusing your mind on the exercise (concentration), controlling your movements, aligning your body precisely, and moving with a steady flow. By practicing the Wall Side Plank regularly, you're not just building physical strength; you're also cultivating a deeper mind-body connection, which is at the heart of Pilates.

Single Leg Wall Squat

The The Single Leg Wall Squat is a more advanced exercise that targets your lower body, specifically your thighs, glutes, and core. Here's how you perform the Single Leg Wall Squat:

Starting Position: Stand with your back against a wall. Your feet should be hip-width apart and about a foot away from the wall.

Prepare: Lift one foot off the floor, straightening it in front of you at about hip height. Your other foot should remain flat on the floor.

Squat Down: Slowly lower your body down into a squat position. Your back should remain flat against the wall. Your standing leg should form a 90-degree angle at the knee. Be sure to keep your knee in line with your toes and not let it go past your toes. Your lifted leg should remain straight and lifted throughout the movement.

Hold and Breathe: Hold the squat position for a few seconds while continuing to breathe deeply and steadily.

Rise Up: Slowly rise back up to the starting position, keeping your lifted leg straight and lifted.

Repetition: Repeat this movement for a set number of repetitions, then switch legs to ensure balanced strength and flexibility on both sides of your body.

The Single Leg Wall Squat is a challenging exercise that requires balance, strength, and control. As with all Wall Pilates exercises, precision is key. This means moving slowly and deliberately, and being aware of the alignment of your body.

This exercise aligns with the Pilates principles of centering, concentration, control, precision, and flow. You're centering by engaging your core, focusing your mind on the exercise (concentration), controlling your movements, aligning your body precisely, and moving with a steady flow. By practicing the Single Leg Wall Squat regularly, you're not just building physical strength; you're also cultivating a deeper mind-body connection, which is at the heart of Pilates.

Remember to always listen to your body and modify the exercise as needed. If you find the Single Leg Wall Squat too challenging at first, you can start with a regular Wall Squat and gradually progress to the single leg version as your strength and balance improve.

Wall Scissors

The Wall Scissors is a powerful exercise that targets your lower body, specifically your glutes, hamstrings, and core. Here's how you perform the Wall Scissors exercise:

Starting Position: Lie down on your back on a yoga mat or any comfortable surface with your legs up against a wall. Your hips should be close to the wall and your legs should be straight and resting against the wall. Your arms can rest by your sides or under your lower back for additional support.

Prepare: Engage your core and lift one leg off the wall while the other leg remains in place.

Scissor Motion: As you lower the lifted leg towards your chest, slowly lift the other leg off the wall, effectively switching their positions. The motion resembles the opening and closing of scissors, hence the name of the exercise.

Controlled Movement: Keep the movement slow and controlled, ensuring you are using your muscles rather than momentum to move your legs.

Repetition: Continue this scissor motion for a set number of repetitions, keeping your core engaged and your movements precise.

This exercise aligns with the Pilates principles of centering, concentration, control, precision, and flow. You're centering by engaging your core, focusing your mind on the exercise (concentration), controlling your movements, aligning your body precisely, and moving with a steady flow. By practicing the Wall Scissors regularly, you're not just building physical strength; you're also cultivating a deeper mind-body connection, which is at the heart of Pilates.

As with all exercises, it's essential to listen to your body and adjust the movement according to your comfort and fitness level. If at any point during the exercise you feel discomfort or strain, modify the movement or take a break. It's always better to perform fewer repetitions with correct form than more with improper form.

Heel Raises

Heel Raises are a simple yet effective exercise that primarily targets your calf muscles but also engages your core and improves balance. Here's how you perform the Heel Raises exercise in the context of Wall Pilates:

Starting Position: Stand up straight with your back and heels against a wall. Your feet should be hip-width apart, and your arms can either be resting by your sides or stretched out in front of you for balance.

Prepare: Engage your core and maintain a straight posture, ensuring that your back remains flat against the wall.

Lift: Gradually lift your heels off the ground, rising onto the balls of your feet. Imagine you're trying to reach something high up with your head, which will help maintain your alignment and stretch upwards.

Controlled Descent: Lower your heels back down in a slow, controlled motion, feeling the stretch in your calf muscles.

Repetition: Repeat this movement for a set number of repetitions, keeping your movements smooth and controlled.

The Heel Raises exercise embodies several Pilates principles. You're centering by engaging your core, focusing on the movement (concentration), controlling your ascent and descent (control), aligning your body against the wall (precision), and maintaining a smooth rhythm (flow).

As with any exercise, it's important to listen to your body. If you feel any discomfort or strain, it's okay to take a break or modify the movement. Consistency and correct form are more important than trying to perform a large number of repetitions. This exercise can be a great way to add some strength training to your routine, improve your balance, and cultivate a stronger mind-body connection.

Wall Core Press

The Wall Core Press exercise is a fantastic way to engage and strengthen your core muscles, particularly the transverse abdominis, which are crucial for stability and support in many movements. Here's how you perform the Wall Core Press:

Starting Position: Stand facing the wall, approximately an arm's length away. Place your palms flat against the wall at about chest level, fingers pointing upwards. Keep your feet hip-width apart.

Prepare: Engage your core, drawing your navel towards your spine. This is crucial for protecting your lower back during the exercise. Keep your spine neutral.

Press: Push your hands against the wall as if you're trying to move it, but without actually moving your body. This action engages your core and upper body. Hold this 'press' for a few seconds.

Release: Slowly release the tension, controlling the movement and maintaining your posture.

Repetition: Repeat this 'press and release' sequence for a set number of repetitions.

This exercise embodies the Pilates principles beautifully. You're focusing on your core (centering), paying attention to the tension and release (concentration), controlling your movements and maintaining your posture (control), ensuring your hands are correctly positioned and your body is aligned (precision), and moving smoothly between tension and release (flow).

As with all exercises, it's essential to listen to your body and modify or stop if you feel discomfort. The Wall Core Press may seem simple, but when performed with the right engagement and control, it can be a powerful tool in your Pilates routine. It's a great way to build core strength, improve stability, and enhance your body awareness.

Arm Circles

The Wall Arm Circles exercise is an excellent move to engage your shoulder muscles and improve your upper body mobility while promoting stability in your core. Here's how you perform the Wall Arm Circles:

Starting Position: Stand facing the wall with your feet hip-width apart, about an arm's length away. Reach out and place your palms flat against the wall at shoulder level, fingers pointing upwards.

Prepare: Engage your core, pulling your navel towards your spine. This will help stabilize your torso during the exercise. Keep your spine in a neutral position, and ensure your shoulders are down and away from your ears.

Move: Slowly start to make circles with your arms. Imagine you're trying to draw a circle on the wall with each hand. Make sure the movement comes from your shoulders, not just your wrists.

Control: Maintain control and smoothness as you circle your arms. You can start with small circles and gradually increase the size as your mobility improves. Keep your body still and only move your arms.

Switch Directions: After a set number of circles in one direction, switch and do the same number of circles in the opposite direction.

The Wall Arm Circles exercise emphasizes the core principles of Pilates: centering through engaging your core, concentration on the movement of your arms and maintaining your posture, control of the movement, precision in the path of your arms, and flow in the smooth circular motion.

Remember to listen to your body and modify or stop if you feel discomfort. This exercise is not just about your arms; it is about integrating your body movement with breath and mindfulness. It can help improve shoulder mobility, promote upper body strength, and enhance body awareness.

Wall Side Leg Circles

The Wall Side Leg Circles is a fantastic exercise for toning your thighs, engaging your core, and improving your balance. Here's how to perform this exercise:

Starting Position: Stand tall and sideways against a wall with your feet hip-width apart. Make sure one of your shoulders and the same side hip is lightly touching the wall for support. Your inside arm should be raised to the wall at shoulder height for balance, while the outside arm rests on your hip.

Prepare: Engage your core by pulling your navel towards your spine. This will help stabilize your torso during the exercise. Make sure your spine is in a neutral position, and your shoulders are down and away from your ears.

Move: Slowly lift the outside leg to hip height, keeping it straight. Start to make controlled circles in the air with this leg. The movement should come from your hip, not your knee or ankle.

Control: Maintain control and smoothness as you circle your leg. You can start with small circles and gradually increase the size as your strength and balance improve. Remember to keep your body still and only move your leg.

Switch Directions: After a set number of circles in one direction, switch and do the same number of circles in the opposite direction.

Switch Sides: Once you've completed your set, turn around and repeat the exercise with the other leg.

The Wall Side Leg Circles exercise emphasizes the core principles of Pilates: centering through engaging your core, concentration on the movement of your leg and maintaining your posture, control of the movement, precision in the path of your leg, and flow in the smooth circular motion.

Remember to listen to your body and modify or stop if you feel discomfort. This exercise is not just about your legs; it is about integrating your body movement with breath and mindfulness. It can help improve hip mobility, promote lower body strength, and enhance body awareness.

Wall Rolling Like a Ball

The "Wall Rolling Like a Ball" exercise is a modification of the traditional Pilates exercise "Rolling Like a Ball". It's an excellent exercise to practice control and enhance core strength. It also helps promote balance and coordination. Here is how to perform this exercise:

Starting Position: Sit on the floor with your back facing the wall. Bend your knees and hold onto your ankles, shins, or the back of your thighs, whichever is most comfortable. Your feet should be lifted off the floor, and your body should be in a tucked position. Your back should be rounded, like a ball, with a small gap between your back and the wall.

Prepare: Engage your core by pulling your navel towards your spine. This will help stabilize your torso during the exercise. Your chin should be tucked towards your chest.

Move: Gently push off the wall using your feet, rolling down your spine until your shoulders touch the ground. Make sure you maintain your rounded "ball" shape throughout the movement.

Control: Use your core muscles to stop the roll at your shoulders and start rolling back up, making sure not to use momentum or swing your body. Roll up until you're back in the starting position, maintaining the space between your back and the wall.

Repeat: Continue the exercise for a set number of repetitions.

This exercise can be quite challenging, so make sure to go at your own pace and only perform the exercise if it feels comfortable for you. The Wall Rolling Like a Ball exercise emphasizes the core principles of Pilates: centering through engaging your core, concentration on the movement of your body, control of the rolling motion, precision in the path of your roll, and flow in the smooth movement up and down.

Remember to listen to your body and modify or stop if you feel discomfort. This exercise is about integrating your body movement with breath and mindfulness. It can help improve spine mobility, promote core strength, and enhance body awareness.

Wall Leg Press

Start Position: Stand with your back flat against a wall. Your feet should be hip-width apart and positioned about 1 to 2 feet away from the wall. Slide down the wall until your hips and knees form a 90-degree angle, as if you're seated in an invisible chair.

The Movement: Begin by pressing your left foot firmly into the ground and extending your left knee. As you do this, lift your right foot off the floor and extend it straight out in front of you. Hold this position momentarily.

Return to Start: Slowly bring your right foot back down to the floor while bending your left knee to return to the initial seated position.

Switch Sides: Repeat the same movement, but this time press your right foot into the ground, extend your right knee, and lift your left foot off the ground. Once again, hold this position for a moment before returning to the start position.

Repetitions: Continue to alternate between sides for your chosen number of repetitions.

Remember to engage your core and maintain your posture throughout the exercise. Your back should remain against the wall, and when bending your knees, ensure they don't extend past your toes. This exercise targets your lower body while also requiring core stability, making it a full-body workout. Always start with a smaller number of repetitions and gradually increase as your strength and endurance improve.

Wall Side Stretches

Start Position: Stand with your right side close to the wall. Extend your right arm and place your hand on the wall at shoulder height, fingers pointing upwards. Your feet should be hip-width apart and parallel to the wall.

The Movement: Lean your body towards the wall while extending your left arm overhead. You should feel a stretch along the left side of your body. Keep your hips and shoulders square, and make sure your left foot remains firmly on the floor.

Hold the Position: Hold the stretch for about 15-30 seconds, breathing deeply and evenly.

Return to Start: Slowly return to the starting position.

Switch Sides: Repeat the stretch on the other side by standing with your left side close to the wall, your left hand on the wall, and leaning towards the wall while extending your right arm overhead.

Repetitions: Continue to alternate between sides for your chosen number of repetitions.

This exercise helps to stretch the obliques and intercostal muscles, improving your flexibility and promoting better posture. Ensure that your movements are controlled and smooth to avoid any injury. If you feel any discomfort, lessen the intensity of the stretch.

Wall Chest Opener

Start Position: Stand facing away from a wall, about one step away. Extend your arms out to the sides and place the back of your hands on the wall.

The Movement: Slowly slide your hands up the wall as far as you comfortably can while keeping your hands in contact with the wall. As you do this, you should feel your chest open up and your shoulder blades come together.

Hold the Position: Hold this position for a few seconds, continuing to breathe deeply and evenly.

Return to Start: Slowly lower your arms back down to the starting position.

Repetitions: Repeat this exercise for your chosen number of repetitions.

The Wall Chest Opener helps to stretch the chest muscles and improve posture. This can be particularly beneficial if you spend a lot of time sitting or hunched over a computer, as these activities can lead to tightness in the chest and shoulders. As with all exercises, ensure your movements are controlled and smooth, and avoid the exercise if it causes discomfort.

Wall Pike

Start Position: Begin in a high plank position with your feet flat against the wall. Your hands should be on the ground directly under your shoulders and your body should be in a straight line from your head to your heels.

The Movement: Push through your hands and use your core strength to lift your hips up towards the ceiling, while your feet slide up the wall. Your body should form an upside-down V shape, similar to a pike position in gymnastics. Ensure your back remains straight and your core is engaged.

Hold the Position: Hold this pike position for a few seconds, feeling the stretch in your hamstrings and the engagement in your core.

Return to Start: Slowly lower your body back down into the high plank position, controlling the movement with your core and arm strength.

Repetitions: Repeat this exercise for your chosen number of repetitions.

The Wall Pike is an advanced exercise that targets the core, shoulders, and hamstrings. It requires significant strength and control, so beginners may need to modify or work up to this exercise. Remember to keep your movements smooth and controlled, and always listen to your body. If you feel any discomfort or strain, stop the exercise and consult with a fitness professional if necessary.

Wall Glute Kickbacks

Start Position: Begin with your hands and knees on the ground in a tabletop position, facing away from the wall. Your hands should be directly under your shoulders, and your knees directly under your hips. One of your feet should be flat against the wall, with your knee bent at a 90-degree angle.

The Movement: Engage your core and glutes to press the foot that's against the wall, straightening your leg and pushing against the wall. Your body should remain stable and your hips should stay square to the ground.

Hold the Position: Hold the position for a second, ensuring your glute muscles are fully engaged.

Return to Start: Slowly bend your knee and lower your leg back down to the starting position, maintaining control throughout the movement.

Repetitions: Repeat this exercise for your chosen number of repetitions, then switch to the other leg.

The Wall Glute Kickbacks exercise targets the glutes and hamstrings, as well as the core muscles for stability. It's important to focus on the mind-muscle connection and really engage your glutes during this exercise. Remember to keep your movements slow and controlled, and always maintain good form. If you feel any discomfort or strain, stop the exercise and consult with a fitness professional if necessary.

Wall Pelvic Tilts

Start Position: Begin by standing with your back against the wall. Your feet should be hip-width apart and about a foot away from the wall. Your head, upper back, and buttocks should be in contact with the wall.

The Movement: Engage your abdominal muscles and gently tilt your pelvis towards the wall. This should cause your lower back to press against the wall. Ensure that you're not using your buttocks or leg muscles to create this movement - it should come from the pelvis.

Hold the Position: Hold this tilted position for a few seconds, keeping your abs engaged and your pelvis tilted.

Return to Start: Slowly release the tilt and return your pelvis to the neutral position. Make sure to keep the movement controlled and maintain contact with the wall.

Repetitions: Repeat this exercise for your chosen number of repetitions.

The Wall Pelvic Tilts exercise targets the lower abs and the muscles of the lower back. It's a subtle movement that requires a lot of control and concentration. By focusing on your pelvic movement, you can help improve your body awareness and control, which is a key aspect of Pilates. Always maintain good form during this exercise and if you feel any discomfort or strain, stop the exercise and consult with a fitness professional if necessary.

Wall Standing Cat-Camel

The Wall Standing Cat-Camel is a great exercise for flexibility and mobility in your spine. Here's how to do it:

1. **Begin by standing up straight** with your feet hip-width apart and your knees slightly bent for balance.

2. **Position your arms** so that your elbows are bent and your hands are in front of your shoulders. Your palms should be facing forward.

3. **On an inhale, engage your back muscles** to pull your shoulder blades together. At the same time, arch your upper and lower back slightly, and lift your gaze upwards.

4. **As you exhale, engage your core and push your palms forward.** Simultaneously, tuck your chin towards your chest, round your upper and lower back, and tuck your tailbone under.

5. **Repeat** the inhale movement, pulling your shoulder blades back together, bending your elbows, and arching your back once more.

6. **Repeat** the exhale movement, pushing your palms forward and rounding your back again.

7. Continue to repeat this sequence at a steady pace, focusing on the movement of your spine and the engagement of your core muscles.

Remember to breathe deeply and evenly throughout the exercise, and move at a pace that feels comfortable for you.

Wall Single-Leg Deadlift

The Wall Single-Leg Deadlift is a fantastic exercise for building strength in your lower body, particularly the hamstrings and glutes, while also improving balance and stability. Here's how to perform the Wall Single-Leg Deadlift:

1. **Stand upright** about an arm's length away from a wall, facing away from it, with your feet hip-width apart.

2. **Shift your weight** onto one foot and slightly bend the knee of the supporting leg for stability. Let's say you are standing on your right foot for this example.

3. **Engage your core** muscles and keep your back straight.

4. **Start to hinge at the hips,** lowering your torso toward the floor while simultaneously extending your left leg behind you. Your left foot should be flexed, and your toes can lightly touch the wall for balance.

5. **As you hinge forward**, extend your arms in front of you, keeping them in line with your body. Your torso and left leg should form a straight line, parallel to the floor.

6. **Maintain a slight bend** in your right knee to avoid locking it out, and keep your hips square to the ground.

7. **Pause for a moment in this position**, then, engaging your glutes and hamstrings, return to the starting position by bringing your torso upright and lowering your left leg back to the floor.

8. **Perform the desired number of repetitions on one leg**, and then switch to the other leg.

9. **Remember to keep your movements controlled,** and focus on keeping your balance throughout the exercise.

This exercise can be challenging, so it's advisable to start with a lighter set and gradually increase the intensity as you get more comfortable. It's also important to keep your back straight and core engaged throughout the movement to avoid any strain on the lower back.

Wall Hamstring Stretch

The Wall Hamstring Stretch is an excellent exercise for stretching the muscles in the back of your thigh, which can help to improve flexibility and reduce the risk of injury. Here's how to do it:

1. **Position Yourself:** Sit down on the floor with your legs extended, and scoot your buttocks all the way against the wall.

2. **Lie Down:** Carefully lie down on your back, and place your legs straight up against the wall. Your body should be in an "L" shape.

3. **Stretch One Leg:** Keep one leg against the wall, and slowly lower the other leg down to the floor, keeping it straight.

4. **Hold the Stretch:** As your leg is lowering, you will begin to feel a stretch in the hamstring of the leg that is up against the wall. Hold this stretch for about 20-30 seconds. Make sure not to force the leg too hard against the wall, and keep the knee slightly bent to avoid hyperextension.

5. **Switch Legs:** Slowly bring the lowered leg back up the wall and lower the other leg.

6. **Repeat:** Repeat the stretch on the other side, holding for the same amount of time.

7. **Relax and Breathe:** Make sure to breathe deeply and relax into the stretch. Avoid bouncing or forcing the stretch.

8. **Practice Regularly:** For best results, incorporate this stretch into your regular fitness routine.

This exercise is particularly beneficial for individuals who have tight hamstrings due to sitting for extended periods or engaging in activities like running or cycling. It's always a good idea to perform stretches like this one after a workout when the muscles are warm, as this can help to improve flexibility more effectively.

Wall Calf Stretch

The Wall Hamstring Stretch is an excellent exercise for stretching the muscles in the back of your thigh, which can help to improve flexibility and reduce the risk of injury. Here's how to do it:

1. **Find a Wall:** First, find a wall with enough space for you to lie down on the floor.

2. **Position Yourself:** Sit down on the floor with your legs extended, and scoot your buttocks all the way against the wall.

3. **Lie Down:** Carefully lie down on your back, and place your legs straight up against the wall. Your body should be in an "L" shape.

4. **Stretch One Leg:** Keep one leg against the wall, and slowly lower the other leg down to the floor, keeping it straight.

5. **Hold the Stretch:** As your leg is lowering, you will begin to feel a stretch in the hamstring of the leg that is up against the wall. Hold this stretch for about 20-30 seconds. Make sure not to force the leg too hard against the wall, and keep the knee slightly bent to avoid hyperextension.

6. **Switch Legs:** Slowly bring the lowered leg back up the wall and lower the other leg.

7. **Repeat:** Repeat the stretch on the other side, holding for the same amount of time.

8. **Relax and Breathe:** Make sure to breathe deeply and relax into the stretch. Avoid bouncing or forcing the stretch.

9. **Practice Regularly:** For best results, incorporate this stretch into your regular fitness routine.

This exercise is particularly beneficial for individuals who have tight hamstrings due to sitting for extended periods or engaging in activities like running or cycling. It's always a good idea to perform stretches like this one after a workout when the muscles are warm, as this can help to improve flexibility more effectively.

Wall Superman

The Wall Superman exercise is a great activity for strengthening your core and improving your posture. Here's how you do it:

1. **Position Yourself:** Stand facing the wall, approximately an arm's length away. Your feet should be hip-width apart.

2. **Initial Movement:** Extend your arms above your head and place your palms against the wall, keeping your fingers spread wide. This is your starting position.

3. **Engage Your Core:** Tighten your core and keep your spine neutral. Your body should form a straight line from your head to your heels.

4. **Extend One Leg and the Opposite Arm:** Lift your right leg off the ground and extend it behind you as you simultaneously slide your left hand up the wall as far as comfortably possible.

5. **Hold the Position:** Hold this 'superman' pose for a few seconds, ensuring your body stays aligned and your core engaged.

6. **Return to the Starting Position:** Slowly lower your right leg and slide your left hand back down to the starting position.

7. **Repeat on the Other Side:** Now, extend your left leg behind you and slide your right hand up the wall.

8. **Complete the Set:** Continue alternating sides for the desired number of repetitions.

Remember to keep your movements smooth and controlled, and ensure your core remains engaged throughout the exercise. The Wall Superman is a great way to work on your balance and stability while also strengthening your core, which can help improve overall body function and performance in other physical activities.

Wall Tricep Dips

The Wall Tricep Dips exercise is an effective way to target your triceps, shoulders, and chest muscles. Here's how to perform it:

1. **Position Yourself:** Stand with your back to the wall and step about two feet away from it. Place your palms flat on the wall behind you at shoulder width apart, with fingers pointing down.

2. **Initial Position:** Bend your knees and lower your body towards the floor. Your arms should be at a 90-degree angle and your back should remain close to the wall. This is your starting position.

3. **Perform the Dip:** Push your body up by straightening your arms, lifting your body away from the floor. Ensure that your elbows don't lock out at the top of the movement, and maintain a slight bend to prevent strain.

4. **Lower Your Body:** Slowly lower yourself back down to the starting position by bending your elbows and allowing your body to move towards the floor again.

5. **Repeat the Movement:** Continue performing these dips for the desired number of repetitions.

Ensure your movements are slow and controlled, and remember to engage your core throughout the exercise. Wall Tricep Dips are an excellent way to target the upper body and can be done virtually anywhere there's a sturdy wall. Always make sure you're using proper form to prevent injury.

Wall High Knees

The Wall High Knees exercise is an excellent way to work your core and lower body while also increasing your heart rate. Here's how to do it:

1. **Position Yourself:** Stand facing the wall with your feet hip-width apart and your arms by your sides.

2. **Initial Position:** Lift your hands and place them flat on the wall in front of you at chest height. This is your starting position.

3. **Perform the Exercise:** Begin to march in place, lifting your knees up towards your chest as high as possible. As you lift each knee, engage your core and maintain an upright posture.

4. **Increase the Pace:** As you become more comfortable with the movement, you can increase your speed, turning the march into a high-speed knee lift or even a jog in place.

5. **Keep Going:** Continue the movement for your desired amount of time or repetitions.

Remember to keep your abdominal muscles engaged throughout the exercise to support your spine and enhance the workout for your core. The Wall High Knees exercise is a good way to add a cardiovascular element to your workout while working your core and lower body muscles. As always, ensure your movements are controlled and consider warming up before starting the exercise to prevent injury.

Wall Dead Bug

The Wall Dead Bug exercise is a fantastic core-strengthening movement that also engages your deep abdominal muscles and helps improve stability. Here's how to do it:

1. **Starting Position:** Lie on your back on a mat or soft surface. Bring your legs up so that your knees are bent at a 90-degree angle, and your thighs are perpendicular to the ground. Your arms should be raised towards the ceiling.

2. **Engage Your Core:** Press your lower back into the ground to engage your core muscles. This is crucial for the effectiveness of the exercise.

3. **Arm Placement:** Extend your arms and place your palms against the wall above your head.

4. **Movement:** Slowly lower your right arm and left leg towards the ground while keeping your lower back pressed to the floor and your left arm and right leg still. Your right hand should move upward on the wall as your left foot moves toward the ground.

5. **Return to Starting Position:** Bring your arm and leg back to the starting position while maintaining your core engagement.

6. **Alternate Sides:** Repeat the movement with the opposite arm and leg (left arm and right leg).

7. **Sets and Repetitions:** Continue alternating sides for the desired number of repetitions or for a set amount of time.

Remember to keep the movements slow and controlled, and ensure that your lower back remains in contact with the ground throughout the exercise. This will help you engage the right muscles and avoid straining your back. The Wall Dead Bug exercise is excellent for improving core stability and strength, which is beneficial for overall posture and preventing back pain..

Wall Windshield Wipers

The Wall Windshield Wipers exercise is a great way to engage your core and improve flexibility in your hips. Here's how to do it:

1. **Starting Position:** Lie on your back on a mat or soft surface, and scoot your hips close to the wall. Extend your legs up against the wall so they're straight and your body forms a 90-degree angle. Extend your arms out to the sides for support.

2. **Engage Your Core:** Tighten your abdominal muscles to help maintain control throughout the exercise.

3. **Movement:** Slowly lower both legs to one side, keeping them together and trying to keep your hips on the floor. Try to lower your legs as close to the ground as you can without discomfort or losing control.

4. **Return to Starting Position:** Slowly lift your legs back up to the center.

5. **Alternate Sides:** Repeat the movement on the other side.

6. **Sets and Repetitions:** Continue alternating sides for the desired number of repetitions or for a set amount of time.

As with all exercises, ensure that your movements are slow and controlled. This exercise is not about speed, but about the range of motion and control. The Wall Windshield Wipers exercise is excellent for targeting your obliques, abs, and hip flexors, and also helps increase flexibility in your lower body.

Wall Side Leg Lifts

The Wall Side Leg Lifts exercise is an effective way to engage your core and tone your outer thighs and hips. Here's how to do it:

1. **Find a Wall:** Choose a clear wall space that's free of obstructions.

2. **Starting Position:** Stand sideways next to the wall, with the side you're going to work facing away from the wall. Place your hand closest to the wall on the wall for balance. Stand tall and engage your core. Your feet should be hip-width apart.

3. **Movement:** Slowly lift your outer leg to the side as high as you can while keeping your leg straight. Ensure that you're keeping your torso upright and not leaning to the side.

4. **Return to Starting Position:** Slowly lower your leg back down to the starting position in a controlled movement.

5. **Repeat:** Perform the desired number of repetitions on one side before switching to the other side.

6. **Sets and Repetitions:** Repeat for the desired number of sets.

Remember to keep your movements slow and controlled, and avoid leaning your torso to the side as you lift your leg. This exercise targets your hip abductors, which include your gluteus medius and minimus, and can help improve balance and stability.

Wall Clamshells

The Wall Clamshells exercise is a fantastic way to engage your glutes, especially the gluteus medius, and the muscles in your outer thigh. Here's how to do it:

1. **Starting Position:** Lie on your side with your back against the wall. Bend your knees and hips to a 90-degree angle, and make sure your feet are in line with your glutes and resting against the wall.

2. **Movement:** Keeping your feet together and against the wall, slowly open your top knee as high as you can, like a clamshell opening. Make sure to keep your hips steady and avoid rocking back as you lift your knee.

3. **Return to Starting Position:** Slowly lower your knee back to the starting position, making sure to maintain control during the movement.

4. **Repeat:** Perform the desired number of repetitions on one side before switching to the other side.

5. **Sets and Repetitions:** Repeat for the desired number of sets.

Remember to keep your core engaged and your back flat against the wall throughout the exercise. This exercise is excellent for strengthening your hip abductors, which can help improve stability and prevent hip, knee, and ankle injuries.

Wall Arm Slides

The Wall Arm Slides exercise is an excellent way to work on your shoulder mobility and upper back strength. Here's how to do it:

1. **Starting Position:** Stand with your back against the wall. Your feet should be hip-width apart, a few inches away from the wall. Place your arms up against the wall in a "W" position, with your elbows and wrists touching the wall.

2. **Movement:** Slowly slide your arms up the wall into a "Y" position, keeping your wrists and elbows in contact with the wall as much as possible.

3. **Return to Starting Position:** Slowly slide your arms back down to the "W" position.

4. **Repeat:** Perform the desired number of repetitions.

5. **Sets and Repetitions:** Repeat for the desired number of sets.

The goal of this exercise is to keep as much of your arms and back in contact with the wall as possible, which can be challenging if you have tight shoulders or a stiff upper back. This exercise can help improve your posture, shoulder range of motion, and upper body strength. Remember to keep your movements slow and controlled, and don't push to the point of pain. If you have any shoulder issues, please consult a physical therapist or trainer before attempting this exercise.

Wall Bicycle Crunches

The Wall Bicycle Crunches exercise is a variation of the traditional bicycle crunches, using the wall as a form of resistance to engage your core more intensely. Here's how to do it:

1. **Starting Position:** Lie down on your back on the floor, with your legs up against the wall. Your hips should be close to the wall, and your legs should be straight. Place your hands lightly on the sides of your head, with your elbows wide.

2. **Movement:** Simultaneously, lift your head, neck, and shoulders off the ground, and bring your right elbow towards your left knee while you extend your right leg out away from the wall, as if you're pedaling a bicycle.

3. **Switch Sides:** Now do the opposite, bringing your left elbow towards your right knee while extending your left leg.

4. **Repeat:** Continue alternating sides in a smooth, pedaling motion for the desired number of repetitions.

5. **Sets and Repetitions:** Repeat for the desired number of sets.

This exercise targets the abs, obliques, hip flexors, and lower back muscles. Remember to keep your movements controlled, and don't pull on your neck with your hands. Breathe out when you twist, and in when you return to the starting position. If you have any lower back or neck issues, please consult a physical therapist or trainer before attempting this exercise.

Wall Marching

Wall Marching is a simple but effective exercise that falls under Wall Pilates. Here's how you can do it:

1. **Position yourself:** Stand with your back against a wall. Your feet should be hip-width apart and approximately two feet away from the wall. Your head, shoulders, and buttocks should be touching the wall.

2. **Start the march:** Slowly raise one knee up towards your chest as high as you comfortably can, without your back losing contact with the wall. As you raise your knee, maintain control and stability through your core. This is not about speed but about control and precision.

3. **Lower and switch:** Lower the raised foot back down to the floor, maintaining control. Then, repeat with the other leg. This is one repetition.

4. **Repeat:** Continue to alternate legs for a set number of repetitions or for a certain amount of time.

Wall Marching is great for engaging the core, working the hip flexors, and improving balance and coordination. It's important to keep your core engaged throughout the exercise to maintain your alignment and stability. This move can be a good warm-up exercise or included as part of a larger Pilates routine.

Wall Reverse Lunges

The Wall Reverse Lunges exercise is another effective move in Wall Pilates. It's a great way to work on your lower body strength, balance, and flexibility. Here's how you can do it:

1. **Position yourself:** Stand about two feet away from a wall, facing away from it. Your feet should be hip-width apart.

2. **Start the movement:** Step one foot backwards towards the wall and lower your body into a lunge position. Your front knee should be bent at a 90-degree angle, and your back knee should be just above the floor. The heel of your back foot should be raised.

3. **Use the wall:** Reach back with your hands and touch the wall for balance. Press your palms flat against the wall and use it to help you maintain your balance and alignment.

4. **Return to the start:** Push off your front foot, bringing your back foot forward to meet it, and stand up straight again. This completes one repetition.

5. **Repeat:** Repeat the movement with the other leg. Continue to alternate legs for a set number of repetitions or for a certain amount of time.

The Wall Reverse Lunges exercise helps to strengthen your quadriceps, glutes, and hamstrings, and it also challenges your balance and core stability. Remember, as with all Pilates exercises, it's important to focus on control, precision, and form.

Wall Toe Touches

Wall Toe Touches is another exercise in Wall Pilates that is great for improving your flexibility and balance while also strengthening your core. Here's how you can do it:

1. **Position yourself:** Stand facing the wall with your feet hip-width apart. Your toes should be touching the wall.

2. **Raise your leg**: Slowly lift one leg up and reach your toes up the wall as high as you comfortably can. Try to keep your leg as straight as possible, but it's okay if you need to bend your knee slightly.

3. **Engage your core:** As you lift your leg, keep your core engaged and maintain a straight posture. Your back should remain straight, and your gaze should be forward.

4. **Touch and lower:** Touch the wall with your toes, then slowly lower your leg back down.

5. **Repeat:** Repeat the exercise with your other leg. This is one repetition. Continue to alternate legs for a set number of repetitions or for a specific amount of time.

Wall Toe Touches is a great exercise for stretching and strengthening your hamstrings and improving your balance. Remember, Pilates is about control and precision, not speed. So focus on maintaining good form and control throughout the movement.

Wall Quadruped Limb Raises

The Wall Quadruped Limb Raises is a Wall Pilates exercise that is great for core stability, balance, and coordination. It also targets the muscles of the back, shoulders, and hips. Here's how you can do it:

1. **Position yourself:** Start by getting into a quadruped (all fours) position with your back against the wall. Your hands should be directly under your shoulders and your knees directly under your hips. The tops of your feet and your shins should be pressed against the wall.

2. **Raise your arm:** Extend one arm straight out in front of you, keeping it level with your body. Make sure to keep your neck in line with your spine and avoid any twisting or turning of your body.

3. **Raise your leg:** At the same time as you are raising your arm, extend the opposite leg out behind you against the wall. Your leg should also be level with your body and your foot flexed, pressing against the wall.

4. **Hold and lower:** Hold this position for a moment, ensuring your core is engaged and your body is in a straight line from your extended hand to your extended foot. Then, lower your hand and knee back to the starting position.

5. **Repeat:** Repeat this process with the opposite arm and leg. This is one repetition. Continue to alternate sides for a set number of repetitions or for a specific amount of time.

The Wall Quadruped Limb Raises can be quite challenging as it requires balance, coordination, and strength. Remember, as with all Pilates exercises, it's important to maintain control and precision throughout the movement.

CHAPTER 5

Building a Pilates Routine

Developing a Routine

Let's imagine a world where a wall isn't just a wall. It's a supportive partner, a stability guide, a quiet instructor nudging us towards perfect alignment and precision. This is the world of Wall Pilates, where the humble wall transforms into a powerful tool for fitness and wellbeing. As we embark on this journey together, remember: each breath, each movement, each moment of stillness is an opportunity for growth.

In Wall Pilates, the wall serves as a constant, providing feedback to our bodies as we move through our routine. It's a tangible reminder of our form, our alignment, and our posture. As we navigate through our exercises, the wall acts as a mirror, reflecting back to us the accuracy of our movements, the depth of our stretches, and the stability of our poses.

When building a Wall Pilates routine, it's essential to start with a warm-up to prepare our bodies for the journey ahead. An effective warm-up can include exercises like Wall Marching, which engages the core, improves balance, and heightens body awareness. As you march in place, your back flush against the wall, take this time to connect with your breath. Feel the rhythm of your steps syncing with your inhalations and exhalations. It's not just about preparing the body, but also about grounding the mind, creating a focused, meditative state that will carry us through our workout.

Once the body is warmed up and ready, we can begin to explore the strength-building aspects of Wall Pilates. Wall Reverse Lunges, for instance, are a fantastic way to strengthen the lower body while challenging your balance. As you step back into a lunge, pressing your palms against the wall for support, imagine the energy flowing from your grounded foot, up through your engaged core, and out through the crown of your head. Each lunge is not just a physical movement, but a potent reminder of our strength and resilience.

Wall Toe Touches, another essential part of our routine, provide an opportunity to enhance flexibility and work on our balance. As we lift our leg, reaching our toes up the wall, we challenge our bodies to maintain stability even as we push our flexibility limits. Picture the leg lifting as a symbol of your daily reach towards your fitness goals, ever higher and more assured.

One of the more challenging but rewarding exercises in our routine is the Wall Quadruped Limb Raises. Here, balance, strength, and coordination converge in a powerful testament to the capabilities of our bodies. Each time we extend an arm and the opposite leg, pressing against the wall's resistance, we're not just building muscle; we're cultivating determination and discipline, qualities that extend beyond the walls of our workout space.

Ending our routine with a cool-down is just as crucial as the warm-up. Slow, controlled movements, perhaps a repeat of our Wall Marching exercise, allow our bodies to gradually return to a state of rest. As we cool down, it's a chance to reflect on our progress, to celebrate our accomplishments, and to set intentions for our next session.

This is the beauty of Wall Pilates. It's more than a series of exercises or a routine of movements. It's a journey of discovery, a pathway to understanding our bodies better, to appreciating our inherent strength, and to celebrating our continual growth. So, the next time you see a wall, see beyond the bricks and paint. See a partner, a guide, a catalyst for change. Because in the world of Wall Pilates, a wall is never just a wall.

Progressing in Your Practice

As we delve deeper into the art of Wall Pilates, it's important to remember that progress isn't always measured in sweat drops or muscle ache. It's found in the subtle shifts in our bodies—the grace of a well-executed Wall March, the ease of a Wall Reverse Lunge, or the control of a Wall Quadruped Limb Raise. Each time we show up on our mats, we're making progress. Each breath, each movement, each session is a step forward on our journey to becoming stronger, healthier, and more in tune with our bodies.

One of the first signs of progress in Wall Pilates is a deeper understanding of our body's alignment. The wall is a brilliant teacher in this regard, its unyielding surface revealing the smallest shifts, the tiniest deviations. As we practice, we become more aware of these subtleties. We learn to adjust, to correct, and to find the alignment that is both challenging and sustainable. The moment when our bodies remember this alignment without the wall's feedback is a milestone worth celebrating.

Next, we start to notice an improvement in our balance and stability. Exercises like the Wall Toe Touches and Wall Quadruped Limb Raises, which seemed so daunting at first, begin to feel more achievable. Our bodies grow more confident in their ability to sustain these poses, to find the delicate equilibrium between effort and ease. We start to move with more grace and fluidity, not just on the mat but in our daily lives.

As we continue our journey with Wall Pilates, our strength and flexibility start to blossom. We find ourselves sinking deeper into our Wall Reverse Lunges, reaching higher in our Wall Toe Touches, holding our Wall Quadruped Limb Raises for just a few moments longer. We feel a newfound power in our muscles, a suppleness in our joints, a resilience in our bodies that wasn't there before.

But perhaps the most profound progress we make in Wall Pilates is not physical, but mental. As we commit to our practice, as we show up day after day, we cultivate a discipline, a dedication, a resolve that seeps into every corner of our lives. We learn to meet challenges with calmness, to embrace discomfort as a path to growth, to see every stumble not as a failure but as an opportunity to learn, to adapt, to rise stronger.

And yet, progress in Wall Pilates isn't a linear path. There will be days when our bodies feel heavy, our movements clumsy. There will be sessions when we struggle to find our balance, our focus, our rhythm. But that's okay. That's part of the journey. What matters is that we keep showing up, keep breathing, keep moving. Because it's in these moments of struggle that we often make the most significant strides.

Progress in Wall Pilates is a dance between patience and perseverance, between accepting our bodies as they are and challenging them to be more. It's about celebrating the small victories, the incremental improvements, the quiet transformations. It's about learning to listen to our bodies, to honor their wisdom, to trust their innate capacity for growth and healing.

So, keep showing up. Keep breathing. Keep moving. Trust in the journey, trust in your body, trust in the transformative power of Wall Pilates. Because every breath, every movement, every moment of stillness is a step towards progress, a step towards a stronger, healthier, more vibrant you. And that's a journey worth embarking on.

Conclusion: Incorporating Pilates into Your Daily Life

As we come to the end of our exploration into the world of Wall Pilates, it's important to remember that the principles and lessons we've learned extend far beyond the mat or the wall. Pilates isn't just a workout—it's a way of life. It's a method of moving, breathing, and being that can enrich our daily lives in countless ways.

Think of Wall Pilates as a conversation between you and your body. It's a dialogue that happens not just during your practice, but all day, every day. When you're sitting at your desk, are your shoulders relaxed and down, your spine long and tall? When you're walking or standing, are you mindful of your alignment, your posture, your breath? These are the questions that Pilates invites us to ask, the mindfulness that Pilates nurtures in us.

Incorporating Pilates into your daily life is about embracing this mindfulness. It's about being present in your body, in your breath, in your movements. It's about noticing the subtleties—the tension in your neck, the slouch in your shoulders, the clench in your jaw—and making conscious choices to move and live more healthily. This awareness, this presence, is the first step in transforming not just your body, but your life.

The beauty of Wall Pilates is that it's accessible to everyone, anywhere, anytime. You don't need a fancy studio or expensive equipment. All you need is a wall and a willingness to explore, to move, to grow. This accessibility makes it easy to incorporate Pilates into your daily routine. You could start your day with a gentle Wall March to wake up your body, take a midday Wall Quadruped Limb Raise break to energize and focus your mind, or wind down with some Wall Toe Touches in the evening to stretch and relax.

But more than the physical exercises, incorporating Pilates into your life is about embodying its core principles. The principles of centering, concentration, control, precision, breath, and flow are not just guidelines for your Pilates practice, they're guidelines for life. When faced with a challenge, can you stay centered and focused? Can you maintain control and precision under pressure? Can you flow with the changes, breathe through the difficulties?

Life, like Pilates, is a balance of strength and flexibility, of effort and ease, of holding on and letting go. The lessons we learn on the mat or against the wall—of resilience, of patience, of self-care—are lessons that can guide us through the ups and downs of life.

So, as you step off the mat, as you walk away from the wall, carry these lessons with you. Carry the strength and flexibility, the balance and stability, the discipline and dedication. Carry the mindfulness, the presence, the connection to your body. Because the true power of Pilates lies not in the exercises we do, but in the way those exercises change us, shape us, inspire us to live healthier, happier, more balanced lives.

Incorporating Pilates into your daily life is a journey, a process, an adventure. It's an invitation to move with grace, to live with intention, to be fully present in your body. It's an opportunity to transform not just your workout routine, but your life. So, embrace it. Explore it. Enjoy it. Because the world of Pilates is not just about the destination, it's about the journey—the journey towards a stronger, healthier, more vibrant you. And that's a journey worth taking.

BOOK 2

Wall Pilates for Beginners

Introduction: Starting Your Pilates Journey

Embarking on the journey of Wall Pilates as a beginner can feel like stepping into a new world. The language is different, the movements are unfamiliar, and the principles might seem complex. Yet, this journey is one of the most rewarding ones you can take for your body and mind. Understanding the basics of Wall Pilates is like unlocking a door to a new understanding of strength, flexibility, and overall wellness.

At its core, Wall Pilates is about mindful movement. It's about understanding how your body works, and using that understanding to move in ways that are efficient, balanced, and harmonious. Each exercise, each pose, each breath is an opportunity to connect with your body, to strengthen it, to stretch it, to challenge it in new and exciting ways.

The wall plays a crucial role in this journey. It provides a tangible, physical point of reference for your body. It helps you understand alignment and positioning, giving you a framework within which to move. As a beginner, the wall is your guide, your teacher, your partner in this exploration of movement and strength.

As a beginner, it's important to approach Wall Pilates with an open mind and a patient heart. It might take time to understand the principles, to learn the exercises, to build the strength and flexibility. But every step you take, every breath you breathe, every movement you make is progress. It's a step towards a stronger, healthier, more vibrant you.

Wall Pilates is more than a workout. It's a way of life, a method of moving and being that can transform your body, your health, and your sense of wellbeing. It's a journey of discovery, of growth, of transformation. As a beginner, you're at the start of this journey. Ahead of you lies the path to strength, to flexibility, to balance. It's a path that's challenging, rewarding, and profoundly empowering.

Remember, every journey starts with a single step. In Wall Pilates, that first step is understanding the basics, embracing the principles, and being open to the possibilities. As you start this journey, remember to be patient with yourself, to listen to your body, and to enjoy the process. After all, Wall Pilates is not just about the destination - it's about the journey. The journey of movement, of strength, of self-discovery. And it's a journey that's worth every step.

CHAPTER 1

Understanding the Basics of Pilates

The Fundamentals of Pilates

Pilates, a system of exercises designed to improve physical strength, flexibility, posture, and mental awareness, has evolved over the years, adapting to modern fitness trends. One such variant, Wall Pilates, stands as a testament to the versatility and enduring relevance of this fitness system. Wall Pilates, as the name suggests, incorporates the use of a wall as a prop to add extra leverage and support to traditional Pilates exercises, opening up a world of new possibilities.

The core of Wall Pilates is its reliance on the wall for stability, allowing you to engage your muscles in unique ways. It's a perfect blend of flexibility, strength, and control, appealing to fitness enthusiasts and professionals alike. The wall serves as a steady, unyielding surface, providing extra support that can help you delve deeper into your stretches and poses, targeting areas that might otherwise be difficult to reach.

Starting with Wall Pilates doesn't require any special equipment. All you need is yourself, a mat, and a sturdy wall surface. This simplicity makes it an accessible form of exercise for anyone, regardless of their fitness level or experience with Pilates. It's also highly adaptable, with exercises ranging from the simple to the complex, allowing you to adjust the intensity to suit your needs and abilities.

One of the first exercises beginners can try is the Glute Bridge. This exercise is perfect for targeting your glutes and hamstrings. By planting your feet hip-width apart on the wall and lifting your hips up and down, you can create a powerful workout for your lower body. Adding a pause and squeeze at the top of the movement or incorporating a resistance band can increase the challenge as you progress.

The Wall Push-Up is another exercise that can be performed using the wall. This movement targets your arms and back, with the challenge level adjustable by the distance of your feet from the wall. The action of pressing your hands into the wall and lowering your body towards it engages your muscles in a new and interesting way, adding variety to your regular push-up routine.

Wall Sits are another excellent exercise that can help improve your posture, engage your core, and work your legs. This exercise requires you to lean against the wall, slide down until your knees are bent at about 90 degrees, and hold the position. It's a static exercise that puts your lower body and core to work, helping you build strength and endurance.

Wall Pilates also offers a unique twist on traditional Pilates exercises like the Hundred. In Wall Hundred, you lie on your back at a distance where your feet just touch the wall. You then lift your arms and shoulders off the mat, reach towards the wall, and begin to pump your arms up and down. This exercise works your core in a different way, providing a challenging workout for your abdominal muscles.

Wall Bicycle Crunches are another dynamic exercise that adds a new dimension to your ab workout. By placing your feet on the wall and performing the bicycle motion, you target your abs from different angles, providing a comprehensive workout for your core.

Adding to the variety of exercises in Wall Pilates, Wall Lunges offer a way to work your legs while also engaging your core. This exercise requires you to stand with the side of your body near the wall, step your inner leg back, and lower into a lunge. The wall provides added support and balance, allowing you to focus on the movement and engage the right muscles.

Exercises like Leg Lifts and Side Kicks add a new layer of complexity to Wall Pilates. They require you to maintain a steady position while performing dynamic movements, enhancing your balance and coordination. The wall provides a steady surface to lean on, allowing you to focus on the movement and engage your muscles effectively.

Lastly, the Roll Down is an exercise that allows you to stretch your back and rejuvenate your body. By standing with your shoulders against the wall and dropping your upper body into a forward fold, you can release tension and stretch your muscles, providing a soothing end to your Wall Pilates session.

In summary, Wall Pilates provides a versatile, accessible, and effective way to engage your muscles, enhance your flexibility, and improve your posture. Whether you're new to Pilates or a seasoned pro looking for a new challenge, Wall Pilates offers an exciting way to revamp your workout routine.

Common Pilates Terms

Embarking on your Pilates journey is like stepping into a new world, one filled with its own language. It's a world where your body and mind unite, leading you to discover strength, flexibility, and balance you never knew you had. One of the first steps is understanding the common Pilates terms, which will enhance your workouts, whether they're traditional Pilates sessions or trending Wall Pilates exercises.

When we speak about Pilates, the conversation often begins with the mention of 'Abduction' and 'Adduction.' The term Abduction refers to your shoulder blades moving away from the spine, a movement also known as protraction[1]. In contrast, Adduction implies your shoulder blades moving towards the spine, similarly known as retraction[1]. These terms are fundamental as they describe the basic movements of our shoulder blades, a key part of numerous Pilates exercises.

Another term you'll frequently encounter is 'C-curve.' It refers to an even rounding of your spine, signifying spine flexion[1]. When we talk about muscle actions, we often discuss 'Concentric Muscle Contraction,' which signifies the shortening of the muscle while it's working, and 'Eccentric Muscle Action,' where the muscle is lengthening while it's working[1]. These terms help us understand how our muscles function during different exercises.

Moreover, 'Dorsiflexion' is a term that represents a flexed foot, reaching away with the heel[1]. It's a common action in various Pilates exercises, especially those targeting the lower body.

When it comes to movements involving the hip, there are several terms to understand. 'Hip Abduction' means the thigh moving away from the midline of the body, while 'Hip Adduction' refers to the thigh moving towards the midline of the body[1]. 'Hip Extension' is the backward movement of the thigh, and 'Hip Flexion' signifies when the thigh bone lifts forward[1]. In addition to these, 'Hip Lateral Rotation' refers to the thigh rotating away from the midline, and 'Hip Medial Rotation' indicates the thigh rotating toward the midline[1]. These terms are crucial for understanding the correct alignment and movement of the body during Pilates exercises.

'Isometric Muscle Action' is another term that is often used in Pilates. It refers to the muscle not changing in length while it's working1. This form of muscle contraction plays a significant role in many Pilates exercises, particularly those focusing on maintaining and improving posture and stability.

Knee movements also have specific terms in Pilates. 'Knee Extension' occurs when the leg is straightened, while 'Knee Flexion' refers to bending the knee, making the angle formed by the back of the leg and thigh smaller1. Understanding these terms helps ensure that the exercises are done correctly to maximize benefits and minimize the risk of injury.

In the world of Pilates, you'll also hear about 'Lateral Flexion,' which means side bending, and 'Plantar Flexion,' which refers to a pointed foot. 'Pronation' signifies when the foot rolls inward, putting more pressure on the arch side of the foot, while 'Supination' refers to when the foot rolls outward, putting more pressure on the outside edge of the foot1. Lastly, 'Supine' is a term used to describe lying on your back.

Understanding foot movements is also crucial in Pilates. The terms "pronation" and "supination" are used to describe the inward and outward rolling of the foot, respectively. Pronation puts more pressure on the arch side of the foot, while supination puts more pressure on the outer edge.

Finally, the term "supine" is used to indicate a position where you're lying on your back. This position is frequently used in Pilates exercises that target the core and lower body muscles.

As we delve deeper into the Pilates world, we encounter a wide range of specialized terms that are crucial for understanding and performing the exercises correctly. Each term carries its own significance and contributes to the overall effectiveness and richness of the practice.

CHAPTER 2

Essential Pilates Exercises for Beginners

Welcome, dear reader, to the transformative world of wall Pilates. A world that blends the strength-building principles of Pilates with the accessibility of a wall, creating a seamless blend of movement and stability. This guide will gently lead you into this unique practice, offering a beginner-friendly journey to core strengthening, flexibility enhancement, and overall well-being.

Let's begin with an invitation to visualize your space. Wall Pilates does not require a studio or specialized equipment. All you need is yourself, a mat for comfort, and a sturdy wall. This simplicity is the beauty of wall Pilates, making it an exercise form accessible to all, regardless of location or resources.

The first step is always the most critical, and in wall Pilates, we begin with an exercise known as glute bridges. This is a fantastic way to engage your lower body while simultaneously introducing the concept of using a wall as a support tool. Plant your feet hip-width apart on the wall, keep your arms and neck neutral on your mat, lift your hips up, then lower them back down. The wall not only provides stability but also helps you to focus on your glutes, the powerhouse muscles that support our daily movements.

Flowing from this exercise, we move into wall push-ups. This workout targets your arms and back, forming a strong foundation for the upper body. Press your hands into the wall, shoulder-distance apart, step your feet back, then lower yourself towards the wall. Here, the wall acts as a supportive partner, guiding your movements and allowing you to explore your strength in a safe and controlled environment.

Next, we transition into wall sits. This exercise is a brilliant way to improve posture and engage your core while working on your legs. With your back against a wall, slide down until your knees are bent about 90 degrees. The wall gives you feedback on your posture and alignment, helping you maintain the correct form and engage the right muscles.

The journey continues with wall 100s, a core workout that not only strengthens your middle but also introduces the concept of rhythm and breath in Pilates. Lie on your back, reach your arms towards the wall, and begin to pump your arms up and down. The wall serves as a reference point, guiding your movements and adding a layer of focus to your workout.

From here, we delve into wall bicycle crunches. In this exercise, the wall acts as a unique prop, adding a new dimension to the traditional crunch movement. Place your feet up on the wall and crunch, bringing an opposite elbow to an opposite knee. This gives you an opportunity to engage with your core in a new and challenging way, all under the secure support of the wall.

The wall lunges are up next. Stand with the side of your body near the wall, keeping one hand on the wall for support. Step your inner leg back, lower straight down into a lunge, then return your leg to start. The wall here acts as a stabilizing force, allowing you to focus on the lunge and the strength-building potential of this movement.

Moving on, we delve into leg lifts. Standing in the center of your mat, reach forward with both hands to press into the wall. Lift one leg back behind you, focusing on squeezing your glute with each rep. The wall allows you to maintain balance, enabling you to focus on the precision and control of the movement.

Sidekicks, a staple in traditional Pilates, take on a new dimension with the wall. Prop yourself up on a diagonal as you lean into the wall and lift your leg out to the side. The wall supports you, allowing you to concentrate on maintaining your body alignment and executing the kicks accurately.

Next, we move to leg circles. Stand with your feet hip-distance apart and about four inches in front of the wall. Press your hips and palms into the wall. Lift one leg in front of you and draw small circles with your toes. The wall provides a secure base that supports your body as you challenge your stability and mobility with this exercise.

Finally, we come to an end with an exercise called roll downs. This workout aims to stretch your back and awaken your body. Stand with your shoulders against the wall and slowly drop your upper body into a forward fold, then roll back up. The wall serves as a tactile reminder to maintain alignment, ensuring you engage the correct muscles and maximize the benefits of this stretch.

As you journey through these exercises, remember that the wall is not merely a prop; it is a partner in your Pilates practice. It provides support when needed, offers resistance when required, and gives you the confidence to explore your strength and flexibility limits. You'll find the wall a silent teacher, guiding you, correcting you, and challenging you, ultimately leading you to a more mindful and present sense of self.

Remember, everybody is unique, and so is every Pilates practice. What works for one might not work for another. Listen to your body and adapt the exercises to your needs. The wall is there to support you, so lean on it, trust it, and let it guide you towards a stronger, more flexible, and healthier version of yourself.

As you embark on this journey of wall Pilates, be patient with yourself. Progress may be slow, but it will be steady. The wall will be there, steadfast and supportive, ready to catch you when you stumble and push you when you're ready to grow. Embrace the process, and remember that each day you show up on your mat is a step towards a healthier, stronger you.

In the world of wall Pilates, every movement is a dialogue between you, your body, and the wall. It's about finding balance, pushing limits, and embracing the beauty of movement. So, step onto your mat, press your palms against the wall, and let the transformative journey of wall Pilates begin. Welcome to the wonderful world of wall Pilates, where strength, flexibility, and mindfulness unite to create a harmonious symphony of movement and health.

Here's a simple wall Pilates workout routine for beginners for each day of the week.

Day	Exercises
Monday	1. Wall Push-Ups (2 sets of 10 reps) 2. Wall Sits (30 seconds, 3 times)
Tuesday	1. Glute Bridges (30 seconds) 2. Wall Bicycle Crunches (3 sets of 15 reps)
Wednesday	1. Wall Lunges (60 seconds each side) 2. Wall 100s (10 rounds)
Thursday	1. Wall Push-Ups (3 sets of 10 reps) 2. Wall Sits (45 seconds, 3 times)

Friday	1. Leg Lifts (60 seconds each side)
	2. Side Kicks (3 sets of 8 reps/side)
Saturday	1. Wall Lunges (60 seconds each side)
	2. Leg Circles (5 circles each side)
Sunday	1. Roll Downs (2 sets of 10 reps)
	2. Wall Sits (60 seconds, 3 times)

Remember, it's important to warm up before starting your workout and cool down afterwards. You can do this by doing some light cardio (like marching in place) and some full body stretches. Also, listen to your body. If any of these exercises cause pain, stop doing them and consult with a healthcare professional. It's normal to feel some discomfort when starting a new workout program, but it's not normal to feel pain.

Finally, be patient with yourself. Progress may be slow, but with consistent practice, you'll start to see improvements in your strength, flexibility, and overall fitness.

CHAPTER 3

Safety Tips for Wall Pilates Beginners

Embarking on a journey into wall Pilates can be an exciting and transformative experience. But before you begin, it's crucial to understand the importance of safety to prevent injury and maximize the benefits of this fantastic workout.

First and foremost, selecting the right environment for your workout is critical. Ensure that the wall you're using for your exercises is sturdy and free of any obstructions. You wouldn't want a picture frame falling mid-workout or a slippery floor surface causing an accident. The area should be clean, spacious, and well-lit, with enough room for you to move freely.

Next, wearing appropriate attire can go a long way in ensuring safety. Opt for comfortable clothing that's not too loose, to avoid getting caught during your movements, but also not so tight that it restricts your mobility. Shoes aren't necessary for wall Pilates, but if you prefer to wear them, select a pair with good grip to prevent slips.

When starting with wall Pilates, it's essential to remember that everyone's fitness level is different. Don't be hard on yourself if you find some exercises challenging initially. Your strength, flexibility, and endurance will improve over time with consistent practice. Start slowly, understand your limits, and gradually increase the intensity of your workouts. Overexertion can lead to injuries, which will set you back in your fitness journey.

Proper form and technique are pivotal to prevent injury and reap the full benefits of wall Pilates. It's easy to get caught up in the number of reps, but it's the quality of each movement that truly matters. Every exercise should be performed with control and precision. If you're unsure about an exercise's correct form, consider seeking advice from a certified Pilates instructor or refer to reliable online resources.

In wall Pilates, many exercises require you to support your body weight, making it crucial to protect your joints, particularly your wrists and knees. Avoid locking your joints and maintain a slight bend to keep them safe. Also, remember to distribute your weight evenly across your hands or feet during exercises.

Breathing plays a crucial role in Pilates. The practice encourages mindful breathing, which helps connect your mind and body, enhance your movements, and maintain a rhythm. It also helps supply your muscles with the oxygen they need during your workout. Always breathe through your nose, fill your diaphragm, and exhale fully.

Regular breaks are necessary, especially for beginners. Listen to your body and take a break if you feel overly tired, dizzy, or experience any sharp pain. These could be signs that your body needs rest. Remember, fitness is not a race but a lifelong journey, and it's important to treat your body with respect and kindness.

Lastly, hydration is key. Even though Pilates may not seem as intense as some other forms of exercise, you're still losing fluids through sweat. Make sure to drink plenty of water before, during, and after your workout to keep your body hydrated.

In conclusion, the key to a safe and effective wall Pilates workout lies in preparation, patience, proper form, and listening to your body. Always remember that it's not about perfection, but progress. Each day you show up is a step closer to your fitness goals. So, take it slow, enjoy the process, and most importantly, have fun on your Pilates journey.

Preventing Injuries

Preventing injuries is an essential aspect of any fitness routine, and wall Pilates is no exception. The sheer joy of engaging your muscles and feeling your body gracefully move through each exercise should never be marred by the specter of injury. With a blend of mindfulness, preparation, and respect for your body, you can create a safe sanctuary for your Pilates practice.

Let's talk about the foundation of your practice - your own body. It's crucial to understand that your body is unique. It has its strengths and limitations. Sometimes, we are so enamored by the grace and flexibility of someone else's practice that we want to dive right in. But remember, Pilates is not a one-size-fits-all. Customizing your routine to fit your body's needs is not just smart, it's essential. Listen to the whispers of your body; it speaks in cues. If a particular movement feels too straining or unnatural, modify it. There's no shame in adaptation.

The core is often considered the powerhouse in Pilates. Engaging your core not only intensifies your workout but also protects your lower back. A strong core acts like a natural corset, keeping your back in alignment and preventing straining. As you press your back against the wall, visualize your abdominal muscles wrapping around your spine like a protective sheath. Embrace that power within you.

Warm-ups are like a heartfelt conversation you have with your body before you ask it to perform. It prepares your muscles and joints for the upcoming physical activity. Spend a few minutes doing gentle stretches and movements before you start with the wall exercises. This isn't just a routine; it's a ritual. A ritual that honors your body's need to prepare.

Technique in wall Pilates is like poetry in motion. Each movement should be fluid, controlled, and deliberate. Jerky or rushed movements are not just ineffective; they are dangerous. Cultivate the art of precision. Even if it means performing fewer repetitions, do them right. This is where the magic lies - in the quality of your movements.

Footwear, or the lack thereof, plays a significant role in preventing injuries. Barefoot is best as it allows for a full range of motion and a better grip. However, if you choose to wear socks, make sure they have grips on the soles. Imagine the ground as an extension of your body and move with the confidence of being connected.

Just like an artist sometimes needs guidance to perfect their art, don't hesitate to seek expert advice. A certified Pilates instructor can be an invaluable resource in guiding you through the nuances of wall Pilates. Sometimes, having an expert eye to watch over your practice can make a significant difference in preventing injuries.

Hydration is like the elixir of life. It's easy to forget to drink water, especially if you're engrossed in a series of exercises. However, muscles need hydration to function effectively. Make a conscious effort to drink water throughout your practice.

Finally, embrace patience as your ally. Progress in Pilates is slow and steady. Don't rush it. Cherish each moment, each breath, and each movement. Your body is your temple, and Pilates is a way to honor it. Be kind, be mindful, and be safe.

Listening to Your Body

Listening to your body is an art, one that requires patience, attentiveness, and empathy. It's like learning a new language, a subtle yet profound dialect that your body uses to communicate with you. In the world of wall Pilates, this dialogue between your mind and body is not just beneficial; it is crucial. It guides you through your practice, whispering the sweet spots of strength and the areas that need caution.

Understanding this language starts with awareness. Awareness of your body, its movements, the way your muscles contract and relax, the rhythm of your breath, the alignment of your spine. It is a journey of discovery. Each time you step onto the mat and press your back against the wall, you are embarking on an adventure within yourself.

Your breath is a vital tool in this exploration. It is not just a life force; it is a barometer that gauges your body's response to each movement. The ebb and flow of your breath harmonizes with the rhythm of your practice. If you find your breath becoming shallow or hurried, it's your body's way of saying that it's time to slow down or modify the movement.

Pain and discomfort are often viewed as adversaries in our fitness journey. But what if we viewed them as allies instead? Pain is your body's alarm system, signaling that something is off balance. It nudges you to pay attention. Don't silence this alarm; heed its call. If a movement causes discomfort, pause, reassess your form, and modify if necessary. Remember, there is strength in yielding.

Fatigue is another signal that your body sends out. It's like your body's way of saying, "I have done my best, now it's time to rest." Honor this need for rest. The space between your workouts, the pause, the recovery is just as important as the workouts themselves. It is in this space that your body heals, recovers, and grows stronger.

Your body also speaks to you through the language of progress. The first time you attempt a wall lunge or a wall push-up, you might feel your muscles trembling, your breath wavering. But as you stay consistent with your practice, one day, you will find yourself moving through these exercises with more ease and control. This progress, however small it may seem, is your body's way of telling you that it is getting stronger, more flexible, and more adept.

Sometimes, our mind is our greatest obstacle. We push ourselves too hard, driven by unrealistic expectations or comparisons. This is where you need to tune in and listen to your body. Your body knows its limits. It knows when to push harder and when to back off. Trust this wisdom.

Listening to your body is also about recognizing its needs off the mat. Nutrition, hydration, and rest play a significant role in how your body performs during your Pilates practice. If you feel sluggish or weak during your workouts, it could be your body's way of telling you that it needs more nourishment or rest.

In the end, listening to your body is about cultivating a relationship with yourself. It's about respect, compassion, and understanding. It's about realizing that your body is not just a vessel but a partner in your Pilates journey. So, the next time you step onto your mat, take a moment to check-in with your body. Ask it how it's feeling. And most importantly, listen. Because in its whispers, you will find the secrets to a safe, effective, and joyful Pilates practice.

CHAPTER 4

Building a Beginner's Wall Pilates Workout Routine

Embarking on your journey into the world of Wall Pilates requires an insightful understanding of not just the exercises involved but how to structure a routine that resonates with your personal fitness goals. Crafting a robust routine that promotes balanced body conditioning is the key to unlocking the full potential of this fitness regimen.

Firstly, let's address the importance of a well-structured workout routine. When we speak of Wall Pilates, or any form of fitness practice for that matter, a well-planned regimen acts as the backbone to your fitness journey. It provides direction, structure, and a measure of progress. It ensures that your workouts are balanced, catering to the overall health of your body, rather than focusing on isolated parts. A well-designed routine eliminates the risk of imbalance, where one group of muscles is overworked while another is neglected.

As you step into this new territory, remember, your routine is not a rigid framework but a flexible guide. It is a tool that will evolve with you as you advance on your path to better health and fitness. It is about finding harmony between challenge and comfort, fostering a sense of achievement, and nurturing your love for the practice.

The initial stages of your Wall Pilates routine should be centered on building a solid foundation. The aim here is to master the correct form and alignment, build endurance, and learn to effectively engage your muscles. Be patient with yourself; this stage is not about the intensity of the workout but about understanding your body and its responses.

Begin with exercises that are fundamental to Wall Pilates, such as the Glute Bridges, Wall Push-Ups, and Wall Sits. These exercises are relatively simple, making them perfect for beginners. They help in strengthening your core, improving your posture, and enhancing your balance, which are crucial for more complex exercises down the line.

The Glute Bridges, for instance, can seem deceptively simple, but when performed with the correct form, they effectively target your posterior muscles. This exercise not only helps sculpt your glutes but also aids in improving your hip mobility, which is often compromised due to prolonged sitting.

Wall Push-Ups, on the other hand, are an excellent exercise for upper body strength. They target your arms, shoulders, and back muscles. This exercise is a great starting point for beginners as it is less challenging than traditional floor push-ups but offers similar benefits.

Wall Sits are another fundamental exercise that works on your lower body strength and endurance. They challenge your quads, glutes, and hamstrings, and also engage your core. The beauty of this exercise lies in its simplicity and versatility. You can easily adjust the intensity by changing the duration of the hold.

After mastering these exercises, you can gradually introduce more complex ones into your routine like the Wall 100s, Wall Bicycle Crunches, Wall Lunges, Leg Lifts, Side Kicks, Leg Circles, and Roll Downs.

A word of caution, though - always remember to listen to your body. It is natural to feel a certain degree of discomfort when you challenge your body with new exercises, but pain is a signal that something is not right. Respect your body's limits and gradually push them as you grow stronger.

Now, onto the structure of your workout. As a beginner, aim for a 20-30 minute workout, three to four times a week. Start with a warm-up to prepare your body for the exercises ahead. This can be as simple as a brisk walk or a few minutes of light cardio. Then move on to your Wall Pilates exercises. Start with two sets of each exercise and as you grow stronger, increase the number of sets or the duration of each exercise. Always wrap up your session with a cool-down. This could be a simple stretching routine or a few minutes of deep breathing. This helps in gradually reducing your heart rate and loosens up your muscles, minimizing the risk of post-workout stiffness and soreness.

Remember that consistency is key in any fitness routine. The more consistent you are with your workouts, the better results you will see. But don't forget to incorporate rest days into your routine. These are just as important as your workout days. They give your body a chance to recover and your muscles to rebuild and strengthen.

One of the most significant parts of creating a Wall Pilates routine is the process of learning to connect with your body. Each exercise should be performed mindfully, paying close attention to your breath and the movement of your muscles. This is not just about physical strength, but also about cultivating a sense of self-awareness and mindfulness.

The power of Wall Pilates lies in its simplicity. You don't need fancy equipment or a gym membership. All you need is a wall, a mat, and the commitment to improve your health and fitness.

As you progress in your Wall Pilates journey, don't hesitate to experiment and adjust your routine. Maybe you want to focus more on your core strength, or perhaps you find your lower body needs more attention. Tailoring your routine to your needs will keep your workouts engaging and relevant.

Wall Pilates is a beautiful journey of self-discovery and growth. Each session is an opportunity to explore your potential, to challenge your limits, and to celebrate your progress.

In the end, remember that this is your journey. There's no need to compare yourself to others. We all have different bodies, different strengths, and different challenges. What matters is that you are making a conscious effort to improve your health and wellbeing. Every small step you take is a victory in itself.

CHAPTER 5

Tracking Your Progress and

Monitoring Your Progress

As an experienced Wall Pilates trainer, one of the most gratifying parts of the journey is watching the progress unfold. There's a unique joy that comes from seeing your strength and flexibility improve, your posture transform, and your mind-body connection deepen. But in order to truly appreciate these changes, it's essential to track and monitor your progress.

The process of monitoring progress is not merely a practice of vanity or self-obsession, but rather a way to engage more deeply in your own personal growth. It's about acknowledging the fruits of your effort, celebrating your achievements, and making data-driven decisions to guide your future practice.

When we talk about tracking progress in Wall Pilates, we're not merely referring to the physical changes you can see in the mirror. Yes, muscle toning and weight management are often the most visible results, but Wall Pilates also improves balance, flexibility, and core strength, which might not be as easily noticeable. Moreover, it fosters mindfulness, breath control, and a sense of inner peace, which, while not visible to the eye, are equally important to track.

So, how can you keep track of such a wide array of benefits? The key is to adopt a holistic approach, which considers both tangible and intangible outcomes.

Physical changes are the easiest to monitor. Take full-body photographs or measure your body parts at regular intervals. You might also notice improvements in your ability to perform certain exercises or hold specific positions for longer periods. Maybe you can do more repetitions, or perhaps you're able to perform exercises that were too challenging before. Remember to celebrate these achievements, no matter how small they seem.

Flexibility and balance improvements can be evaluated by seeing how far you can stretch in certain exercises or how long you can maintain balance-dependent poses. For example, if you can reach further down your leg in a hamstring stretch or hold a single-leg stance for longer, you are becoming more flexible and balanced.

As for the mental and emotional benefits, maintaining a journal can be incredibly helpful. Write about your experiences after each workout. How do you feel? Are you becoming more aware of your breath and body? Do you feel calmer and more centered? Look back on these entries over time to understand your mental and emotional journey better.

Another way to track your progress is by setting goals. Goals give you a target to aim for and make it easier to notice improvements. However, ensure that your goals are SMART: Specific, Measurable, Achievable, Relevant, and Time-bound. They could be as simple as holding a wall sit for a minute or as ambitious as mastering a complex routine.

While tracking your progress, it's crucial to be patient and kind to yourself. Change takes time, and progress isn't always linear. Some days you'll feel stronger and more flexible, and other days, you might feel like you're regressing. That's completely normal. Don't let these fluctuations discourage you. Instead, use them as reminders that progress is a journey, not a destination.

In the beginning, the process of tracking progress can feel daunting. You might wonder if you're doing it right, or if you're making enough progress. But rest assured, every little bit of progress counts. And over time, you'll start to see the fruits of your labor. You'll notice changes in your body, in your mindset, and even in your outlook on life.

Additionally, avoid the temptation to compare your progress with others. Wall Pilates is a personal journey, and everyone progresses at their own pace. Comparisons can only lead to unnecessary pressure and frustration. Focus on your own journey and celebrate your unique progress.

At the same time, remember that tracking should not become an obsession. While it's important to acknowledge your progress, don't let it steal the joy and mindfulness inherent in the practice of Wall Pilates. Your ultimate goal should be to improve your health and well-being, not merely to achieve certain numbers or targets.

In conclusion, monitoring your progress in Wall Pilates is an empowering process. It gives you a clear picture of where you are, where you're going, and how far you've come. It motivates you to keep going, even on the tough days, and it allows you to celebrate your victories, both big and small. But more than anything, it deepens your connection with yourself. It makes you more mindful of your body, more appreciative of your abilities, and more compassionate towards yourself.

Remember, every time you step onto the mat to practice Wall Pilates, you are making progress. Every breath you take, every move you make, brings you one step closer to your goals. By tracking this progress, you are not just charting your physical journey, but also your journey of personal growth and self-discovery.

As you continue on this path, you'll find that Wall Pilates is not just about building strength or flexibility, but also about cultivating resilience, self-confidence, and inner peace. It's about learning to navigate life's challenges with grace and balance, just as you navigate the complex poses and movements of Wall Pilates.

So, keep showing up for yourself. Keep breathing, moving, growing. And as you do, remember to pause, observe, and appreciate how far you've come. Because every step forward, no matter how small, is a testament to your strength, your dedication, and your incredible capacity for growth.

Celebrating Small Victories

Celebrating small victories is an essential part of the Wall Pilates journey. It's the joyful acknowledgment of the progress made, regardless of how small it may seem. Every single step forward, every time you reach a little higher, push a little harder, or hold a pose for a little longer, is a cause for celebration.

Each one of us begins our Wall Pilates journey at a different point, and progress is unique to each of us. You might take pride in mastering a new move, holding a difficult pose for a few more seconds, or simply completing a routine without losing your balance. These are all victories, and they deserve to be celebrated.

When you celebrate your small victories, you're not just acknowledging the physical progress you're making. You're also celebrating your resilience, your determination, and your unwavering commitment to your health and wellbeing. These are powerful attributes, ones that deserve to be recognized and honored.

Remember, the journey towards mastery in Wall Pilates is not a sprint, but a marathon. It's a path filled with ups and downs, challenges and victories. But every step you take on this path, no matter how small, is a victory in itself. It's a sign of your dedication, your resilience, and your commitment to your health and wellness.

One way to celebrate these small victories is to savor the moment. When you reach a milestone, no matter how small, take a moment to reflect on your achievement. Let it sink in. Bask in the feeling of accomplishment. This moment of reflection not only boosts your morale but also strengthens your resolve to push further.

You could also share your victories with others. Sharing your success, no matter how small, creates a positive feedback loop that motivates you to keep going. It also helps build a sense of community, a shared understanding that we are all on this journey together, each of us striving, succeeding, and celebrating in our own unique way.

Another way to celebrate is by treating yourself. This doesn't have to mean indulging in something lavish or extravagant. It could be as simple as taking a few extra minutes of relaxation after a tough routine, enjoying a healthy treat, or spending time in nature. The idea is to reward yourself in a way that brings you joy and reinforces your commitment to your Wall Pilates practice.

Remember, every victory, no matter how small, is a step towards a stronger, healthier, and more resilient you. So, take the time to celebrate these moments. Let them fill you with pride and joy. Let them serve as a reminder of how far you've come and how much more you're capable of achieving.

In Wall Pilates, as in life, it's the small victories that make the journey worthwhile. They remind us of our strength, our resilience, and our capacity for growth. So, celebrate these victories. Savor them. Share them. And most importantly, let them inspire you to keep pushing, keep growing, and keep striving towards your goals.

Because in the end, it's not just about the big goals or the final destination. It's about the journey, the small steps you take each day, the little victories that make you smile, make you proud, and make you fall in love with the process. So, here's to your journey, to your victories, and to the wonderful world of Wall Pilates. May it bring you strength, joy, and endless growth.

Conclusion: Your Next Steps in Pilates

As we journey towards the closing stages of our exploration into the transformative world of Wall Pilates, it's important to look ahead to what comes next. You've embarked on this rewarding path, dedicating time and effort to your practice, and now it's time to delve deeper and expand your horizons.

Wall Pilates is not just a fitness routine; it's a lifestyle, a mindset. It requires patience, commitment, and a deep sense of self-awareness. As you continue on this path, there are countless possibilities for growth and exploration. The beauty of this practice is that it's adaptable to your needs and capabilities. It grows with you, always offering new challenges to conquer and new heights to reach.

One possible next step is to deepen your understanding of the practice. There's always more to learn, more to explore. This could mean delving into the principles of Pilates, understanding the nuances of each movement, or exploring the many variations of each exercise. You could take a deeper dive into the anatomy and physiology behind the movements, enhancing your knowledge about the way your body moves and functions.

This deeper understanding will not only enrich your practice but also empower you to be more in tune with your body, enabling you to adjust and modify your routines to better suit your needs and goals. It's about cultivating a relationship with your body that's based on respect, understanding, and love.

Another path you might consider is sharing your passion for Wall Pilates with others. Sharing your journey can be an incredibly rewarding experience. Whether you choose to do this informally, by introducing a friend to Wall Pilates, or more formally, by pursuing a certification to become a Pilates instructor, spreading the joy of Pilates can add a new layer of fulfillment to your practice.

One of the most important next steps, however, is to maintain consistency. Wall Pilates, like any other form of exercise, requires regular practice to reap its full benefits. Make it a part of your daily routine, even if it's just for a few minutes each day. Consistency is the key to progress, to transformation.

Lastly, always remember to be patient and kind to yourself. Progress in Pilates, as in life, is not always linear. There will be days when the exercises feel more challenging, when balance seems elusive, or when your body simply needs rest. On these days, remember to listen to your body, to respect its signals, and to be gentle with yourself.

As you move forward in your Wall Pilates journey, let these words be your guide: patience, persistence, and compassion. With these by your side, you're poised to explore new depths, reach new heights, and uncover new strengths. Your journey in Wall Pilates has just begun, and the possibilities are boundless.

So, here's to your next steps in this exciting journey. May they bring you deeper understanding, greater strength, and immeasurable joy. And remember, every step, no matter how small, is a step forward. So, keep moving, keep exploring, and keep growing. Your Wall Pilates journey awaits.

BOOK 3

Wall Pilates Transformation: A 45-Day Journey to Enhanced Mobility, Strength, and Vitality for All Ages

Introduction: Why Wall Pilates?

Welcome to your journey into Wall Pilates, a transformative practice that offers enhanced mobility, increased strength, and a revitalized sense of vitality. Over the next 45 days, we're going to embark on an adventure that can change the way you move, feel, and perceive your body, regardless of your age. But why Wall Pilates? What makes it a worthy companion for this journey? Let's delve into that.

Wall Pilates stands tall in the world of fitness, not as a fleeting trend but as a grounded, accessible, and effective approach to wellbeing. It is built on the principles of classical Pilates, a method celebrated for its power to develop strength, flexibility, and body awareness. However, Wall Pilates takes these principles a step further by incorporating the use of a wall, transforming it from a mere architectural structure into a supportive tool for your fitness journey.

The wall serves a dual purpose: it acts as a gentle guide, helping you align your body correctly, and a steadfast partner, supporting you as you explore the boundaries of your strength and flexibility. It is a constant, reliable presence that allows you to focus on the precision and control that are the hallmarks of Pilates.

Wall Pilates is for everyone. Yes, it's true. It doesn't discriminate based on age or fitness level. Whether you're a sprightly teenager, a busy middle-aged professional, or a senior citizen looking to maintain mobility and strength, Wall Pilates can be tailored to your needs. It offers a range of modifications and progressions, meaning you can adjust the intensity and complexity of the exercises to match your current capabilities. It's a practice that grows with you, respects your pace, and celebrates your progress, no matter how small.

This accessibility does not come at the cost of effectiveness. On the contrary, Wall Pilates offers a comprehensive workout that targets your entire body. It challenges your core stability, promotes good posture, enhances flexibility, and builds muscular strength and endurance. Furthermore, it encourages mindfulness, inviting you to tune in to your body and breath, thus fostering a deeper connection between your mind and body.

In a world where quick fixes and extreme routines often take the spotlight, Wall Pilates offers a refreshing alternative. It's not about punishing your body or striving for an unattainable ideal. It's about embracing your body as it is, acknowledging its capabilities, and nurturing its potential for growth and change.

Over the next 45 days, as we journey together through this Wall Pilates transformation, you will witness firsthand the power of this practice. You'll see changes not just in your body, but also in your mindset. You'll cultivate a sense of self-confidence that extends beyond the mat, empowering you in all areas of your life.

So, why Wall Pilates? Because it's more than just a workout. It's a journey of self-discovery, a celebration of what your body can do, and a commitment to nurture your wellbeing. It's a path that leads not just to better fitness, but to a better relationship with your body and yourself. And that, dear reader, is a journey well worth embarking on.

CHAPTER 1

Benefits of Wall Pilates

The transformation you experience over the course of 45 days with Wall Pilates will make you realize that each day brings something unique to cherish. Each day you connect with your body and the wall, you'll observe the benefits that extend well beyond just a toned physique. The magic of Wall Pilates lies in the rich tapestry of benefits it bestows upon your overall well-being.

Imagine waking up each morning and feeling the newfound strength in your muscles, not just the external ones that mirror our physical progress, but also those deep within. The deeper, often overlooked muscles that are so essential to our posture and daily movements. The first thing you'll notice during your 45-day journey is the improvement in your strength and endurance. These exercises, though seemingly simple, target multiple muscle groups simultaneously, making them extraordinarily efficient. As a result, you will find your capacity for other physical activities increased, and tasks that once fatigued you will seem less daunting.

But the benefits of Wall Pilates aren't limited to physical strength alone. As you move through your journey, you'll notice an improvement in your overall flexibility and mobility. The gentle, focused movements of Wall Pilates allow for a gradual increase in the range of motion in your joints. This enhanced mobility can reduce the risk of injury and increase your overall performance in other physical activities. You'll begin to move through your daily life with a newfound ease and fluidity that feels just as good as it looks.

Balance is another key area where you'll see significant progress. Wall Pilates provides an excellent platform for improving balance and coordination, as many of the exercises require you to maintain stability while performing controlled movements. With time, you'll find yourself moving with greater confidence and grace, even when away from the wall.

101

While the physical improvements are tangible and gratifying, the benefits of Wall Pilates extend beyond the physical realm. The mental benefits are just as profound. Pilates is known for its emphasis on mindfulness and breath control. Each session invites you to focus on the present moment and the movement of your body. This focus helps to quiet the mind, reducing stress and promoting a sense of inner calm. Over 45 days, this can lead to significant improvements in mental clarity and a reduction in anxiety levels.

Furthermore, each Wall Pilates session is an opportunity to enhance your mind-body connection. As you move through each exercise, you'll be encouraged to focus on how your body feels and responds. This heightened awareness of your body can lead to improved body confidence and overall self-esteem. You'll become more in tune with your body, understanding its capabilities, recognizing its progress, and appreciating its strength.

In the end, the 45-day transformation with Wall Pilates is not just about changing your body, it's about changing your relationship with yourself. It's about recognizing your strength, celebrating your progress, and cherishing the journey. Each day, each exercise, each breath brings you closer to a healthier, stronger, and more vibrant version of yourself. It's a journey that begins with the wall but extends far beyond it, into every facet of your life. Embrace the transformation, enjoy the journey, and cherish the benefits that Wall Pilates brings to your life.

Increased Strength and Flexibility

Wall Pilates, the art of integrating the support of a wall into traditional Pilates, carries with it a profound potential to amplify your physical strength and flexibility. As you embark on this journey, you'll gradually uncover the transformative power these exercises have in helping you reach new heights of physical prowess.

The concept of strength is multifaceted, involving not only our muscles but also our endurance, our balance, and our capacity to harmonize different parts of our body in unison. Wall Pilates, with its unique exercise repertoire, embraces this holistic perspective on strength. From glute bridges that engage your posterior chain, to wall push-ups that target your upper body, each exercise is designed to challenge and strengthen various muscle groups.

As you progress through your Wall Pilates journey, you'll notice an incremental increase in strength that transforms your daily experiences. Tasks that once seemed challenging may become more manageable. Carrying groceries, climbing stairs, or even maintaining good posture during long periods of sitting can become noticeably easier. And in those moments, you'll truly appreciate the power of Wall Pilates.

But Wall Pilates is not just about building strength. It also enhances flexibility, a critical component of physical fitness that is often overlooked. Flexibility plays a vital role in our everyday movements, and improved flexibility can enhance performance in other physical activities. Whether it's reaching for something on a high shelf or bending down to tie your shoelaces, the importance of flexibility permeates our daily lives.

Wall Pilates exercises like leg lifts, leg circles, and roll downs, gently stretch and lengthen your muscles, promoting improved flexibility. These movements, performed consistently and with mindful attention, can increase your range of motion, making your body feel more open and less restricted. As you deepen your Wall Pilates practice, you'll notice a fluidity in your movements that you may not have experienced before.

In the midst of this physical transformation, there's also an emotional transformation that takes place. As you become stronger and more flexible, you'll also become more confident. With each Wall Pilates session, you'll learn to trust your body's capabilities, to push beyond perceived limitations, and to appreciate your body for its strength and resilience.

As you continue your Wall Pilates journey, remember to celebrate each step forward, no matter how small. Each day, each exercise, each breath brings you closer to a stronger, more flexible you. Embrace the progress, cherish the journey, and remember: the wall is not just a prop; it's a tool for transformation. And with Wall Pilates, that transformation reaches beyond physical strength and flexibility, into a realm of improved confidence, self-esteem, and overall well-being. Enjoy the journey, and celebrate each moment of increased strength and flexibility. It's your journey, and it's one worth cherishing.

Improved Posture and Alignment

If we were to consider the body as a symphony, posture and alignment would be the maestro leading the orchestra. Proper alignment is the cornerstone of a well-functioning body, and Wall Pilates is an exceptional tool to orchestrate this.

As you delve into the world of Wall Pilates, you will quickly understand its compelling power to transform your posture. The wall, a simple yet profound prop, offers an external reference point to help you understand and better align your body. With each session, the wall becomes your mirror, reflecting the way you stand, move, and engage your muscles.

The first benefactor of improved alignment is your spine. Wall Pilates exercises such as wall sits, roll downs, and wall push-ups promote a healthier alignment of the spine. They encourage you to lengthen your back, open your chest, and engage your core, leading to a more upright and confident posture.

The transformation doesn't stop there. As your spine finds its alignment, the rest of your body follows suit. Your shoulders relax away from your ears, your hips align with your knees and ankles, and your body starts to move more efficiently and effortlessly. The transformation can be so profound that you may start to feel taller, stronger, and more grounded.

With improved alignment, you will also notice a change in the way you carry yourself outside of your Wall Pilates practice. Walking, sitting, even standing still, each action will be a testament to the improved posture and alignment you've achieved. You'll find a renewed sense of confidence in your stride, a boldness in your stance, and an overall sense of well-being that radiates from the inside out.

But the journey to improved posture and alignment is not merely a physical one. It's also a journey of self-discovery and self-awareness. Each time you press your body against the wall, you learn something new about yourself. You discover areas of tension you weren't aware of, you notice imbalances that had gone unnoticed, and you learn to listen to your body's subtle cues. This heightened sense of body awareness is one of the most valuable gifts Wall Pilates has to offer.

As you continue your Wall Pilates journey, remember that improving posture and alignment is a journey in itself. It's a process of learning, unlearning, and relearning how to hold and move your body. Be patient with yourself, celebrate your progress, and know that with each Wall Pilates session, you are one step closer to a more aligned, better-postured version of yourself.

Your journey with Wall Pilates is not just about the destination, it's about the transformation that happens along the way. So, here's to better posture, improved alignment, and the beautiful symphony that is your body, playing its music more harmoniously than ever before.

CHAPTER 2

The 45-Day Wall Pilates Program: Overview

Immerse yourself in the transformative power of Wall Pilates with our specially designed 45-Day Wall Pilates Program. This program is crafted to guide you gently yet steadily into the world of Wall Pilates, helping you unlock the extraordinary potential within your body. As you embark on this journey, you can expect to experience enhanced body awareness, improved posture, and increased strength and flexibility.

The 45-Day Wall Pilates Program isn't just about the movements you'll perform; it's about establishing a nurturing relationship with your body. Over the course of 45 days, you'll be introduced to exercises that challenge and support your body, pushing you to grow while respecting your individual limitations.

The program begins with a focus on foundational exercises. During the first week, you'll familiarize yourself with basic Wall Pilates exercises such as glute bridges, wall push-ups, and wall sits. The wall will serve as your guide, assisting you in performing these exercises with precision and alignment. By the end of the week, you'll have a better understanding of your body and how it interacts with the wall.

As the program progresses, we will gradually introduce more challenging exercises into your routine. These exercises will build on the foundational movements, adding complexity and depth to your practice. You'll explore exercises like wall bicycle crunches, wall lunges, and leg lifts. Each of these exercises will challenge your strength, flexibility, and endurance in a new way.

Throughout the program, you'll also engage in targeted workouts aimed at specific areas of the body. One day you might focus on your core, the next on your lower body, and another on your upper body. This approach ensures a balanced workout regime, preventing overuse of any single muscle group and promoting overall body strength and resilience.

An integral part of the program is rest and recovery. Scheduled rest days will give your body a chance to recuperate and adapt to the new demands being placed upon it. These days are just as important as the workout days, as they allow your body to heal and grow stronger.

Beyond the physical, the 45-Day Wall Pilates Program is also a journey of mental resilience. You'll cultivate patience as you learn new movements, perseverance as you push through challenging exercises, and mindfulness as you tune into your body's needs and responses. These skills will benefit you not just in your Wall Pilates practice, but in your day-to-day life as well.

By the end of the 45 days, you will have not only a new set of exercises in your fitness repertoire but also a deeper understanding of your body and its capabilities. You'll stand taller, move with more grace and fluidity, and carry a newfound confidence that extends beyond the wall.

In essence, the 45-Day Wall Pilates Program is not just a fitness program; it's a journey of self-discovery and transformation. It's about learning to respect your body, challenge it, and ultimately, understand it better. So, as we begin this journey together, let's commit to being present, being patient, and most importantly, being open to the transformative power of Wall Pilates.

What to Expect

Embarking on the 45-day Wall Pilates program is a commitment to personal growth, self-care, and physical development. It's a promise to yourself that over the next month and a half, you will prioritize your wellness, dedicating time each day to enhance your strength, flexibility, and mental resilience. Here is what you can expect from this transformative journey.

The first sensation you will likely experience is a deepening connection with your body. Wall Pilates is a discipline that demands concentration and precision. As you practice these exercises, you will cultivate a heightened awareness of your body, its movements, and the subtleties of each muscle contraction and release. This body awareness is not confined to your workout sessions; it will permeate into other areas of your life, improving your posture, movement, and overall physical well-being.

As you progress through the program, you'll notice your strength building, quite literally, from the ground up. The exercises are designed to activate and engage different muscle groups, each one building on the previous one. You'll feel your core becoming stronger, your legs more powerful, and your upper body more defined. This strength isn't just about aesthetics; it's about functionality. A stronger body is a more capable body, equipped to handle everyday tasks with more ease and less strain.

Flexibility is another key benefit of the program. Wall Pilates exercises, with their focus on controlled, elongated movements, will gradually increase your flexibility. This can lead to better mobility, improved athletic performance, and a decreased risk of injuries. You might find that you're able to move in ways you didn't think were possible, and this can be an incredibly empowering experience.

However, the changes are not just physical. Pilates is as much a mental practice as it is a physical one. Throughout the program, you will be honing your focus, patience, and perseverance. You'll learn to stay present even when the exercises become challenging, and to push through even when your muscles are asking you to stop. These mental skills are invaluable, and they'll serve you well beyond the confines of your workout space.

Of course, any fitness program comes with its challenges, and it's important to go into this with open eyes. There will be days when your body feels sore, when the exercises feel particularly tough, or when you struggle to find the motivation to continue. It's in these moments that your commitment to the program and to yourself will be tested. But remember, it's often in the face of these challenges that we experience the most significant growth.

In terms of time commitment, you can expect to dedicate around 30-45 minutes per day to the program. The beauty of Wall Pilates is its flexibility; you can fit it around your schedule, and since you only need a wall and a mat, you can do it almost anywhere.

In the end, the 45-day Wall Pilates program is a comprehensive, challenging, and rewarding journey. It offers you the opportunity to transform your body, strengthen your mind, and discover a new level of physical capability. And most importantly, it's a step towards a healthier, more balanced, and more fulfilling lifestyle. As you step into this journey, remember to be patient with yourself, to celebrate your progress, and to enjoy the process. After all, this journey is all about you.

How to Prepare

Embarking on a new fitness journey, like the 45-day Wall Pilates program, is a thrilling endeavor. But it's also one that requires a bit of preparation to ensure you can make the most of the experience and set yourself up for success. Here's how you can ready yourself for this exciting journey.

First and foremost, clear a space in your home where you can perform your workouts undisturbed. You'll need an area with a sturdy wall, enough space for a mat, and enough room for you to stretch out and move freely. This should be a space that feels calm, inviting, and free from distractions. Remember, this is your sanctuary for the next 45 days, a space where you'll be pushing your limits and exploring new strengths.

Next, invest in a good quality Pilates mat. A thick, cushioned mat will provide the necessary support for your body, especially your spine and joints, during the exercises. While there's no need for fancy equipment with Wall Pilates, a comfortable and supportive mat is non-negotiable.

Beyond the physical space and mat, you should also prepare your body. Start hydrating more regularly, and consider incorporating more protein into your diet to support muscle recovery and growth. If you're new to regular exercise or have any health concerns, it's a good idea to check in with your doctor and ensure that it's safe for you to embark on this program.

It's also essential to prepare mentally. Starting a new fitness program can be challenging, and there will be days when your resolve is tested. It can be helpful to set clear, realistic goals for what you want to achieve during these 45 days. Whether that's improving your flexibility, building strength, or simply dedicating a certain amount of time each day to focus on your physical well-being, having a goal can keep you motivated and committed.

Finally, consider keeping a journal of your progress. This doesn't have to be anything elaborate - a simple notebook will do. Document how each session makes you feel, any challenges you faced, and the victories you achieved, no matter how small. This can be a powerful tool for tracking your progress, reflecting on your journey, and celebrating your achievements along the way.

As you prepare for this program, remember that the most important thing is to approach it with an open mind and a commitment to your personal growth. This is your journey, and every step you take is a step towards a stronger, more capable, and healthier you. Embrace the challenge, celebrate your victories, and above all, enjoy the process. You're about to embark on an incredible journey, and I can't wait to see where it takes you.

CHAPTERS 3

Day 1 to Day 45 Exercises, Daily Routines and Reflections

Navigating through the 45-Day Wall Pilates program will be a journey of discovery and self-improvement. Every day will bring new challenges and opportunities to strengthen your body, enhance your flexibility, and elevate your overall health. Here's what you can expect.

For the first week, let's focus on getting familiar with the basic exercises. Day 1 will start with glute bridges and wall push-ups, aimed at activating your lower body and upper body muscles. On Day 2, introduce wall sits to challenge your lower body endurance further. Wall 100s, designed to engage your core, will be the focus of Day 3. On Day 4, add wall bicycle crunches to the mix, and on Day 5, you'll be introduced to wall lunges. Day 6 will be all about leg lifts, and Day 7 will bring your first week to a close with sidekicks. You'll be doing three sets of each exercise daily, taking care to maintain proper form and alignment.

In Week 2, you'll add a new exercise each day to the ones you've already learned. Day 8 will introduce leg circles, and Day 9 will bring in roll downs. For the rest of the week, you'll be focusing on enhancing your proficiency in these exercises, increasing the number of sets gradually.

Week 3 will be about upping the intensity. Continue with the exercises you've learned, but now, start increasing the time spent on each one. Aim for more reps and longer hold times. This week, you'll also introduce the concept of progressions and variations to keep the workouts challenging and engaging.

Week 4 marks the halfway point of the program. By now, you'll be feeling stronger and more confident in your ability to perform the exercises. This week, focus on mastering the form and alignment of each exercise, ensuring that you're getting the most out of every movement. Keep challenging yourself with increased reps and longer hold times.

Week 5 is all about endurance. By now, your body has adapted to the regular exercise, and it's time to push your limits. Increase the duration of your workouts, try advanced variations of the exercises, and keep focusing on your form.

Week 6 brings with it a renewed focus on flexibility. You'll continue with your regular exercises, but now, you'll also spend more time on stretches and mobility exercises. This will help your body recover, increase your range of motion, and improve your performance.

In the final week, Week 7, you'll be doing a mix of all the exercises you've learned, but with an added twist. Each day, you'll focus on one specific exercise and do an intense, focused workout around it. This will test your strength, endurance, and flexibility, and it's a great way to finish the program strong.

On Day 45, the last day of the program, you'll do a comprehensive workout incorporating all the exercises. It will be a celebration of all the hard work you've put in, a testament to your strength and perseverance.

Remember, everyone's journey is different. Listen to your body, take rest days as needed, and adjust the program as necessary. The goal is to challenge yourself, but also to enjoy the process. Each day of this program brings you one step closer to a stronger, healthier you. Embrace the journey and celebrate your progress every step of the way.

Here's a detailed breakdown of the exercises to be performed each day in the 45-day Wall Pilates program:

Week 1: Introduction to Basic Exercises

- Day 1: Glute Bridges
- Day 2: Wall Push-Ups
- Day 3: Wall Sits
- Day 4: Wall 100s
- Day 5: Wall Bicycle Crunches
- Day 6: Wall Lunges

- Day 7: Leg Lifts

Week 2: Adding New Exercises

- Day 8: Add Side Kicks
- Day 9: Add Leg Circles
- Day 10 to 14: Continue with the exercises from Days 1-9

Week 3: Increasing Intensity

- Day 15 to 21: Continue with exercises from Days 1-9, increase the number of reps or sets

Week 4: Mastering Form and Alignment

- Day 22 to 28: Continue with exercises from Days 1-9, focus on form and alignment

Week 5: Building Endurance

- Day 29 to 35: Continue with exercises from Days 1-9, increase duration and intensity

Week 6: Focus on Flexibility

- Day 36 to 42: Continue with exercises from Days 1-9, spend more time on stretching and mobility exercises

Week 7: Intense Focus Workouts

- Day 43: Intense Glute Bridges workout
- Day 44: Intense Wall Push-Ups workout

Celebration of Progress

- Day 45: Comprehensive workout incorporating all the exercises

Remember to always warm up before starting the exercises and cool down afterwards. Listen to your body throughout the program and adjust the intensity and reps as needed. The goal is to challenge yourself but also to enjoy the process and celebrate your progress every step of the way.

Each Day's Routine and Reflection

Here's a detailed breakdown of the routine and reflection for each day in the 45-day Wall Pilates program:

Day 1 - Glute Bridges: Begin your Wall Pilates journey with Glute Bridges. This exercise is perfect for activating and strengthening your glutes and hamstrings. After the workout, reflect on how your body feels. Did you feel the burn in your glutes? Make sure to record these reflections in a journal or notebook.

Day 2 - Wall Push-Ups: Add Wall Push-Ups to your routine. This exercise will engage your arms and back. Reflect on your form and alignment. How did the wall support you? How do your arms and back feel?

Day 3 - Wall Sits: Introduce Wall Sits. This exercise will help to improve your posture and work your legs and core. Reflect on your posture and core engagement. Did you keep your back straight against the wall?

Day 4 - Wall 100s: Time to work on your core with Wall 100s. Reflect on your breath control and core engagement. How did the small movements feel? How was your breath control?

Day 5 - Wall Bicycle Crunches: Add Wall Bicycle Crunches for a dynamic core workout. Reflect on your coordination and core strength. Did you manage to bring your opposite elbow to your opposite knee smoothly?

Day 6 - Wall Lunges: Incorporate Wall Lunges into your routine. Reflect on your balance and leg strength. How did it feel to keep one hand on the wall for support while lunging?

Day 7 - Leg Lifts: End the first week with Leg Lifts. Reflect on your glute engagement and body alignment. Did you keep your spine neutral as you lifted your leg back?

As you move into the second week, continue to add new exercises while reflecting on your progress and how your body feels. Remember, the aim of this program is not only to improve your strength and flexibility, but also to enhance your body awareness and appreciation for what it can do.

Day 8 - Side Kicks: Begin the second week with the addition of Side Kicks. This exercise will challenge your balance and work your outer thighs. Reflect on your balance and body alignment. Did you keep your body aligned as you lifted your leg out to the side?

Day 9 - Leg Circles: Add Leg Circles to your routine. This exercise will challenge your control and stability. Reflect on your control and balance. Were you able to draw small circles with your toes without shifting your weight?

Days 10 to 14: Continue with the exercises from Days 1-9. Each day, focus on one exercise and reflect on your form, control, and the sensations in your muscles.

Continue to follow this pattern of reflection throughout the rest of the program. With each week, you will increase the intensity and duration of your workouts, focus on your form and alignment, build endurance, and enhance your flexibility.

By **Day 45**, you will have completed a comprehensive workout incorporating all the exercises, marking a significant milestone in your Wall Pilates journey. Reflect on your overall progress and how your body has changed over the course of the program. You've come a long way since Day 1, and it's a moment to celebrate your commitment, perseverance, and all the progress you've made.

Conclusion: Maintaining Your Progress Post-45 Days

After reaching the remarkable milestone of 45 days in your Wall Pilates journey, you've undoubtedly experienced a transformation. Not only physically, through increased strength, flexibility, and overall better body awareness, but also mentally, as the consistent commitment to your health and well-being has likely brought a sense of accomplishment and confidence.

Now, standing at the threshold of this significant achievement, it's essential to take a moment to honor the journey and celebrate your accomplishment. Remember that each day you committed to this practice, you were making a choice to prioritize your health and well-being. Be proud of your dedication, the progress you've made, and the strength and resilience you've built.

As you move forward, it's important to maintain the progress you've made. The key lies in the beautiful simplicity of the principle that underpins Pilates: consistency. Just as the steady, regular practice of these exercises brought you to this point, it is the continued application of the same principle that will ensure your progress is maintained.

Consider incorporating the exercises you've learned into your daily routine, treating them not as tasks to be accomplished, but as an ongoing commitment to your body. Maybe some mornings, it's a series of Glute Bridges and Wall Push-Ups, or an evening routine of Wall Sits and Wall Lunges. Perhaps it's a mid-day break with Wall 100s and Wall Bicycle Crunches to reenergize your body and mind. The beauty of these exercises is their versatility; they can be done anywhere, anytime, fitting seamlessly into your day-to-day life.

It's also important to continue with the habit of reflection you've cultivated during these 45 days. Recognize how each exercise makes you feel, both during the activity and afterward. By maintaining this dialogue with your body, you'll continue to foster a deeper connection with yourself, promoting not only physical strength but also mental and emotional well-being.

Embrace the principle of progression. Remember that Pilates, like any other fitness practice, is not a destination but a journey. Feel free to explore more advanced exercises or variations, challenge yourself with longer hold times or more repetitions. The aim is not to strain or push to the point of pain, but to continually challenge your body, maintaining the strength and flexibility you've worked so hard to build.

Remember, the benefits of Pilates extend beyond the physical. It's a holistic practice that fosters a connection between body and mind, enhancing not only your physical health but also promoting a sense of calm and well-being. By continuing with your practice, you're not only investing in your physical health but also nurturing your mental and emotional well-being.

In your journey ahead, let the lessons you've learned during these 45 days guide you. May the strength, flexibility, and body awareness you've cultivated be your companions, and the wisdom you've gained through reflection be your guide. Here's to your continued health and well-being, and to the many milestones yet to come in your Pilates journey.

Incorporating Wall Pilates into Your Routine

As you transition from the focused 45-day Wall Pilates program into a more integrated practice, it's important to approach this new chapter with the same intentionality and dedication that you've shown over the past month and a half. Incorporating Wall Pilates into your daily routine doesn't need to be a daunting task; rather, it's an opportunity to seamlessly blend these movements into the rhythm of your life, allowing you to continue reaping the benefits of this powerful practice.

One of the most appealing aspects of Wall Pilates is its simplicity. All you need is a wall and a bit of floor space, and you have everything required for a robust workout. This means that it's an exercise regime that can be done anywhere, at any time, whether it's first thing in the morning to kick start your day, during a lunch break to re-energize your body, or in the evening to unwind after a long day. The accessibility of Wall Pilates makes it an ideal choice for anyone looking to maintain a regular fitness routine amidst the hustle and bustle of everyday life.

As you begin to incorporate Wall Pilates into your routine, it's important to listen to your body and allow it to guide you. Remember that it's not about how many exercises you do, but rather the quality of each movement. One day, you might feel energized and ready to tackle a series of different exercises. Another day, you might choose to focus on just one or two movements, paying close attention to your form and the sensation in your muscles. There is no right or wrong approach - what matters is that you're staying active and honoring your body's needs.

Over time, you'll likely find that Wall Pilates becomes more than just an exercise routine. It becomes a time to connect with yourself, to quiet your mind, and to pay attention to your body's strengths and areas for improvement. You might start to notice subtle changes in your body, such.

Setting New Goals

At the conclusion of your 45-day journey into the world of Wall Pilates, you've not just been nurturing your body, you've been fostering the growth of your inner self as well. Goals were set, challenges were faced, and you've emerged victorious, stronger, and more in tune with your body than ever before. As you transition into your post-45-day routine, it is important to consider setting new goals to keep your journey alive and continue to challenge yourself.

One goal could be increasing the intensity of your Wall Pilates workouts. This could mean holding the positions for longer periods, adding more repetitions, or incorporating more challenging movements. It's not about pushing yourself to the point of discomfort, but rather, exploring the edges of your comfort zone and expanding them little by little. The stronger and more confident you become, the more capable you will be of tackling more complex exercises.

Another goal might be to focus on improving your flexibility. Wall Pilates offers a great platform for enhancing your body's range of motion and fluidity. You could aim to improve your posture, work on achieving deeper stretches, or focus on movements that enhance your mobility. This kind of goal is not only beneficial for your Pilates practice, but it also contributes to your overall well-being, reducing the risk of injuries and enhancing your body's functionality in day-to-day activities.

Don't forget about the mental aspect of Pilates as well. Consider setting goals that target your mindset, such as improving your mind-body connection, enhancing your focus during workouts, or cultivating a more positive attitude towards exercise and fitness in general. Pilates is a holistic discipline that targets both the body and the mind, so incorporating mental goals can greatly enhance your overall experience.

Lastly, remember that goals should inspire and motivate you, not create stress or pressure. It's important to set realistic, achievable targets, and to celebrate every small victory along the way. And remember, the ultimate goal is to cultivate a lifelong love for Wall Pilates and the benefits it brings to your health and well-being. With every goal you set and achieve, you're not just improving your fitness, you're enhancing your life.

BOOK 4

The 28-Day Wall Pilates Challenge

Introduction: Embarking on the 28-Day Challenge

Welcome to the exciting start of your 28-Day Wall Pilates Challenge. As you stand on the precipice of this new adventure, you're not just committing to a physical endeavor, but also embarking on a journey of self-discovery. Wall Pilates, with its unique blend of strength, flexibility, and mindfulness, provides an ideal platform to explore your personal potential and elevate your fitness level.

Getting started with the 28-Day Wall Pilates Challenge is like opening a new chapter in your fitness journey. This challenge is designed to provide you with a unique opportunity to push your boundaries, broaden your horizon, and discover new dimensions of your physical capabilities. The beauty of Wall Pilates is its adaptability and scalability, making it accessible to everyone from complete beginners to seasoned fitness enthusiasts.

The journey you're about to embark on is not just about the physical aspect of Wall Pilates. There's a certain mental and emotional transformation that comes along with it. As you challenge your body with new movements and postures, you'll also be challenging your mind to stay focused and present. The wall doesn't just provide physical support, it acts as a metaphorical anchor, reminding you to stay grounded and balanced amidst the challenges.

The 28-Day Challenge is structured to gradually introduce you to the world of Wall Pilates, easing you into its concepts and techniques. Each day presents a new opportunity to learn, grow, and improve. Your body will adapt, your confidence will blossom, and your understanding of your own capabilities will expand. This challenge is not about achieving perfection, but about the ongoing pursuit of progress, no matter how small.

As you embark on this 28-Day Challenge, remember that this is your journey. Listen to your body, honor your limits, and celebrate your victories, no matter how small. The goal is not to be the best, but to be better than you were yesterday. That's the real essence of the 28-Day Wall Pilates Challenge. It's more than just a fitness routine, it's a journey of self-discovery and personal growth.

Welcome aboard the 28-Day Wall Pilates Challenge. Embrace the journey, trust the process, and enjoy every moment. Here's to a stronger, more flexible, and more empowered you. Let's get started!

CHAPTER 1

Preparing for the Challenge: Equipment and Safety

As your guide on this thrilling journey, I want to ensure that you feel confident, prepared, and safe while engaging in the 28-Day Wall Pilates Challenge. Adequate preparation is not merely a precursor to your success but a cornerstone of it.

Firstly, the beauty of Wall Pilates lies in its simplicity. The essential equipment you require is a wall and a mat. Yes, it's that straightforward. The wall you choose should be smooth, sturdy, and free of any obstructing furniture or décor. It will act as your partner throughout this challenge, providing support and resistance in equal measure. Your mat should be comfortable and non-slip to ensure a firm grounding while performing the exercises.

While the wall and mat form the core of your setup, you might find it beneficial to have a few additional items on hand. A towel can be useful for cushioning any movements that may cause discomfort to your back or joints. A water bottle is a must-have, keeping hydration within arm's reach. Remember, your body performs best when it's well-hydrated.

Now, onto safety – the invisible thread that weaves through every successful fitness journey. In Wall Pilates, as with any physical activity, understanding and adhering to safety protocols is crucial. Each exercise should be performed with mindful precision, a keen awareness of your body, and respect for its limitations. It's not a race or a competition, so feel free to adjust the pace and intensity to suit your comfort level.

Warm-ups and cool-downs are your trusted allies in preventing injuries. They prepare your body for the workout ahead and help it recover afterward. Don't skip these vital bookends to your Pilates sessions. They're as much a part of the process as the exercises themselves.

Listen to your body at all times. If a movement causes discomfort or pain, stop immediately. Wall Pilates, when done correctly, should challenge but not strain your body. There's no shame in modifying exercises to match your abilities. It's far more important to perform an exercise correctly at a modified level than to force your body into positions it's not ready for.

Throughout this challenge, maintain an open line of communication with your body. It will tell you when to push harder and when to ease off. Your safety and well-being are the top priorities. Remember, this challenge is about cultivating strength, flexibility, and balance in a manner that's sustainable and respectful of your body's unique needs and capabilities.

So, with your equipment ready and safety guidelines etched in your mind, you stand on the cusp of an exhilarating journey. The 28-Day Wall Pilates Challenge awaits. Let's take this step forward together, embracing the excitement, the challenges, and the triumphs that lie ahead.

What You Need

To perform the 28-Day Wall Pilates Challenge, you'll need a few key items:

1. **A Suitable Wall:** The wall will be your main prop throughout the challenge. It should be sturdy, with a smooth surface and free of any obstacles like hanging pictures or furniture.

2. **Exercise Mat:** A good-quality, non-slip exercise mat will provide cushioning for your body during the exercises. It will also offer you the necessary grip to perform movements safely and effectively.

3. **Comfortable Clothing:** Wear clothes that are comfortable and allow you to move freely. Opt for breathable, stretchy fabrics that won't restrict your movements during the exercises.

4. **Water Bottle:** Staying hydrated is essential when engaging in any form of exercise. Keep a water bottle nearby to ensure you're drinking enough throughout your workout.

5. **Towel:** A towel can be handy to wipe away sweat during your workout, and can also provide additional cushioning for certain exercises if needed.

6. **Determination and Patience:** Lastly, but most importantly, bring along a healthy dose of determination and patience. Progress might be slow at times, but remember that every bit of effort counts. Stay committed to the challenge and be patient with your body as it adjusts to the new routine.

Optional:

1. **Resistance Band:** This is not a must-have but can add variety and intensity to some exercises. If you choose to use one, make sure it's suitable for your fitness level.

2. **Mirror:** If available, a full-length mirror can be useful to check your form and alignment during the exercises. However, it's not essential.

Remember, the most crucial requirement for this challenge is your commitment and willingness to explore new ways of strengthening and toning your body. This journey is as much about patience and consistency as it is about physical strength and flexibility. So, equip yourself with a positive mindset and embark on this exciting Wall Pilates adventure!

Safety Tips

Safety is paramount when engaging in any form of exercise, including the 28-Day Wall Pilates Challenge. Here are a few important safety tips to keep in mind:

Check With Your Doctor: Especially if you're new to exercise or have any health concerns, it's always a good idea to consult with your doctor before starting any new exercise regimen. They can provide guidance based on your specific health conditions and fitness level.

Warm-Up: Start each session with a warm-up to prepare your body for the exercises to come. This can help increase your heart rate, warm up your muscles, and reduce the risk of injury.

Maintain Proper Form: Form is key in Pilates. Always strive for quality of movement over quantity. Listen to your body and don't rush through the exercises. Prioritize maintaining a correct posture and alignment to maximize the benefits of each exercise and to avoid unnecessary strain or injury.

Hydrate: Staying hydrated is important, especially when you're exercising. Drink water before, during, and after your workout to keep your body hydrated.

Cool Down: Just as warming up is important, cooling down after each session helps your body recover and reduces the risk of muscle soreness. Include stretches in your cool-down routine to help relax the muscles you've worked.

Listen to Your Body: This is perhaps the most important tip. While a certain level of discomfort is normal when trying new exercises or pushing your limits, sharp or persistent pain is a sign to stop. If an exercise causes pain, stop doing it and consult a fitness or health professional.

Create a Safe Environment: Make sure the area where you're exercising is clear of any objects that you could potentially trip over. Also, ensure your wall is sturdy and your exercise mat is secure and not likely to slip.

Modify As Needed: If an exercise is too challenging or causes discomfort, modify it to suit your current fitness level. Over time, as your strength and flexibility improve, you'll be able to perform the full version of the exercise.

Remember, the goal of the 28-Day Wall Pilates Challenge isn't to push your body to the point of pain or exhaustion, but rather to gradually increase your strength, flexibility, and overall fitness level in a safe and sustainable way. Enjoy the journey and respect your body's limits..

CHAPTER 2

Week 1: Establishing Basics

This is an essential time for you to become familiar with the core exercises and techniques that will form the basis of your practice in the weeks to come. Embrace this as a time of learning and exploration, a time to connect with your body in new and exciting ways.

Our program for the first week will consist of five workout days and two rest days. Rest is just as important as exercise in any fitness regimen, as it allows your body to recover and grow stronger. On rest days, take the time to engage in gentle stretching or relaxation techniques to further enhance your overall wellbeing.

On **Day 1**, we'll start with the Glute Bridges. Position yourself with your feet hip-width apart on a wall and your arms and neck neutral on your mat. Lift your hips up and then lower them back down, repeating this for 30 seconds. The goal is to engage your core and glutes, and to familiarize yourself with the sensation of using the wall as a support.

Day 2 will introduce Wall Push-Ups. Place your hands on the wall about shoulder-distance apart, and step your feet back to a comfortable distance. Lower yourself towards the wall, keeping your elbows at a 45-degree angle, then press into the wall to rise back up. Aim for four sets of 10 reps. This exercise will work your arms and back, getting your upper body involved in the workout.

On **Day 3**, we'll add Wall Sits to our routine. Lean your back against a wall and slide down until your knees are bent at about 90 degrees. Press your back into the wall and engage your quads, glutes, and hamstrings to stay steady. Hold this position for anywhere from 10 to 60 seconds and repeat three times. This is a great exercise for improving your posture and strengthening your legs.

Day 4 is for Wall 100s. Lie on your back at a distance where your feet just touch the wall. Reach your arms straight up, take a breath, then exhale as you lower your arms and lift your shoulders off the mat. Reach your arms towards the wall and begin to pump your arms up and down, inhaling for five counts and exhaling for five counts as you pump. Keep going for 10 rounds. This exercise is designed to work your core and get your heart rate up.

On **Day 5**, we'll bring everything together. Start with the Glute Bridges, move on to the Wall Push-Ups, then to the Wall Sits, and finally, the Wall 100s. This is your chance to see how far you've come in just a few days and to feel the synergy of all these exercises working together.

Days 6 and 7 are your rest days. Use them to relax, stretch, and prepare yourself for the week to come. You've made great strides in your first week, and you should be proud. Keep that momentum going, and get ready to tackle Week 2 with all the strength and confidence you've built up.

Remember, everyone's journey with Wall Pilates is unique. Listen to your body and adjust the exercises as needed. The most important thing is to stay consistent and to keep enjoying the process. You're doing something wonderful for your body and mind, and every step of the journey is valuable. So keep going, and know that with every session, you're becoming stronger, more flexible, and more in tune with your body. Here's to a fantastic first week of Wall Pilates!

Daily Routines for Week 1

Here, we'll lay the groundwork with fundamental exercises that will become part of your daily routine.

Day 1: Introduction to Wall Pilates - Glute Bridges

Your Wall Pilates journey begins with Glute Bridges. This exercise targets your glutes and core, providing a gentle introduction to using the wall as a support. Place your feet hip-width apart on the wall, keeping your arms and neck neutral on your mat. Lift your hips up and then lower them back down, repeating this for 30 seconds. By the end of this session, you'll feel a deeper connection to your core and a newfound appreciation for the strength of your glutes.

Day 2: Upper Body Focus - Wall Push-Ups

On Day 2, we turn our attention to the upper body with Wall Push-Ups. Position your hands shoulder-width apart on the wall and step your feet back. The further your feet are from the wall, the more challenging the exercise. Lower yourself towards the wall, keeping your elbows at a 45-degree angle, then push away from the wall to return to your starting position. Aim for four sets of 10 repetitions. You'll feel this exercise in your arms and back, as it helps to build strength and stability in these areas.

Day 3: Lower Body and Core Engagement - Wall Sits

Day 3 introduces Wall Sits, a powerful exercise to improve your posture, strengthen your legs, and engage your core. Position your back against a wall and slide down until your knees form a 90-degree angle. Press your back into the wall, engaging your quads, glutes, and hamstrings. Hold this position for 10 to 60 seconds, repeating three times. By the end of this day, you'll notice an improvement in your overall balance and core strength.

Day 4: Cardio and Core Activation - Wall 100s

On Day 4, we raise our heart rate with Wall 100s, a dynamic exercise that works your core. Lying on your back, position yourself so your feet just touch the wall. Reach your arms straight up, inhale, then exhale as you lower your arms and lift your shoulders off the mat. Pump your arms up and down as you inhale for five counts and exhale for five counts. Continue for 10 rounds. This exercise not only strengthens your core but also gets your blood pumping, offering a cardio component to your Pilates routine.

Day 5: Complete Wall Pilates Routine

Day 5 is a cumulative day where you'll put all of the exercises together in a comprehensive Wall Pilates routine. Start with Glute Bridges, move on to Wall Push-Ups, then Wall Sits, and finally Wall 100s. This is a great way to end the working week and see how far you've come in just five days.

Day 6 and Day 7: Rest and Recover

After five days of introducing new exercises and putting them into practice, your body deserves some rest. On Days 6 and 7, engage in light activities such as walking or stretching, or perhaps try some mindfulness techniques. This is also a good time to reflect on the past week, noting your progress and any areas where you'd like to improve.

This is just the beginning of your Wall Pilates journey. Remember, it's not about perfection, but about progress. Enjoy these daily routines and take one step at a time. Your commitment in this first week lays a strong foundation for the weeks to come!

CHAPTER 3

Week 2: Increasing Intensity

As dawn breaks on Week 2, you may start to feel a sense of harmony between your body and mind. You've established a rhythm, and it's time to pump up the intensity. This week, we'll add some zest to your routine, challenging your muscles and inspiring your soul.

Day 1: Let's kick things off with a burst of energy – Wall Bicycle Crunches! There's something so liberating about this exercise. Get close to the wall, place your feet up, and crunch as you bring an opposite elbow to an opposite knee. You'll feel like you're cycling through the clouds. The sheer dynamism of this exercise not only works your core but also sends a wave of energy through your entire being. Aim for three to four sets of 15, and remember to smile – you're doing something wonderful for yourself.

Day 2: On the **second day**, let's indulge in some Wall Lunges. Stand gracefully, with the side of your body near the wall. With poise, keep one hand on the wall for support as you step your inner leg back, lower down into a lunge, and then return. Imagine yourself as a dancer, moving fluidly and with purpose. Lift your leg in front of you to waist height to challenge yourself, and repeat for 60 seconds on each side. This exercise instills a sense of balance, as your muscles work in unison like a finely tuned orchestra.

Day 3: As we glide into the third day, let's focus on the often-overlooked muscles with Leg Lifts. Stand at the center of your mat and reach forward with both hands to press into the wall. As you lift one leg behind you, picture yourself as a figure skater, gliding effortlessly across the ice. The elegance and poise in this movement are matched only by the strength it builds in your glutes. Focus on the power of your movements, repeating for 60 seconds on each side.

Day 4: Day four will have you channeling your inner martial artist with Side Kicks. In this version, prop yourself up on a diagonal as you lean into the wall. Lift your leg out to the side, keeping your body aligned. Imagine you are a warrior, strong and fierce.

This exercise not only tones your legs but also fortifies your spirit. Aim for three sets of eight reps per side, and remember that you are a force to be reckoned with.

Day 5: Towards the end of the week, let's combine grace and strength with Leg Circles. Stand tall with your feet hip-distance apart and press your hips and palms into the wall. Lift one leg in front of you and draw small circles with your toes, like a painter creating a masterpiece. This exercise is a testament to the beauty that is within you and the strength that you possess. Trace five times in one direction, then reverse, and repeat on both sides.

Days 6 and 7: As the week comes to a close, take some time to appreciate the symphony of movements you've created. Your body has been both the canvas and the paintbrush, creating art through movement. Dedicate the last day of Week 2 to Roll Downs. Stand with your shoulders against the wall and fold your upper body forward. As you roll back up, imagine each vertebra as a note in a melody, creating a beautiful tune as you move.

Congratulations on completing Week 2. Your dedication and the intensity you brought to each movement have made this week an invigorating and soulful experience. Take the weekend to reflect on the elegance and strength you've displayed, and prepare yourself for the wonders Week 3 will bring. You are not just working out; you are painting a canvas with your body, and it is simply breathtaking.

Daily Routines for Week 2

As we embark on Week 2, the energy shifts. Your body is adjusting to the rhythm of movement, and now we increase the intensity. Each day offers a new opportunity to push your boundaries and discover your strength.

On **Day 1**, we introduce Wall Bicycle Crunches. This is a dynamic exercise that not only engages your core but also injects a sense of vitality into your routine. Aim to complete three to four sets of 15 reps. Remember, it's not just about the number of crunches, but the quality of each movement.

Day 2 brings the elegance and strength of Wall Lunges. Stand beside the wall, step your inner leg back, and descend into a lunge. For an added challenge, lift the leg in front of you to waist height. Perform this movement for 60 seconds on each side. This exercise not only tones your legs but also helps develop your balance and coordination.

On **Day 3**, we focus on Leg Lifts. Stand in the center of your mat, press both hands into the wall, and lift one leg back behind you. Keep your spine neutral and focus on engaging your glutes with each lift. Repeat this for 60 seconds on each side. This exercise is a wonderful way to strengthen your glutes and improve your posture.

Day 4 invites the power and poise of Side Kicks. Lean into the wall on a diagonal, and lift your leg out to the side while maintaining body alignment. Try for three sets of eight reps per side. This exercise not only engages your core but also strengthens your hip abductors, providing stability to your movements.

On **Day 5**, we explore the grace of Leg Circles. Stand with your feet hip-distance apart, press your hips and palms into the wall, and lift one leg. Draw small circles with your toes, tracing five times in one direction, then reverse. Repeat on both sides. This exercise not only works your hip flexors but also promotes flexibility and range of motion in your hips.

Day 6 is dedicated to Roll Downs. Stand with your shoulders against the wall, and gently roll your upper body down into a forward fold. Then, roll back up. This exercise stretches your back and encourages spinal mobility.

Take **Day 7** to rest, reflect on your progress, and prepare for the week ahead. You've done an incredible job in increasing the intensity of your exercises while maintaining control and elegance. Remember to take some time to appreciate your progress, and prepare yourself for the adventures of Week 3.

CHAPTER 4

Week 3: Mastering Precision and Control

The third week is a critical juncture in our journey. It's the week where we seek to master precision and control, two core principles of Pilates. This week, we revisit the exercises of the previous weeks, but with a new perspective and an added touch of complexity. Every movement, every breath, and every pose is an opportunity to exercise precision and control.

Day 1: The dawn of Day 1 brings us back to Glute Bridges. As familiar as they might be by now, we want to infuse them with even more control. Focus on the lift of your hips, the alignment of your body, and the engagement of your glutes. Challenge yourself by holding at the top for a moment longer, feeling the burn in your muscles, the tension that speaks of strength and endurance.

On **Day 2**, we revisit Wall Push-Ups. By now, your arms and back are stronger, and your technique is improved. Try to step your feet a bit further from the wall, increasing the challenge. As you lower your body, imagine yourself as a feather, light but controlled. Each push-up should feel like a testament to your strength and your determination.

With the arrival of **Day 3**, we return to Wall Sits. This exercise is all about endurance and control. Hold the position for a little longer this time, focusing on pressing your back into the wall and engaging your quads, glutes, and hamstrings. Embrace the effort, the pull of gravity, the whisper of challenge that makes you stronger.

Day 4 takes us back to Wall 100s. Your core will be put to the test once more, but you're ready for it. Be precise with your breaths and controlled in your movements. Each round should be a rhythmic dance of inhale-exhale, a testimony to your resilience.

On **Day 5**, we will tackle Wall Bicycle Crunches again. Ensure your movements are slow and controlled, engaging your core with each crunch. As you bring your opposite elbow to your opposite knee, visualize a line of energy, aligning your body with your intentions.

Day 6 presents us with the challenge of Wall Lunges once again. However, this time, we aim for more precision in our movements. Pay attention to your form as you lower into the lunge, ensuring your knee doesn't go over your toes. As you lift your leg, engage your core and maintain your balance.

On **Day 7**, we rest and reflect. As you look back on the week, consider your journey of precision and control. Be proud of your progress and the strength you've discovered. Every sweat drop, every muscle ache, every breath was worth it. You've not only improved your physical strength but also your mental resilience. The road ahead is exciting, and you are more than ready to conquer it. You're not the same person you were three weeks ago. You're stronger, more balanced, and empowered. You're a Pilates warrior, ready for the next challenge. The journey continues, and you're prepared to face it with a smile.

Daily Routines for Week 3

Day 1: Glute Bridges

- Warm up with some light stretching.
- Perform Glute Bridges with an emphasis on control and precision. Pay close attention to the lift of your hips, the alignment of your body, and the engagement of your glutes.
- Challenge yourself by holding at the top for a moment longer, really feeling the burn in your muscles. Aim for three sets of 15-20 reps.
- Follow with a cool down and stretching.

Day 2: Wall Push-Ups

- Begin with a warm up.
- Perform Wall Push-Ups with focus on precision. Try to step your feet a bit further from the wall, increasing the challenge.

- As you lower your body, control your descent as if you were a feather, light but controlled. Each push-up should be a testament to your strength and your determination. Aim for four sets of 10 reps.
- Cool down and stretch to finish.

Day 3: Wall Sits

- Start with a warm up.
- Perform Wall Sits focusing on endurance and control. Hold the position for a little longer than you did the previous week, focusing on pressing your back into the wall and engaging your quads, glutes, and hamstrings.
- Embrace the effort and aim to hold for anywhere from 20 to 90 seconds and repeat three times.
- Cool down with stretching.

Day 4: Wall 100s

- Warm up.
- Revisit the Wall 100s exercise. Be precise with your breaths and controlled in your movements. Each round should be a rhythmic dance of inhale-exhale. Aim for 10 rounds.
- End with a cool down and stretching.

Day 5: Wall Bicycle Crunches

- Start with a warm up.
- Perform Wall Bicycle Crunches. Ensure your movements are slow and controlled, engaging your core with each crunch. As you bring your opposite elbow to your opposite knee, visualize a line of energy, aligning your body with your intentions. Aim for three to four sets of 15.
- Cool down with stretching.

Day 6: Wall Lunges

- Warm up.
- Perform Wall Lunges once again. Pay attention to your form as you lower into the lunge, ensuring your knee doesn't go over your toes. As you lift your leg, engage your core and maintain your balance. Repeat for 60 seconds on each side.
- Cool down and stretch to finish.

Day 7: Rest and Reflect

- Take this day to rest your body and reflect on your progress. Consider how you've improved in terms of precision and control, and how these principles have been applied throughout the week.
- Use this time to perform some light stretching or yoga, focusing on breath control and mindful movement.
- Prepare for the upcoming week by setting new goals and revisiting the previous week's challenges.

Remember that during this week, the focus is on control and precision in every movement. This is an opportunity to improve your technique and deepen your understanding of each exercise. You're doing fantastic! Keep up the great work!

CHAPTER 5

Week 4: Enhancing Endurance and Flexibility

As the first rays of the sun herald the beginning of week 4, a sense of exhilaration envelops you. The dedication and hard work of the past three weeks have forged a newfound strength within. Week 4 is an ode to endurance and flexibility - the twin pillars that will elevate your Pilates journey to new heights.

Day 1 of this week is graced by the serene elegance of Leg Lifts. Stand in the center of your mat, pressing both hands into the wall. As you lift one leg back behind you, relish the symphony of your muscles harmonizing. Picture the waves of the ocean as you lift and lower your leg, embracing the ebb and flow of strength and grace.

Day 2 welcomes the dynamic spirit of Side Kicks. Prop yourself up on a diagonal as you lean into the wall, and lift your leg to the side. This exercise is not just a physical movement; it is an echo of your will. Every kick tells a story of the barriers you have shattered and the mountains you have scaled.

The dawn of **Day 3** is painted with the hues of Leg Circles. Stand near a wall, lift one leg in front of you, and draw small circles with your toes. As you trace these circles, envision yourself painting your canvas of dreams. Each rotation is a brushstroke, a commitment to creating a masterpiece that is your well-being.

On **Day 4**, you are reunited with the ethereal Roll Downs. Stand with your back against the wall, and as you roll down, imagine yourself shedding layers of doubt and inhibitions. As you roll back up, you're collecting fragments of hope and courage. This exercise is more than a stretch; it's a journey of rediscovery.

Day 5 brings along the grace of Wall Planks. Place your forearms on the wall and step your feet back. Hold this position, channeling the poise of a ballet dancer on the grand stage. The Wall Plank is a testament to your fortitude, a declaration of the endurance that pulsates through your being.

Day 6 is adorned with the beauty of Wall Arabesques. Stand facing the wall, place one hand for support, and extend the opposite leg back. Imagine yourself as a bird spreading its wings, soaring through the skies. This exercise is a symphony of balance, strength, and flexibility.

As the curtain falls on **Day 7**, take a moment to bask in the golden silence. It is a day for reflection, a day to let the waves of gratitude wash over you. The whispers of your muscles, the symphony of your breath, and the tapestry of your spirit have woven together an opus of change.

Week 4 has been a waltz of endurance and flexibility. You have painted your dreams, soared through the skies, and danced with grace. This week has not just been a chapter in your Pilates journey; it has been a verse in the ballad of your life.

With an open heart and a soul enriched by the echoes of your strength, you stand on the precipice of boundless possibilities. The journey thus far has been exhilarating, and as you stride forward, know that the winds of change are with you.

Daily Routines for Week 4

Week 4 focuses on enhancing your endurance and flexibility. Here's a detailed day-to-day guide for this week:

Day 1: Leg Lifts: To start off the week, stand in the center of your mat with both hands pressed into the wall. Maintain a neutral spine and focus your gaze towards the floor. Lift one leg back behind you, focusing on engaging and squeezing your glute with each rep. Perform this action for 60 seconds on each side.

Day 2: Side Kicks: On the second day, perform Side Kicks by propping yourself up on a diagonal as you lean into the wall. Lift your leg out to the side, ensuring that your body remains aligned. Avoid sagging down in the middle. Do this exercise for three sets of eight reps per side.

Day 3: Leg Circles: Day 3's routine will be Leg Circles. Stand with your feet hip-distance apart and around four inches in front of the wall. Press your hips and palms into the wall, lift one leg in front of you and float it a few inches off the floor. Start drawing small circles with your toes, tracing five times in one direction, then reverse it. Repeat this on both sides.

Day 4: Roll Downs: On the fourth day, Roll Downs will help stretch your back and awaken your body. Stand with your shoulders against the wall and drop your upper body into a forward fold. Slowly roll back up and repeat.

Day 5: Wall Planks: Day 5 will test your endurance with Wall Planks. Place your forearms on the wall and step your feet back, maintaining a straight line from your head to your heels. Hold this position for 30 seconds, rest for a bit, and repeat.

Day 6: Wall Arabesques: For Day 6, stand facing the wall, place one hand on the wall for support, and extend the opposite leg back, creating an arabesque-like shape. Hold this position for a few seconds, then switch sides.

Day 7: Rest: After six days of rigorous exercises, take the seventh day to rest and reflect on the progress you've made over the week. Use this time to prepare yourself for the next week of the program.

Conclusion: Life After the Challenge

As you stand at the precipice of this moment, having braved the challenges and risen through the ranks of your own limitations, take a moment to soak in the elation of accomplishment. The sweat, the strain, the unyielding resolve that has carried you through this Wall Pilates journey is not just a testament to your physical prowess, but a melody of your soul's symphony.

Now that you have completed the challenge, it is important to remember that this is not an end but rather a beautiful beginning. The world of Wall Pilates has been a vessel, and the lessons you've learned are the winds in your sails. You've gained strength, flexibility, and an inner balance that can only come from listening to the whispers of your body.

As you move forward, make Wall Pilates your steadfast companion. Integrate it into your daily routine. Maybe some days it's only for ten minutes, and other days you delve deeper. The wall, which once seemed like an inanimate slab of indifference, is now a dear friend. It supports you, challenges you, and dances with you in the rhythm of your movements.

But don't let the wall be a boundary. Let it be a gateway to exploring other dimensions of fitness and well-being. Perhaps, indulge in the soft whispers of yoga, or the passionate cries of dance. There is a wide spectrum of colors waiting to be painted on the canvas of your fitness journey.

And in this odyssey of self-discovery, remember to be kind and compassionate to yourself. There will be days when the tempests of life may sway your ship. Your body may not always be the same; it is an ever-changing temple. Honor it with your efforts but also with your forgiveness and love.

Share your journey, too. The paths we walk are illuminated by the lights we carry, and when shared, they can light the ways for others. Be an inspiration. Perhaps, you can be the reason someone finds the strength they didn't know they had.

Finally, as you walk this endless path, know that every step is a note in the opus that is your life. Let each movement, each breath, be a song of love to the wondrous creation that is you.

Continuing Your Practice

As the curtain falls on this chapter of your Wall Pilates journey, a new dawn awaits. Embrace it with open arms and a heart full of passion. The path forward may not always be a straight one; it twists and turns, creating a beautiful mosaic of experiences that shape you, mold you, and ultimately guide you. But how do you continue practicing and maintaining the rhythm that you've established over the past weeks?

First and foremost, listen to your body. It is a symphony, with each part playing its unique role. Recognize the days when you need to push, and the days when you need to rest. Your body is not just a vessel but a partner in this journey, so treat it with respect and kindness. Every stretch, every twist, every moment of rest is a conversation between you and your body. Engage in this dialogue with attentiveness and care.

Building a routine is of paramount importance. Wall Pilates, as we've learned, is a dance between the body and the wall. It is a dance that needs to be practiced consistently to perfect. Perhaps you find solace in the quiet of the morning, or maybe the calm of the night resonates with you. Find a time that sings to you and make it a sacred space for your practice.

Remember, consistency doesn't mean rigidity. Explore and experiment with your routine. Some days, you might want to focus more on strength, other days on flexibility, and some days might call for focusing on balance. The beauty of Wall Pilates is its adaptability. It can be as gentle or as challenging as you need it to be.

In your continuous journey, don't hesitate to revisit the exercises you've learned during the challenge. They are your foundations, the roots from which your practice will grow. But also, don't be afraid to learn new movements. The world of Wall Pilates is vast and beautiful, full of variations that can add color to your routine.

Community can be a beacon of motivation. Connect with others who share your passion. You might find that their triumphs inspire you, and their struggles resonate with yours. Share your experiences, your victories, your struggles. In this shared space, you might find friendships that go beyond the wall, beyond Pilates.

The journey of Wall Pilates, like life, is a constant dance of growth and learning. Each day presents an opportunity to learn something new about your body, about your strength, about your resilience. Embrace these lessons with an open heart and a curious mind. And in this journey, remember to carry the light of joy, for the path of fitness is not just about the destination, but also about the joy of the journey.

Setting New Goals

There's a certain magic in setting new goals, an electrifying mix of anticipation and excitement. The world of Wall Pilates is vast, offering a myriad of opportunities to grow, to challenge oneself, and to discover new layers of strength and flexibility. But where should one start when setting new goals?

The first step is to look inward. Reflect on your journey so far. What elements of your practice brought you the most joy? Where did you find the most challenge? What aspects would you like to improve? The answers to these questions form the cornerstones of your new goals.

Perhaps you've found a newfound love for the strength-building elements of Wall Pilates. In that case, your new goal could be to increase your strength. This could mean performing more repetitions of strength-focused exercises, adding resistance bands to your routine, or learning new, more challenging strength-based movements.

Alternatively, you might have discovered a passion for the flexibility that Wall Pilates offers. Your new goal, then, could be to enhance your flexibility. This might involve incorporating more flexibility-focused exercises into your routine, holding your stretches for longer, or working on more advanced flexibility movements.

Remember, goals are not a one-size-fits-all deal. They're deeply personal, reflecting not just your desires, but also your unique journey. Craft your goals with the same love and attention you give your practice.

But while setting goals, it's essential to ensure they're realistic and achievable. Setting a goal that's too ambitious can lead to frustration and burnout. On the other hand, a goal that's too easy may not provide the challenge necessary for growth. Striking a balance is key. A well-set goal should ignite a spark of challenge but should also be within the realm of possibility.

Lastly, don't forget to celebrate your progress along the way. Every step towards your goal, no matter how small, is a victory worth celebrating. These moments of celebration nourish your motivation, making the journey towards your goal a joyous one.

The process of setting new goals is a beautiful dance of reflection, aspiration, and determination. As you step onto this dance floor, let your heart guide you. After all, the most rewarding goals are those that resonate with your innermost passions. And with these new goals, you'll find that your Wall Pilates journey is not just a path of fitness, but a path of self-discovery and growth.

BOOK 5

Wall Pilates for Pain Management and Enhanced Well-being

Introduction: Understanding Pain and the Role of Exercise

Let us embark on a journey of understanding, a journey where we delve into the nature of pain and the remarkable role that exercise, specifically Wall Pilates, can play in managing it, and enhancing our overall well-being. Pain is a complex and deeply personal experience. It is our body's way of communicating that something is not quite right. However, chronic pain, pain that persists for weeks, months, or even years, can be a disruptive force, diminishing our quality of life.

Pain can originate from various sources such as injury, disease, or even stress. Regardless of its origin, chronic pain can affect our mental and physical health, our relationships, and our ability to lead fulfilling lives. However, hope is not lost. In the fight against pain, we are not powerless. In fact, one of our most potent weapons can be found in the world of exercise, in the realm of Wall Pilates.

Wall Pilates, a variation of traditional Pilates that utilizes a wall for support and balance, offers a gentle yet effective way to engage our bodies, strengthen our muscles, and increase our flexibility. These physical improvements can play a significant role in managing pain.

When we engage in Wall Pilates, we work on a variety of muscles throughout our bodies. This balanced approach to exercise can help to correct muscular imbalances, a common cause of pain. For instance, a person with a desk job might experience back pain due to weakened back muscles and tight chest muscles. By strengthening the back muscles and stretching the chest muscles, Wall Pilates can help restore balance, alleviating the back pain.

Moreover, the focus on core strength in Wall Pilates can lead to better overall posture, which can alleviate pain related to poor posture. The core is our body's powerhouse, its center of gravity, and it plays a crucial role in maintaining posture. A strong core can help ensure that our bodies are aligned properly, reducing strain on our muscles and joints and, thus, reducing pain.

Wall Pilates can also aid in managing pain by increasing flexibility. Tight, inflexible muscles can lead to a limited range of motion, which can result in pain. The stretching elements of Wall Pilates can help to increase our flexibility, allowing our muscles to move more freely and reducing the likelihood of pain.

However, the benefits of Wall Pilates extend beyond the physical. Chronic pain can take a toll on our mental health, leading to conditions like anxiety and depression. The mindful nature of Wall Pilates, with its focus on controlled, intentional movements and deep, rhythmic breathing, can have a calming effect, reducing stress and promoting mental well-being. This can help break the cycle of pain and negative emotions, leading to a better quality of life.

When we engage in Wall Pilates, we are not just exercising our bodies, we are also caring for our minds. We are not just building strength and flexibility; we are also cultivating resilience and peace of mind. In this way, Wall Pilates can help us manage pain and enhance our overall well-being.

The Physiology of Pain

The human body is a marvel of intricate systems and processes, all working harmoniously to create the remarkable abilities we often take for granted. Among these systems is the complex and multifaceted pain response—an important signal to our brain that something is wrong. But what happens when this signal misfires, or becomes chronic? Understanding the physiology of pain is the first step towards managing it effectively.

Pain is, fundamentally, a survival mechanism. It's the body's way of alerting us to injury or illness, demanding our immediate attention. Our nervous system is the vehicle for these messages, carrying signals from the site of damage to our brain, which interprets these signals as pain. This intricate process involves a variety of receptors, nerves, and brain regions, all working in concert to produce the experience we know as pain.

When we experience a physical injury, for instance, specialized nerve endings called nociceptors are activated in the affected area. These nociceptors respond to various forms of damaging stimuli, such as heat, cold, pressure, or chemical changes, and send signals through peripheral nerves to the spinal cord. From there, the signals ascend to the brain, where they are processed and perceived as pain.

Acute pain, as unpleasant as it may be, is crucial for our survival. It's a stark warning that prompts us to withdraw from harmful situations and protect ourselves from further harm. A burn, a cut, a broken bone—these all-trigger acute pain responses that make us instinctively recoil and protect the injured area.

However, not all pain is a direct result of obvious physical damage. Sometimes, pain can persist long after an injury has healed, or arise in the absence of any discernible injury at all. This type of pain, known as chronic pain, can be far more challenging to understand and manage.

Chronic pain is often linked to conditions such as fibromyalgia, arthritis, migraines, and neuropathy, among others. The mechanisms behind chronic pain are complex and not entirely understood, but research suggests it involves changes in the nervous system that cause it to become overly sensitive to pain signals. In essence, the body's pain system gets stuck in the "on" position, leading to persistent discomfort or even intense pain.

This is where the importance of understanding pain's physiology becomes clear. By comprehending the mechanisms of pain, we can develop strategies to manage it more effectively. Exercise, for example, has been shown to be a powerful tool in the battle against chronic pain.

Engaging in regular physical activity, like wall Pilates, can have a host of benefits for individuals dealing with chronic pain. For starters, exercise stimulates the release of natural pain-relieving substances in the body, such as endorphins. These chemicals interact with the same receptors in the brain as opioids do, effectively reducing the perception of pain.

Moreover, exercise can help combat some of the secondary effects of chronic pain. It can increase strength and flexibility, improve sleep, boost mood, and reduce feelings of stress and anxiety—all of which can contribute to a better overall quality of life for those living with chronic pain.

Wall Pilates, in particular, can be an excellent choice for individuals dealing with pain. Its focus on gentle, controlled movements and deep, mindful breathing can help to relax tense muscles and promote a sense of calm and well-being. Furthermore, many wall Pilates exercises can be modified to accommodate individual abilities and pain levels, making it a versatile and accessible option for many people.

The journey of understanding and managing pain can be a long and winding one. It requires patience, resilience, and a willingness to try various strategies to see what works best for you. By understanding the physiology of pain and the role of exercise, you've taken the first important steps on that journey.

It's crucial to remember that pain is a deeply personal experience. What works for one person might not work for another. That's why it's essential to approach pain management with an open mind and a sense of curiosity. Try different strategies, listen to your body's responses, and be patient with yourself. It's a process, and every step forward, no matter how small, is a victory.

In the end, understanding the physiology of pain isn't just about knowing the biological mechanisms at play. It's about embracing a holistic approach to health and well-being. It's about acknowledging the interconnectedness of our body systems and recognizing the influence of our mental and emotional state on our physical health. It's about learning to tune into the unique language of our bodies and responding with kindness, compassion, and care.

Pain can be a challenging teacher, but it's also an opportunity. It's an invitation to deepen our understanding of ourselves, to cultivate resilience, and to discover new strategies for health and well-being. It's an invitation to engage with our bodies in a new way, with mindfulness, respect, and a commitment to self-care.

So, while the physiology of pain might seem complex, remember this: you are not alone on this journey. There are resources available, strategies to try, and people who understand what you're going through. There's a wealth of knowledge to explore, and every bit of understanding you gain is another tool in your toolbox.

In essence, understanding the physiology of pain is a way of reclaiming your power. It's a way of saying, "I am not just a passive recipient of this experience. I can understand it. I can manage it. I can navigate my way through it." And that, ultimately, is an incredibly empowering thing.

Exercise as a Pain

Exercising the body and pushing its limits is a fundamental aspect of human life. Our bodies are designed to move, to stretch, to flex, and to feel the sweet satisfaction of physical exertion. However, there's an interesting dichotomy at play: while exercise is an essential component of health and well-being, it can also bring about discomfort and pain. This isn't a deterrent; rather, it's a profound invitation to understand the language of our bodies better.

Let's explore this through the lens of Wall Pilates, a form of exercise that has gained popularity for its unique approach of using a wall as a prop for support and leverage. Wall Pilates, like other forms of exercise, can bring about a sense of discomfort or even pain, especially for beginners. But is this something to fear? Or is it something to understand, to work with, and ultimately to embrace as part of our fitness journey?

Pain and discomfort during exercise, including Wall Pilates, can often be an indicator of muscles being pushed beyond their comfort zone. It's the body's way of signaling that it's being challenged, that it's working hard, that it's growing stronger. Consider the first time you attempted a Wall Push-Up or a Glute Bridge. The strain in your arms or the burn in your glutes wasn't just a signal of discomfort; it was a testament to your body's remarkable capacity to adapt, to grow, and to overcome challenges.

Pain can also be an effective communicator, alerting us to potential issues in our technique or posture. In the world of Wall Pilates, precision is paramount. The alignment of the body, the positioning of the limbs, the engagement of the core - every detail matters. If you're feeling excessive pain or discomfort, it might be your body's way of telling you that something is off. Listen to it. Adjust. Align. And then try again.

But let's be clear, not all pain is the same. There's a distinct difference between the burn of a challenging workout and the sharp, persistent pain of an injury. The former is a part of the process, a sign that you're pushing your limits and getting stronger. The latter is a warning, a signal that something is wrong. Understanding this difference is crucial. It's the difference between growth and damage, between pushing on and knowing when to stop.

So, how do you differentiate between the two? It's about tuning into the nuances of your body's language. Paying attention to the type of pain, its intensity, its duration, and any accompanying symptoms. A Wall Pilates session might leave your muscles sore and tired, but this should subside with time and rest. On the other hand, a sharp, severe pain that persists or worsens over time should not be ignored. It's your body telling you that something isn't right.

Yet, exercise and pain are not always adversaries. There is a transformational side to this relationship. When approached mindfully and with an understanding of the body's language, exercise can become an empowering tool to manage and alleviate chronic pain. Movement can help reduce stiffness, increase flexibility, improve blood flow, and strengthen the muscles that support our joints. Furthermore, the endorphins released during exercise can act as natural painkillers, providing a sense of relief and well-being.

Consider Wall Pilates as a perfect example of this transformative potential. With its focus on gentle, controlled movements, this form of exercise can be an excellent choice for those managing chronic pain. Its emphasis on proper alignment and core engagement can help strengthen the body and improve posture, reducing the strain on painful joints and muscles. Moreover, the wall's support can make exercises more accessible, allowing individuals tomove at their own pace and within their comfort levels.

Embracing the discomfort that comes with physical exertion can teach us invaluable lessons about our strength, resilience, and capacity for growth. It invites us to face our fears, to step out of our comfort zones, and to push our limits. Yet, it also reminds us of the importance of balance, of listening to our bodies, and of knowing when to rest and recover.

However, it's essential to remember that every individual's experience with exercise, pain, and Wall Pilates will be unique. What might be a challenging but manageable discomfort for one person might be unendurable for another. It's crucial not to compare your pain or your progress with others. This is your journey, and it's about listening to your body, understanding its signals, and responding with compassion and care.

The journey with Wall Pilates or any form of exercise is not always smooth. There will be days of discomfort, of struggle, of pain. But remember, this is not a signal to stop;

it's a call to listen, to understand, and to adapt. It's an invitation to learn more about your body, its strengths, its limitations, and its incredible capacity for growth and healing.

Pain is not just a discomfort to be avoided; it's a powerful teacher. It pushes us to grow, to adapt, and to become stronger. It teaches us to listen to our bodies, to respect their signals, and to respond with care and understanding. It forces us to be present, to be mindful, and to be patient with ourselves and our progress.

The relationship between exercise and pain is complex, layered, and deeply personal. It's a dance - sometimes challenging, sometimes graceful, but always enlightening. As you navigate this journey, remember to listen to your body, to respect its signals, and to respond with kindness and care. After all, it's not just about building strength or flexibility; it's about cultivating a deep, loving, and understanding relationship with your body.

As you continue your journey with Wall Pilates, embrace the discomfort. Welcome the burn. Celebrate the soreness. But also, listen to your body. Rest when you need to. Adapt your movements. Keep your focus on the journey, not just the destination. And remember, every twinge, every ache, every moment of discomfort is a sign of growth. It's your body's way of saying, "I'm here. I'm strong. And I'm capable of so much more than I thought."

In the end, remember that the essence of Wall Pilates, like all forms of exercise, is not about enduring pain but about embracing the journey. It's about understanding your body, challenging your limits, and growing stronger with each session. It's about learning to see discomfort as an opportunity for growth, as a teacher, as a guide on your journey to better health and well-being.

Exercise is not merely a physical act; it's a profound dialogue between the body and the self. It's a journey of growth, of understanding, of self-love. So, the next time you find yourself wincing at the burn of a Wall Lunge or aching after a challenging Wall Push-Up, remember this: The pain is not a signal to stop; it's an invitation to listen, to understand, and to grow. And that, at its core, is the true essence of Wall Pilates and the transformative power of exercise.

CHAPTER 1

The Connection Between Pilates and Pain Management

As an experienced Wall Pilates instructor, I have witnessed firsthand the transformative power this discipline can have, not only on our physical strength and flexibility but also on our overall well-being. One particularly striking aspect of Wall Pilates is its potential for managing and mitigating pain. Whether it's chronic pain from an injury or ailment, or acute discomfort from tension and stress, Wall Pilates offers a holistic approach to pain management that goes beyond mere symptom relief.

Pilates is, at its heart, a mind-body practice. Founded by Joseph Pilates in the early 20th century, it's designed to align the body, strengthen the core, and improve flexibility. But more than that, it's a discipline that encourages us to listen to our bodies, to pay attention to their signals, and to respond with compassion and understanding. It's this mindful aspect of Pilates that makes it such a powerful tool for pain management.

When we experience pain, it's easy to fall into a cycle of fear and avoidance. We tense up, resist, and withdraw from the source of our discomfort. But this reaction often exacerbates the pain, leading to a cycle of tension, stress, and more pain. Wall Pilates offers a different approach. Rather than avoiding the pain, we're encouraged to engage with it, to explore it, and to understand it.

This isn't about pushing through the pain or ignoring it. Quite the opposite. It's about creating a safe space where we can explore our discomfort, understand its source, and find ways to alleviate it. It's about learning to work with our bodies, rather than against them. It's about cultivating a relationship with our bodies that's based on trust, respect, and compassion.

In Wall Pilates, the wall serves as a supportive partner. It provides stability, feedback, and a point of reference as we explore our movements and our discomfort. It allows us to practice our exercises with control and precision, reducing the risk of injury and strain. But more than that, it invites us to lean into our discomfort, to understand it, and to work with it.

The physical benefits of Wall Pilates for pain management are clear. The exercises are designed to strengthen the core, improve posture, and enhance flexibility. They help to alleviate tension, correct muscular imbalances, and promote better alignment. Over time, this can lead to a significant reduction in pain and discomfort.

But the benefits of Wall Pilates go beyond the physical. The practice encourages mindfulness, relaxation, and stress reduction. It invites us to slow down, to focus on our breath, and to connect with our bodies. This mindful approach can have profound effects on our perception of pain. By slowing down and tuning into our bodies, we can begin to shift our relationship with pain. We can learn to understand it, to manage it, and ultimately, to alleviate it.

Managing pain with Wall Pilates is not about quick fixes or instant results. It's a journey, a process of exploration, understanding, and growth. It's about learning to listen to our bodies, to respect their signals, and to respond with kindness and care. It's about finding balance, strength, and flexibility, not just in our bodies, but in our approach to pain.

Wall Pilates offers an empowering approach to pain management. It allows us to take an active role in our healing process, to understand our bodies, and to work with them to alleviate discomfort. It's not a cure-all, but it can be an effective tool in our pain management toolkit.

In my experience as a Wall Pilates instructor, I've seen how this practice can transform people's relationship with pain. I've witnessed the shifts in their bodies, their attitudes, and their lives. But what strikes me the most is the sense of empowerment that comes from understanding and managing their own pain. When we understand our pain, we are no longer at its mercy. Instead, we can approach it with knowledge, compassion, and a sense of control.

Wall Pilates encourages us to connect with our bodies on a deeper level, to appreciate the signals they send us, and to respond to them in a mindful and intentional way. The focus on core strength, alignment, and flexibility is more than just a physical workout - it's an exercise in self-awareness and body consciousness. This newfound understanding of our bodies and their capabilities often extends beyond the Pilates studio, influencing our daily lives and our approach to pain and discomfort.

The importance of breath in Wall Pilates should not be underestimated either. The act of conscious breathing during our workouts has a profound effect on our perception of pain. Breathing deeply and mindfully helps us to relax, to let go of tension, and to release the grip of pain on our bodies and minds. It becomes a soothing rhythm that grounds us, aligns us, and guides us through each movement. The breath becomes a bridge between our physical bodies and our mental state, linking the two in a powerful dance of wellness and relief.

The beauty of Wall Pilates lies in its adaptability. The exercises can be modified to suit each individual's needs, allowing everyone, regardless of their fitness level or physical condition, to benefit from the practice. For those dealing with chronic pain, this adaptability is crucial. It allows them to engage in physical activity without fear of exacerbating their pain or causing further harm. It gives them the freedom to explore their movement within a safe and supportive framework.

Wall Pilates does not promise a life free of pain, but it does offer the tools to manage it effectively. It teaches us to understand our bodies, to respect their boundaries, and to work with them, rather than against them. It encourages us to take charge of our own wellness, to engage with our pain, and to find ways to alleviate it. It's a holistic, empowering, and compassionate approach to pain management.

As an instructor, it is deeply rewarding to witness the transformative journey of individuals as they navigate through their pain using Wall Pilates. Each breath, each movement, each moment of understanding is a step towards better pain management and improved quality of life. The journey might not be easy, but it is undoubtedly empowering.

Through Wall Pilates, we learn that pain is not something to fear or fight. Instead, it's a signal from our bodies, a form of communication that asks for our attention. By engaging with it mindfully, by exploring it with curiosity, and by responding to it with compassion, we can transform our experience of pain. We can move from a place of suffering to a place of understanding, from a place of fear to a place of empowerment.

The beauty of Wall Pilates as a method for pain management is that it is a journey that respects the individual. It recognizes that each of us is unique, that our experiences of pain are personal, and that our paths to wellness will be as varied and unique as we are. It's a practice that celebrates our individuality, our strengths, and our potential. It's a practice that invites us to lean into our discomfort, to learn from it, and to grow.

In the end, the connection between Wall Pilates and pain management is one of understanding, compassion, and empowerment. It's about learning to work with our bodies, to understand their signals, and to respond with care. It's about finding balance, strength, and flexibility, not just in our bodies, but in our approach to pain. And above all, it's about recognizing that we have the power to manage our pain, to improve our quality of life, and to thrive, regardless of the challenges we face.

In the world of Pilates, there is a saying: "Movement heals." This is a testament to the power of our bodies to heal and restore themselves through deliberate and mindful movement. But it's more than just a catchy phrase; it's a philosophy that guides the practice of Wall Pilates. This belief in the healing power of movement is particularly relevant when it comes to managing pain. When we move, we stimulate blood flow, we strengthen our muscles, and we enhance our flexibility. All of these are key to reducing pain and promoting overall wellness.

In addition to its physical benefits, Wall Pilates also offers psychological benefits that can significantly improve our experience of pain. The practice promotes a sense of calm and relaxation, helping to alleviate stress and anxiety, which are often associated with chronic pain. The mindful nature of Wall Pilates, the focus on breath and body awareness, fosters a state of mental clarity and tranquility. This can help us better manage our pain, as we learn to separate the physical sensation of pain from the emotional and psychological distress it can cause.

Wall Pilates also fosters a sense of self-efficacy, the belief in our ability to manage our own health and wellbeing. As we grow stronger, more flexible, and more in tune with our bodies through our Wall Pilates practice, we become more confident in our ability to manage our pain. This sense of self-efficacy can be incredibly empowering for individuals dealing with chronic pain, providing a much-needed boost of optimism and hope.

One of the most profound ways Wall Pilates assists in pain management is by enhancing body awareness. With improved body awareness, we become more attuned to our bodies' needs and signals, allowing us to respond to pain in a more proactive and informed way. This heightened sense of body awareness also helps us avoid movements and postures that might exacerbate our pain, further aiding in pain management.

On a deeper level, Wall Pilates helps us redefine our relationship with pain. Instead of viewing pain as an adversary to be defeated, we learn to see it as a guide, a messenger that alerts us when something is amiss in our bodies. This shift in perspective can have a profound impact on our experience of pain. It empowers us to approach pain with curiosity and openness, rather than fear and resistance.

Moreover, Wall Pilates encourages a compassionate and accepting approach towards our bodies and our pain. Instead of criticizing ourselves for our limitations or comparing ourselves to others, we learn to embrace where we are in our journey and to appreciate our bodies for their strength and resilience. This compassionate approach can reduce the emotional distress often associated with chronic pain, further aiding in pain management.

So, the question is not whether Wall Pilates can aid in pain management - the evidence is clear on that front. The real question is how we can best utilize this powerful tool to enhance our own wellness. The answer to that will be different for everyone, but the starting point is always the same: by stepping onto the mat, by taking a deep breath, and by being willing to listen to our bodies. From there, the possibilities are endless.

In conclusion, Wall Pilates offers a holistic, empowering, and compassionate approach to pain management. By combining physical exercise with mental focus, it enhances our overall wellness and gives us the tools to effectively manage our pain. But perhaps most importantly, it teaches us that we are not defined by our pain. We are not passive victims of it. We are active participants in our own health and wellbeing. And that is a lesson worth learning.

How Pilates Helps in Pain Management: A Scientific Perspective

When we talk about pain management, it is essential to look beyond the confines of traditional medicine and embrace the diverse methods that have been proven to be effective. Wall Pilates, a variation of the classic Pilates method, is a shining example of this diversity. It's not just a form of exercise; it's an amalgamation of mindful movements that has a powerful impact on pain management.

Delving into the science behind Wall Pilates, we uncover the mechanisms that make this practice so effective. As you align yourself against a wall, engaging your muscles and focusing on your breath, you're doing much more than just physical activity. The wall offers an additional layer of support and resistance, which is pivotal in targeting the deeper muscles that are often overlooked. The activation of these muscles, especially around the spine and pelvis, plays a crucial role in alleviating pain, particularly in the lower back region.

One of the fundamental principles of Pilates is the focus on the core. Wall Pilates takes this a step further by allowing for a greater range of motion and a deeper engagement of the core muscles. A strong core acts like a corset for your trunk, supporting your spine. This is extremely beneficial for individuals suffering from chronic back pain. The muscles surrounding the spine are strengthened, which provides better support and stabilization, reducing the strain on the back.

Now, let's address the role of blood flow in pain management. Enhanced circulation is one of the many benefits of Wall Pilates. When your muscles are activated through the various movements, there is an increase in blood flow to those areas. This is significant because blood carries oxygen and nutrients that aid in the healing of damaged tissues. For someone experiencing pain due to inflammation or injury, this accelerated healing process is a boon.

Furthermore, Wall Pilates is also about the mind-body connection. The practice demands concentration and mindfulness. This mental aspect is not to be underestimated. When you're focused on your movements and breath, you're practicing a form of meditation. This meditative state has been shown to reduce the levels of cortisol, a stress hormone, in the body. Chronic pain is often linked to high levels of stress and anxiety. By reducing cortisol levels, Wall Pilates can contribute to a reduction in the sensation of pain.

Let's also explore the role of endorphins. These are chemicals in the brain that act as natural painkillers. Physical activity, including Wall Pilates, triggers the release of endorphins. These endorphins bind to receptors in the brain that decrease the perception of pain. This is often referred to as the "feel-good" effect of exercise.

Beyond just the perception of pain, endorphins also contribute to a sense of well-being and happiness, which can be transformative for individuals dealing with chronic pain.

Another aspect of Wall Pilates that is particularly beneficial for pain management is the emphasis on flexibility and range of motion. Often, pain is a result of stiffness and lack of mobility. Through the stretches and movements in Wall Pilates, you can work on increasing your flexibility. This not only helps in pain reduction but also aids in preventing future injuries.

Wall Pilates is also adaptable, making it accessible to people of different fitness levels and abilities. For individuals with pain, it's essential that exercise routines can be modified to accommodate their specific needs. Wall Pilates allows for such customization. The wall serves as a prop that can either increase or decrease the level of difficulty, ensuring that you can find a variation of the exercise that is both safe and effective for your pain management needs.

Wrapping it all up, Wall Pilates is a multifaceted approach to pain management. It's not just exercise; it's therapy for the mind and body. Through the strengthening of core muscles, enhancement of blood flow, stress reduction, increased endorphin levels, and improvement in flexibility, Wall Pilates addresses pain from multiple angles. The beauty of this practice lies not only in its effectiveness but also in its simplicity. All you need is a wall and the willingness to embrace the movements.

It's also important to remember that Wall Pilates, as effective as it is, should be a part of a broader pain management plan. While it can significantly contribute to reducing pain, it's crucial to consider other aspects such as proper nutrition, adequate sleep, and, if necessary, consultation with healthcare professionals.

In a world where pain has become all too common, it's refreshing to find solace in a practice that is both gentle and powerful. Wall Pilates doesn't ask for much; it only asks for your presence - both physical and mental. As you press your hands against the wall and feel your muscles engaging, take a moment to connect with yourself. Each breath, each movement is a step towards not just a stronger body, but a life with less pain.

This is not just science; it's the art of understanding and listening to your body. It's about taking ownership of your well-being and recognizing that within you lies the power to manage and alleviate pain. Wall Pilates is more than a set of exercises; it's a journey of self-discovery and healing. Through this practice, you're not only building a stronger body but also cultivating an inner sanctuary of peace and balance.

So, as you stand against the wall, ready to embark on this journey, know that with each movement, you're weaving the tapestry of your health. Let Wall Pilates be the thread that brings not just strength, but also relief and peace into the fabric of your life.

CHAPTER 2

Wall Pilates Exercises for Specific Types of Pain

The journey of Wall Pilates does not stop at general pain relief. Its versatility is one of its most distinguishing features. The practice can be tailored to address specific types of pain. You may be grappling with a stiff neck from hours of sitting at a computer, or perhaps you are dealing with chronic lower back pain. Whatever the case may be, Wall Pilates offers exercises targeted at these specific discomforts. In this chapter, we will delve deeper into the world of Wall Pilates, exploring how it can serve as a gentle yet effective antidote for various types of pain.

Neck and shoulder pain is a common affliction in the modern world. Many of us spend long hours hunched over computers or straining our necks to look at smartphones. This constant strain on the neck and shoulders can lead to chronic discomfort and even impact our quality of life. Wall Pilates offers a way to gently stretch and strengthen these muscles, thereby alleviating pain. Exercises such as Wall Push-Ups and Roll Downs can be particularly beneficial. They encourage proper alignment of the spine and neck, reducing strain and promoting healthier posture. As you engage in these movements, you are not just working on your physical well-being but also learning to cultivate mindfulness about your posture and alignment.

Lower back pain is another pervasive issue. It can stem from a variety of factors, including sedentary lifestyles, improper lifting techniques, or even stress. Wall Pilates comes to the rescue here as well. An exercise like the Glute Bridge, performed against the wall, can strengthen the lower back muscles and glutes, offering pain relief. The Wall Sit is another powerful exercise. It targets the core, glutes, and back muscles, fostering strength and stability that can safeguard against future discomfort.

There are other forms of discomfort that Wall Pilates can address. For instance, knee pain can often be the result of weak or imbalanced leg muscles. Wall Lunges and Wall Sits are two exercises that can help strengthen the surrounding muscles and provide relief. Likewise, for those grappling with hip pain, Leg Lifts and Wall Bicycle Crunches can help stretch and strengthen the hip flexors and extensors, thereby easing discomfort.

But, Wall Pilates is not just about the exercises. It is about understanding and listening to your body. It's about recognizing the signals your body sends you and responding to them with care. It's about acknowledging your pain, not as an enemy, but as a messenger signaling that something needs attention. When you engage in Wall Pilates, you are not just following a set of exercises. You are engaging in a dialogue with your body, seeking to understand its language and respond with love and care.

As we delve into these Wall Pilates exercises, it's essential to remember that each body is unique. What works for one person may not work for another. Therefore, it's crucial to listen to your body and modify exercises as needed. This is not about pushing through pain or forcing your body into positions it's not ready for. Instead, it's about nurturing a kind and patient relationship with your body, meeting it where it is, and gently guiding it towards increased strength and flexibility.

So, whether you're dealing with neck, back, knee, or hip pain, know that Wall Pilates can offer you a path towards relief. These exercises, combined with the philosophy of kindness and respect for your body, can help you manage and even alleviate your pain. But more importantly, they can empower you to take charge of your health, to become an active participant in your healing journey.

As you lean against the wall, ready to embark on your Wall Pilates practice, remember that this is not just about physical movement. It's about cultivating an inner dialogue with your body. It's about learning to listen, to respond, and to respect your body's wisdom. It's about discovering the strength that lies within you and the incredible capacity your body has for healing and transformation. With each push-up, each bridge, each lunge, you are saying to your body, "I hear you. I respect you. I am here for you."

This journey is not just about pain relief, though that is a significant part. It's about cultivating a deeper relationship with your body, about learning to see it not as a machine that needs fixing but as a partner in your journey towards health and well-being.

Remember that patience is key in this journey. Pain did not develop overnight, and it won't disappear instantly either. Each day that you dedicate to your Wall Pilates practice is a step towards healing. Every exercise is a message of care and respect that you send to your body. Over time, these messages accumulate, transforming not just your physical condition but also your relationship with your body.

In the quiet moments of practice, as you press your hands against the wall or lower your body into a lunge, you may experience a shift. A shift from viewing your body as a source of pain to seeing it as a source of strength. From feeling at war with your body to feeling in harmony with it. From feeling frustrated with your pain to feeling grateful for the signals your body sends you, guiding you towards the care it needs.

This is the power of Wall Pilates. Yes, it can help alleviate various types of pain. Yes, it can help strengthen your muscles and improve your flexibility. But perhaps most importantly, it can transform your relationship with your body. It can empower you to shift from a mindset of frustration and resistance to one of understanding, compassion, and respect.

So, as you embark on this journey of Wall Pilates for specific types of pain, remember this: you are not just practicing a set of exercises. You are engaging in a practice of love and respect for your body. You are taking a stand against the modern culture of pushing through pain and instead choosing a path of kindness and understanding. And in doing so, you are not just relieving your pain. You are transforming your relationship with your body and, ultimately, with yourself.

With each Wall Pilates exercise, you are sending a powerful message to your body. A message that says, "I see you. I hear you. I care for you." And in the end, isn't that what true healing is all about?

Wall Pilates for Back Pain

Ah, the back - the canvas of our body's masterpiece. It holds us upright, supports our movements, and carries the weight of our daily lives. However, when back pain strikes, it's like the paint on that canvas starts to crack. The beauty of our movements becomes hindered, and we long for the days when our back was strong and pain-free. Wall Pilates, my friend, is like the art restorer for your back's canvas. With gentle strokes and a keen eye for detail, it brings back the luster and vitality to your back. So, let's explore the magnificent world of Wall Pilates exercises designed for back pain relief.

Imagine yourself walking into an art studio, where the walls are your canvas and your body the paintbrush. The first exercise we are going to paint on this canvas is the 'Wall Roll Down'. Stand with your back against the wall. Feel the cool surface against your skin. It's like the touch of an old friend. As you inhale deeply, let your body feel the support of the wall. As you exhale, start rolling down, vertebra by vertebra. This exercise stretches your back, releasing the tension that builds up like layers of paint. When you come back up, imagine the negativity and pain rolling off your shoulders.

Next, let's paint the 'Wall Angels'. This exercise is like the gentle wings of an angel guiding your back to the heavens, free from pain. Stand against the wall with your feet slightly away from it. As you breathe in, raise your arms with your elbows bent, and as you exhale, glide them upwards. Feel the grace in your movements, and imagine your back pain dissolving like clouds parting for the sun.

Now, let's add some depth to our painting with 'Wall Supported Leg Extensions'. This exercise adds a touch of Renaissance to our canvas, as it's classical yet transformative. Sit down with your back against the wall, your knees bent and feet flat on the floor. Extend one leg out and bring it back in. With each extension, picture your leg as a paintbrush, stroking away the back pain.

Let's not forget the 'Wall Plank', a modern abstract piece in our gallery. Place your forearms against the wall and step back, engaging your core. This exercise is like balancing the colors on the canvas. It strengthens the core, which in turn supports the back. Feel the energy flowing from your heels to the crown of your head, as if you're channeling the strength of a warrior.

Now, for the final touch, the 'Wall Supported Bridge'. This is the crescendo, the final flourish in our painting. Lie down on the floor with your feet against the wall. Press down through your heels and lift your hips. The bridge is the metaphorical bridge between pain and relief. As your hips rise, envision the weight of your pain being lifted, leaving room for peace and relief.

Throughout these exercises, the wall is your ally, your guide, and your support. It's the canvas that captures the essence of your journey from pain to power. Wall Pilates is not just a set of exercises; it's an art form that speaks to the soul. It's the tender kiss of a loved one on a wound, the soft lullaby that puts a restless mind to sleep, and the ray of sunshine that breaks through a stormy cloud.

As you go through each exercise, remember that this is a sacred time between you and your body. Listen to its whispers, honor its needs, and paint your canvas with love and respect.

You are not just alleviating back pain; you are creating a masterpiece that tells the story of strength, resilience, and healing. So, let's nurture your back with the tenderness it deserves. Like an artist who spends days giving life to a canvas, give yourself the gift of time. Be patient and gentle. Let your back immerse in the euphony of movement and stillness.

As you walk out of the studio, your body might feel lighter, maybe even a bit euphoric. Carry that feeling with you. Let it be a reminder that the art of healing is within you. Your body is the canvas, Wall Pilates the paint, and your spirit the artist.

Feel the joy in knowing that with each stroke, you're not just relieving pain - you are painting the portrait of the renewed, magnificent you. Through Wall Pilates, you are embracing the whispers of your body, dancing in the rhythm of your breath, and creating a symphony that sings the song of healing.

Your back, the keeper of your body's secrets, has now a renewed strength and a quiet, knowing smile. Through Wall Pilates, you have given it a voice, a language to express itself. As you move through life, let this be the guiding light that illuminates your path, the gentle embrace that keeps you warm, and the sacred whisper that reminds you of the boundless strength within.

Now, go forth and paint the world with the colors of your spirit, for you are an artist, and your life is a canvas waiting to be adorned with the beauty of your being.

Wall Pilates for Neck and Shoulder Pain

In the tapestry of life, our neck and shoulders are the threads that often bear the weight of our worries and stress. We carry the world on our shoulders, and sometimes, that weight becomes too heavy. Through Wall Pilates, let's learn the art of unraveling the knots of tension and breathe life into the tired threads.

As dawn breaks, let the Wall Pilates studio be your sanctuary. Imagine the sun rays that peek through the window as gentle whispers, telling you that today is the day you take charge. So, with hope in your heart and dreams in your eyes, let's begin the journey.

Begin by standing against the wall. Feel the cool surface kiss your skin. Close your eyes and take a deep breath. As the air fills your lungs, imagine it carrying away the tension from your neck and shoulders. Now, place your arms against the wall at shoulder height, palms facing forward. Slowly slide them up as you breathe in and down as you breathe out. This simple Wall Angel exercise is like the first brushstroke on your canvas, releasing tension and improving mobility.

Now, let's add more colors to our painting. Place your right hand against the wall at shoulder height. Gently turn your head to the left and feel the stretch in your neck and shoulder. This is the Wall Neck Stretch. Be mindful of your breath, and let it guide you. Imagine the air as a gentle breeze, caressing your skin, and carrying away the knots of stress.

As you slowly come back to center, let's transition into the Wall Chest Stretch. Bring your right arm to the wall at a 90-degree angle with your elbow at shoulder height. Gently turn away from the wall, feeling your chest and shoulder open up like a blossoming flower. This stretch is like adding warm colors to your painting, bringing light and life to the canvas that is your body.

Next, let us move to the Wall Shoulder Rolls. Stand with your back against the wall, feet hip-width apart. Imagine you are holding a brush in each hand, painting circles with your shoulders. Roll them up, back, down, and forward. This is not just an exercise; it is a dance, a celebration of your newfound freedom from pain.

As you paint your circles, let's transition into the Wall Supported Warrior. Stand sideways with your right side against the wall. Extend your right arm, and let it rest against the wall. Reach your left arm overhead, and feel the stretch through your side, neck, and shoulder. Like a warrior who battles the storms, let this pose be your armor against pain.

Finally, let's add the finishing touches to our masterpiece with the Wall Shoulder Squeeze. Stand with your back to the wall and bend your elbows at 90 degrees. Gently squeeze your shoulder blades together and release. This is like sealing your painting with a protective layer, strengthening the muscles that guard your neck and shoulders.

As you complete your session, stand still for a moment. Feel the symphony of your breath, the colors of your spirit dancing on your canvas. You have just created not just art, but magic. Through Wall Pilates, you have breathed life into your neck and shoulders. You have turned the pages of an old story and written a new chapter.

So, as you step out into the world, carry this magic with you. Let your shoulders be not just a bearer of burdens but wings that soar. Let your neck be the pillar that holds your dreams. In Wall Pilates, you have found a sanctuary, a haven where your body and spirit can paint stories untold.

Your neck and shoulders, once weary, now wear a cloak of strength and grace. They are the unsung heroes of your daily life, carrying your head high through storms and sunshine. Treasure them, for they are a part of your beautiful tapestry.

And remember, Wall Pilates is not just an exercise; it is a conversation with your body. It's a gentle whisper to your muscles that they are loved, cherished, and valued. Like a painter who speaks through colors, let every movement be your body's voice, singing the songs of freedom from pain.

So, as you leave the Wall Pilates studio, let the door be a gateway to a world where neck and shoulder pain is but a distant memory. A world where your shoulders are strong, your neck is long, and your spirit is unshakable.

May Wall Pilates be the paintbrush that colors your canvas, the melody in your song, and the wind beneath your wings.

Wall Pilates for Knee Pain

In the dance of life, our knees are the most diligent of dancers. They bend and flex to the rhythm of our strides, bearing the weight of our dreams and ambitions. As we waltz through the pages of this book, let us set our sights on Wall Pilates and its tender embrace in healing knee pain. The symphony of movements will guide us to a place where grace meets strength, and pain bows out of the dance.

Imagine a serene morning, with the golden light painting the walls of your Pilates space. In this sanctum, you find solace from the throbbing pain in your knees. As you lay your mat against the wall, you feel the steadfast support it offers, just like a trusted friend. The magic begins with gentle leg slides. With your back on the floor and feet against the wall, you begin to slide one leg down and then the other. The beauty of this exercise lies in its simplicity, as the delicate sliding motion invites your hamstrings and quadriceps to waltz together. This harmonious dance helps to alleviate the pressure on your knees.

Now, let's glide into Wall Squats. As your back nestles against the wall, your feet welcome the floor with a gentle caress. Slowly, descend into a squat, as if an invisible chair awaits your grace. In this regal seated position, your knees bend with poise, and your thighs embrace the strength. The wall is the guardian that ensures you do not overextend your knees, while the thighs work in concert to fortify the supporting muscles around the knee joints.

As you rise from the imaginary chair, a sense of accomplishment envelops you. We now flow into the realm of Wall Angels. With your back against the wall, your arms ascend as if to touch the heavens. The movement is akin to making snow angels, but this time, the soft flakes are the tenderness of the wall against your back. As you raise and lower your arms, your knees are subtly engaged, fostering balance and stability. Wall Angels whisper to the knee joints, "You are safe, and you are cherished."

The ballet continues with the Standing Calf Raises. Your feet firmly planted on the ground, the wall supporting your back, you lift your heels in a gentle crescendo. The muscles around the knees awaken, like a chorus in a symphony. The calf raises are like the gentle plucks of a harp, each movement stringing together notes of relief and comfort for the knees.

As we near the finale, the stage is set for the Wall Hamstring Stretch. One foot rests high against the wall, as if reaching for the stars. The other leg lays outstretched on the floor, grounded and stable. The beauty of this stretch is the way it echoes through the back of the leg, giving a standing ovation to the hamstrings and extending gratitude to the knees.

As you transition from one exercise to the next, it's as if you're choreographing a ballet. Each movement is a step, each breath is a note, and the wall is your partner, leading you through the dance with grace and strength. The ballet of Wall Pilates is a testament to the art of movement as a healer, a comforter, and a friend to your knees.

As you perform these exercises, remember that every bend and stretch is a tribute to your knees, the unsung heroes in your body's symphony. They are more than joints; they are the keepers of your stride, the pulse in your step, and the beat in your dance. With Wall Pilates, you gift them a melody that heals and rejuvenates.

So, let this chapter be a reminder that in the midst of pain, there is grace. In the whispers of discomfort, there is the song of healing. Wall Pilates is not just a collection of exercises; it is a dance of strength and elegance, a ballet where your body is the dancer and the wall is your partner. Together, you waltz through the pain, and as the curtain falls, you bow to the applause of relief and the standing ovation of newfound strength.

With each day, as you return to the mat, let your heart be light. Know that the wall, your silent companion, is there to guide and support you. And your knees, oh, your precious knees, are dancing the dance of healing. In the sanctuary of your Pilates space, a transformation is taking place - a transformation that is mending the worn-out tapestry of muscles and sinews that have served you tirelessly.

In this journey, you are never alone. Your breath, the wall, and the spirit of Pilates are your companions. They dance with you through the low ebbs of pain and the high waves of relief. They hold your hands and your heart as you rediscover the joy of movement without the shackles of pain.

And as you close your eyes at the end of each session, take a moment to thank your body, for it is a vessel of miracles. Thank your knees for bearing the weight of your world. Thank the wall for being the unwavering support you needed. And thank yourself, for taking the steps toward healing, toward dancing again.

In Wall Pilates, you have found more than just exercises; you have found a symphony for the soul, a ballet for the body, and a healing balm for the knees. May your dance be light, your steps be strong, and your heart be filled with the grace of movements that sing the songs of healing.

In the quietude that follows, listen closely, for the gentle whispers of your heart will tell you tales of strength and tales of grace; and your knees, relieved of their pain, will join in the chorus, dancing once again in the grand ballet of life.

Wall Pilates for Hip Pain

There is something about hip pain that makes it unlike any other pain. Perhaps it's because our hips are the cradle of our bodies, the very foundation upon which we move, live, and thrive. When this foundation is shaken by pain, it's as if the rhythm of our lives has been interrupted. But here, my friend, is where the soothing embrace of Wall Pilates comes to our rescue. It whispers sweet nothings to the aggrieved hips and tells them, "I am here for you."

As you stand in front of that wall, your companion in this healing journey, let's take a deep breath together. Feel the air filling your lungs and envision it as the energy that will fuel your movements. This is your moment of reconnection with your body; a sacred moment where every motion brings you one step closer to healing.

We begin with Wall Lunges. Stand with the side of your body near the wall, one hand resting on it for support. Feel the texture of the wall, it's sturdiness. This very texture and sturdiness are what your hips will soon regain. Step your inner leg back, lower into a lunge, and then gracefully return your leg to the start. As you do this, imagine the pain in your hips being wrung out with each motion. Gradually, you'll feel your hips regain their fluidity, like a stream that flows freely after the removal of a dam.

Now, let's transition to Leg Lifts. Stand in the center of your mat, reaching forward with both hands pressed against the wall. Gently lift one leg behind you, focusing on the glute muscles. This is where you will feel the nurturing touch of Wall Pilates on your hips. Like a mother cradling her child, the movements cradle your hips, caressing away the pain and discomfort.

As you proceed, let's not forget the magic of Leg Circles. Stand with your feet hip-distance apart, pressing your hips and palms into the wall. Lift one leg and draw small circles. Oh, the beauty of these circles! They are like a potter's wheel, shaping and molding your hips, crafting them into vessels of strength and mobility.

The Roll Downs are waiting for you next. Stand with your shoulders against the wall, and slowly roll down, dropping your upper body into a forward fold. This is more than just a movement; it's a release. With every roll, the pain in your hips is being unshackled, leaving behind a lightness that makes your heart sing.

Now, close your eyes for a moment. Imagine a world where your hips are free of pain. A world where you can dance, walk, and move with the grace of a gazelle. Can you see it? That, my dear friend, is the world that Wall Pilates is leading you to.

There's a symphony in your movements, a ballet where pain pirouettes into relief, and stiffness pliés into flexibility. The wall, your partner, leads you in this dance with the grace of a seasoned maestro. With every step, every lift, and every circle, you are dancing away from the world of hip pain and into a world of freedom.

Your hips, which have borne so much, are now being borne on the wings of Wall Pilates, soaring towards a horizon where the sun of relief rises to greet them. And as you stand here, with your hand on the wall and your heart in the dance, know that you are not just moving; you are reclaiming the rhythm of your life.

This is Wall Pilates for hip pain; a dance, a song, a poem where the verses are woven with strength, the chorus is sung with relief, and every word is a testament to theresilience and grace of the human spirit.

Imagine yourself as a mighty oak tree, with roots grounded deep in the earth and branches reaching out to embrace the sky. Your hips are the trunk of this tree, and just like how the trunk supports the tree, your hips support your body. This is why it is imperative to nurture and care for them. Wall Pilates is the gentle breeze that rustles the leaves of this mighty oak, invigorating it with life and vitality.

Now, let's continue this graceful dance by introducing Hip Abduction and Adduction. Stand with your side to the wall, your hand lightly touching it. As you lift your leg away from the body, feel the space you're creating - the opening of possibilities. This is Hip Abduction. Now bring your leg back towards the body, feeling the control and strength in your movement - this is Hip Adduction. Through this elegant dance of the legs, the hips are serenaded into a state of harmony, where pain gives way to peace.

Hip Lateral and Medial Rotations are the next steps in this ballet of healing. With one hand on the wall, lift your leg and gently rotate it away and then towards your body. Like the tender turn of a page, each rotation tells a story - a story where the hero, which is you, triumphs over the adversary that is hip pain.

As the crescendo of this symphony approaches, let's not forget the element of balance in our composition. The Wall Sits are next. With your back against the wall, slide down until your knees are at a 90-degree angle. Feel the power coursing through your thighs and hips, as if you are drawing strength from the Earth. Hold, and as you do, let the wall absorb all the pain, all the fatigue, and all the frustration.

Finally, let's end this chapter with an ode to gratitude - the Glute Bridges. Plant your feet on the wall and lift your hips. As you do, think of all the things your hips have allowed you to do - walk, run, dance, and so much more. Let this be a thank you note from your soul to your hips.

As you lay on the mat, your breath syncing with the rhythm of your heart, feel the newfound freedom in your hips. The pain that was once an unwelcome guest is now a distant memory. Your hips have found their melody, and it is one of strength, grace, and boundless possibilities.

Wall Pilates is not just an exercise; it's a brush with which you paint the canvas of your health. It's a melody that strings the chords of wellbeing. It's a flame that rekindles the fire of vitality within you.

So, dear friend, as you step away from the wall, carry the strength and grace you've found today in your every step. Let every stride be a dance, let every movement be a song, and let your hips be the harbingers of the symphony of your life.

And in moments of doubt, remember this - your body is the most incredible instrument you'll ever own. Play it with love, play it with joy, and let the music it creates be your anthem of healing and hope.,

CHAPTER 3

Mind-Body Connection: Pilates and Mental Well-being

The union of mind and body is an ancient concept, long embraced by holistic practices around the world. From the serene temples of the East to the bustling gyms of the West, this marriage of the physical and the mental is celebrated in every corner of the globe. Pilates, with its sublime grace, is a testament to this union, a bridge that connects the shores of the physical and mental, and a path that leads to a destination of holistic well-being.

Pilates, at its core, is more than an exercise regime; it is an invitation to connect with oneself, a journey inward. Each movement, each breath, each posture in Pilates is a step toward self-awareness. As you move through the physical poses, you are also journeying through the landscape of your mind. The exploration of this internal terrain is as valuable as the physical benefits derived from the practice.

When you focus on your breath during a Pilates session, you are not just oxygenating your body; you're also bringing your attention to the present moment. This focus on the 'now' anchors the wandering mind, providing an escape from the relentless chatter of past regrets and future anxieties. It's a moment of respite, a sanctuary of serenity amidst the chaos of life.

Practicing Pilates is an act of self-care, and each session is an appointment with oneself. As you roll out your mat and settle into the opening poses, you're setting aside dedicated time for self-reflection and introspection. This commitment to oneself fosters a sense of self-worth, an acknowledgment of one's own value, and an affirmation of self-love.

Moreover, Pilates encourages patience and perseverance. The journey to mastering a pose or perfecting a sequence is often long and challenging. There are moments of struggle, of self-doubt, and of failure. But each time you get back on the mat, you are embodying resilience, acknowledging that progress is a dance with ebbs and flows. This resilience nurtures mental strength, fortifying the mind against life's adversities.

The physical benefits of Pilates – strength, flexibility, balance – are also metaphors for qualities of the mind. A strong body echoes a strong mind, resilient against the winds of change. Flexibility in movement mirrors the ability to adapt, to bend without breaking in the face of life's challenges. And balance, the elusive goal of many a Pilates pose, is a reflection of the equilibrium we seek in our lives, between work and leisure, between self and others, between giving and receiving.

There's a rhythm to Pilates, a harmony that resonates with the melody of life. As you flow from one pose to another, you're dancing to the symphony of existence. This dance is a celebration of life, an expression of joy, and a testament to the human spirit's resilience. It's a reminder that life, like Pilates, is a balance of holding on and letting go, of striving and surrendering, of challenging and cherishing.

As the session draws to a close, and you sink into the final relaxation, you're not just resting your body; you're also stilling your mind. This quietude is a fertile ground for reflection, a canvas for self-discovery, and a mirror reflecting the depth of your being. It's a moment of connection, not just with yourself, but with the world around you.

So, dear reader, as you embrace the practice of Pilates, remember that each pose is a pledge of presence, each breath is a whisper of self-love, and each session is a journey toward holistic well-being. The mat is not just a space for physical exercise; it's asanctuary for mental rejuvenation, a platform for personal growth, and a testament to the power of the mind-body connection. It is a place where the physical and mental not only meet but dance in harmony, creating a symphony of wellness that resonates within and beyond.

The beauty of Pilates lies in its simplicity – the notion that through concentrated and conscious movements, you can explore the depths of your own strength, both physical and mental. Each stretch, each contraction, each moment of holding your body against the pull of gravity is also a moment of triumph for your mind over the clatter of external distractions. It's a dialogue between your body and mind, a conversation that fosters self-understanding and self-appreciation.

As you navigate the ebb and flow of life's challenges, Pilates becomes more than a set of physical exercises; it becomes a tool for mental resilience. The confidence you gain from mastering a difficult pose, the patience you cultivate when progress seems slow, the mindfulness you practice with each controlled breath – these are gifts from Pilates that extend far beyond the mat. They are skills for life, equipping you to face the world with a balanced mind and a resilient spirit.

In the grand tapestry of life, Pilates is a vibrant thread, weaving together the physical and the mental into a pattern of holistic well-being. It's not just about building muscles or enhancing flexibility; it's about nurturing a mind-body connection that fosters mental peace and emotional balance. It's about discovering the strength within, the peace within, the joy within. Through Pilates, you're not just sculpting a body; you're also shaping a mindset, a perspective, a way of life.

Pilates is more than a path to physical fitness; it's a journey to mental well-being. It's a dance between strength and grace, between effort and relaxation, between the physical and the mental. As you embark on this journey, remember to savor each step, to cherish each breath, and to celebrate each moment of connection with yourself. For in this connection lies the essence of Pilates, the magic of the mind-body union, and the secret to holistic well-being.

In the end, Pilates is not just a practice; it's a philosophy, a lifestyle, a celebration of the human potential. It's a testament to the power of the mind-body connection, a tribute to the strength of the human spirit, and a beacon of hope for holistic well-being. So, as you step onto the mat, remember, you're not just exercising; you're embarking on a journey of self-discovery, self-love, and self-transformation. And this journey, dear reader, is the true essence of Pilates.

The Science of the Mind-Body Connection

At the heart of our exploration into the world of Pilates lies the intriguing science of the mind-body connection. It's a concept that has fascinated philosophers, psychologists, and scientists alike, and it's integral to our understanding of Pilates.

At its core, the mind-body connection is the intimate relationship between our mental and physical states. This is not a new concept; ancient practices such as yoga and meditation have long recognized and harnessed the power of this connection. But it is only in recent decades that modern science has begun to unravel its mysteries, providing a fascinating perspective on the profound impact our minds can have on our bodies, and vice versa.

Neuroscience has made significant strides in illuminating the complex pathways that link our thoughts, emotions, and physical sensations. The brain, it turns out, is not a solitary commander issuing directives to a passive body. Instead, it is a part of an intricate, bi-directional communication system, where signals from the brain can influence the body, and feedback from the body can impact the brain.

Take, for example, the phenomenon of 'fight or flight,' a primal response to stress or danger. When we perceive a threat, our brain sends signals to various organs in our body, triggering a cascade of physiological responses. Our heart rate increases, our breathing quickens, our muscles tense up – all orchestrated by the brain to prepare us for a potential fight or flight situation. This is a classic illustration of how our mental state, in this case, the perception of a threat, can elicit a tangible physical response.

Conversely, our physical state can also influence our mental well-being. It's common knowledge that physical exercise can boost mood and alleviate symptoms of depression and anxiety. The act of physical movement can trigger the release of endorphins, often referred to as 'feel-good hormones', which can promote feelings of happiness and relaxation. This is the flip side of the mind-body connection – the ability of our physical actions to influence our mental state.

As we delve deeper, we find this connection extends beyond the brain and the body. It also involves the mind and the 'body' of our thoughts and emotions, an aspect of our being that is as real and as impactful as our physical body.

Emotions, for example, are not just fleeting feelings; they are complex physiological and psychological responses that can significantly affect our physical health. Chronic stress or anxiety can lead to high blood pressure, heart disease, and a host of other health issues. On the other hand, positive emotions like happiness and love can boost our immune system, enhance our resilience to pain, and even improve our longevity.

Mindfulness, a key component of Pilates, is a powerful tool that can help us harness the benefits of positive emotions. By bringing our attention to the present moment, we can cultivate a sense of calm and contentment, mitigating the harmful effects of stress and negative emotions.

Even our thoughts, intangible as they are, can produce physical changes in our bodies. This is the premise of cognitive-behavioral therapy, a psychological treatment that works on the principle that changing maladaptive thought patterns can lead to improvements in behavior and emotional state.

What does all this mean for Pilates? The practice of Pilates is a beautiful embodiment of the mind-body connection. Each pose, each movement in Pilates is not just a physical exercise; it's an opportunity to bring our attention to our bodies, to tune into our physical sensations, to cultivate mindfulness, and to foster positive emotions.

By consciously engaging our minds in our workouts, we can maximize the benefits of Pilates, not just for our bodies, but for our mental well-being too. The strength, flexibility, and balance we gain from Pilates are not just physical attributes; they are also reflections of the mental resilience, clarity, and equanimity we cultivate through the practice.

The conscious control we exercise in Pilates, where every movement is performed with full awareness and intent, helps to bridge the gap between the mind and the body. It trains us to listen to our bodies, to respect its limits, and to understand its signals. At the same time, it helps us to harness the power of our minds, to focus our attention, to manage our stress, and to foster positive thoughts and emotions.

Moreover, Pilates encourages us to slow down, to take a break from the fast-paced hustle and bustle of our daily lives. It invites us to create a space for stillness and silence, where we can tune into our inner selves, connect with our emotions, and cultivate a sense of inner peace. This, in turn, can have profound effects on our physical health, boosting our immune system, improving our sleep, and reducing our risk of various health conditions.

Another significant facet of Pilates is the breath. Breathing is a unique physiological process that straddles the voluntary and involuntary realms. We can control it when we want to, and it continues automatically when we don't. In Pilates, we learn to harness this unique characteristic of breath, using it as a tool to enhance our mind-body connection.

The conscious control and synchronization of breath with movement in Pilates can have a calming effect on the mind, helping to reduce stress and anxiety. Moreover, the deep, diaphragmatic breathing encouraged in Pilates can improve oxygenation, promote better circulation, and enhance overall physical health. Thus, breath acts as a bridge between the mind and the body, linking our mental state with our physical well-being.

In conclusion, the science of the mind-body connection offers us a profound understanding of the interconnectedness of our mental and physical states. It sheds light on how our thoughts, emotions, and physical sensations interact, influence each other, and ultimately shape our overall health and well-being.

The practice of Pilates, with its focus on conscious control, breath, and mindfulness, beautifully embodies this mind-body connection. It offers us a practical, accessible, and powerful way to harness the benefits of this connection, helping us to enhance not just our physical health, but our mental and emotional well-being as well.

As we continue our journey through the world of Pilates, let us bear in mind this profound mind-body connection. Let us approach each pose, each breath, each moment of mindfulness, not just as a physical exercise, but as an opportunity to strengthen this connection, to enhance our overall well-being, and to cultivate a sense of balance and harmony in our lives.

How Pilates Enhances Mental Well-being

Pilates, at its core, is more than just a physical workout—it's a comprehensive approach to health that considers the intricate interplay between the mind and the body. As we delve into the exploration of how Pilates enhances mental well-being, we uncover a treasure trove of benefits that have a profound and lasting impact on our mental health.

Joseph Pilates, the creator of this holistic practice, believed in the power of movement to heal, not just the body, but the mind as well. His practice, underpinned by this philosophy, aims to foster a strong connection between the mind and the body, a connection that subsequently aids in enhancing mental well-being.

When we practice Pilates, our focus is drawn towards the precision of each movement, the rhythm of our breath, and the alignment of our bodies. This concentration on the present moment resembles a form of moving meditation. The calming effect of this focused attention can be remarkably therapeutic, helping to reduce stress and anxiety levels, while fostering a sense of tranquility and inner peace.

Furthermore, the rhythmic and controlled movements of Pilates require not only physical strength and coordination but also mental discipline and focus. This dual engagement of the mind and body can help improve mental clarity, boost memory, and enhance cognitive function. It's a mental workout that keeps the mind active, alert, and engaged.

Stress is a common factor in our lives. The gentle, flowing movements in Pilates, combined with deep, controlled breathing, can help activate the body's relaxation response, counteracting the negative effects of stress. This not only helps to alleviate stress-related symptoms such as insomnia, tension headaches, and high blood pressure, but it also promotes a positive mood and a sense of well-being.

Feeling strong and confident in one's body can significantly impact one's mental health. Pilates, with its emphasis on core strength, flexibility, and body awareness, fosters a strong sense of self. It can help improve body image, boost self-esteem, and enhance self-confidence. This newfound confidence can permeate other areas of life, fostering a more positive outlook and a healthier relationship with oneself.

As we engage with Pilates, we also learn to honor our bodies, respecting its limits, and acknowledging its abilities. This practice of self-care and self-love can promote a healthier self-image and cultivate a more positive mental state.

Pilates is also a practice of self-discovery. As we move through the poses, we become more attuned to our bodies, learning to listen to its cues and respond to its needs. This heightened body awareness can help us recognize and manage our emotions better, enhancing our emotional intelligence and promoting emotional health.

Finally, the practice of Pilates can foster a sense of community and belonging. Whether it's practicing in a group class or sharing experiences and progress with a friend, the social aspects of Pilates can contribute to a sense of connectedness and social well-being. This sense of community can provide emotional support, reduce feelings of loneliness, and enhance overall mental health.

In essence, the benefits of Pilates extend far beyond the physical. It's a practice that nurtures the mind, heals the spirit, and fosters a sense of peace, happiness, and well-being. As we continue our journey with Pilates, let's remember to honor this powerful mind-body connection and the profound impact it can have on our mental health.

Conclusion: Crafting a Personalized Wall Pilates Pain Management Plan

As we reach the end of our exploration into the world of Wall Pilates, it's now time to bring together all the knowledge and insights we've gleaned to create our own personalized pain management plan. Remember, the journey to health and wellness is personal and unique for each one of us. There's no one-size-fits-all approach, but a carefully crafted, personalized plan can make all the difference in managing and overcoming pain.

We've learned how Wall Pilates, with its gentle, controlled movements, can be a potent tool in managing and alleviating various types of physical discomfort. From lower back pain to neck strain, from shoulder discomfort to knee aches, Wall Pilates offers a wealth of exercises that target and strengthen specific muscle groups, enhancing flexibility, improving posture, and reducing pain.

The beauty of Wall Pilates lies in its adaptability. It can be tailored to suit your personal needs, capabilities, and goals. But where do you start? The first step is to listen to your body. Recognize the areas of discomfort and observe how certain movements affect your pain levels. This will help you identify the exercises that bring relief and those that need to be modified or avoided.

Next, remember the importance of consistency. Like any exercise regimen, the benefits of Wall Pilates come with regular practice. Start with a routine that's manageable and aligns with your lifestyle. This could be as simple as a 10-minute routine every morning or a 30-minute session three times a week. The key is to make it a part of your daily life, a routine that you look forward to and enjoy.

Now, let's not forget the power of progress. As you continue with your Wall Pilates practice, keep track of your progress. Notice how your strength and flexibility improve, how your posture changes, and most importantly, how your pain levels decrease. This record of your progress can be incredibly motivating and a testament to the effectiveness of your personalized plan.

A successful Wall Pilates pain management plan also considers the mental aspect of pain. As we've discovered, Wall Pilates is not just a physical exercise. It's a mindful practice that connects the body and mind, helping us manage not just the physical symptoms of pain, but also the emotional and mental toll it takes.

Incorporate mindfulness into your practice. Concentrate on your breath, focus on the precision of each movement, and stay present in each moment. This mindful approach to Wall Pilates can help reduce stress, alleviate anxiety, and improve mental clarity, all of which can significantly impact our perception of pain.

Lastly, be patient with yourself. Healing takes time, and progress may be slow. But remember, each small step takes you closer to your goal. Celebrate every milestone, every pain-free day, every successful exercise. Every step forward, no matter how small, is a victory.

Your journey with Wall Pilates doesn't end here. Consider it as the beginning of a lifelong relationship with your body, a commitment to listening to it, caring for it, and nurturing it. So as you embark on this journey, remember to be gentle with yourself, celebrate every progress, and enjoy the process. After all, the journey towards health and wellness is just as important as the destination.

Assessing Your Pain: Identifying Triggers and Patterns

Navigating the path to pain management begins with a critical first step - understanding your pain. Gaining clarity on the nature of your discomfort, its triggers, and patterns plays a vital role in crafting an effective pain management plan. This understanding isn't something that happens overnight, but with time, patience, and a keen observation of your body's signals, you can decode your pain and use this knowledge to your advantage.

Pain is a complex phenomenon. It's not just a physical sensation; it's a multi-dimensional experience that has emotional and cognitive components too. It's your body's way of communicating that something isn't right. It's an alert system designed to protect you. So when pain surfaces, it's essential to stop, listen and engage in a meaningful dialogue with your body.

The first step in this dialogue is to pinpoint the location of your pain. Is it concentrated in a specific area, like the lower back or neck? Or is it more diffused, spreading across a larger area like the entire back or the full length of a leg? Identifying the exact area of discomfort can guide you towards exercises that target these zones, bringing much-needed relief.

Next, consider the quality of your pain. Is it sharp and stabbing, or is it more of a dull ache? Does it throb, or is it a constant pressure? Understanding the quality of your pain can provide insights into its possible causes and guide you towards appropriate management strategies.

Now, let's turn our attention to triggers. These are specific circumstances or actions that intensify your pain. Triggers can vary greatly from person to person. For some, it could be prolonged periods of sitting or standing. For others, it could be certain movements or positions, like bending over or lifting heavy objects. Identifying these triggers is crucial as it helps you understand what actions to avoid or modify to manage your pain effectively.

Just as triggers can intensify pain, certain factors can alleviate it as well. Maybe you've noticed that your pain eases after a warm bath, or when you're lying down. Or perhaps gentle stretches bring some relief. Recognizing these pain-relieving factors can provide you with immediate strategies for pain management.

Pain also often has a pattern. It may be worse at certain times of the day, like first thing in the morning or late at night. It may be influenced by your menstrual cycle or even the weather. Recognizing these patterns can help you anticipate periods of increased pain and adjust your schedule or routine accordingly.

In assessing your pain, it's also essential to acknowledge its emotional component. Chronic pain can lead to feelings of frustration, anxiety, and depression. These emotions, in turn, can intensify the perception of pain, creating a vicious cycle. Acknowledging these feelings and seeking appropriate emotional support is as crucial in managing pain as addressing its physical aspects.

Remember, understanding your pain is a journey, not a destination. It's a continuous process of listening, learning, and adapting. It requires patience and a willingness to engage in a deep, compassionate conversation with your body. So as you embark on this journey of understanding, remember that every insight you gain, no matter how small, brings you one step closer to effective pain management.

Building Your Personalized Wall Pilates Pain Management Plan

Embarking on a journey to manage your pain through Wall Pilates is akin to crafting a personal narrative. Each individual's experience with pain is unique, as is their body's response to different movements and exercises. There is no one-size-fits-all approach to pain management.

Instead, it is a tailored tapestry, woven from threads of careful observation, patient experimentation, and compassionate self-awareness.

To begin, let's revisit the concept of understanding your pain. The information you've gathered about the location, quality, triggers, and patterns of your pain is the foundation upon which your personalized Wall Pilates plan will be built. This knowledge forms the blueprint for your plan, guiding you towards the exercises that may be most beneficial for your specific pain points.

Wall Pilates offers a plethora of exercises, each designed to target different muscle groups and areas of the body. The beauty of this approach is that it allows you to customize your workout routine to address your unique needs. For example, if you've identified your lower back as a source of pain, exercises like Wall Glute Bridges or Wall Lunges might be particularly beneficial. If neck pain is a concern, exercises like Wall Push-Ups could help to strengthen your neck and shoulder muscles.

As you begin to incorporate Wall Pilates exercises into your routine, it's crucial to listen to your body. Pain is a communication tool your body uses to tell you if something is wrong. If an exercise exacerbates your pain, take it as a sign that the movement might not be suitable for you at the moment. It's important to respect your body's boundaries and not push through pain. Remember, Wall Pilates is about facilitating healing, not inducing more pain.

Equally important is the concept of gradual progression. Starting small and gradually increasing the intensity or duration of your exercises can help prevent additional strain or injury. It's not about how many exercises you can do or how quickly you can progress. Instead, it's about the quality of each movement and the connection you foster with your body during each session.

Incorporating regular rest periods into your plan is another key aspect of a sustainable pain management approach. Rest is when your body heals and recovers. It's an integral part of the process, not a sign of laziness or lack of progress.

In your journey of managing pain, remember to be patient with yourself. Progress may not always be linear. There may be days when the pain seems worse, or when certain exercises feel more challenging. It's during these times that self-compassion becomes essential. Remind yourself that it's okay to have bad days, and that they do not negate the progress you've made.

Lastly, don't forget to celebrate your victories, no matter how small. Every step you take towards managing your pain, every new insight you gain about your body, is a victory worth celebrating. You're not just managing pain; you're also cultivating a deeper relationship with your body and reclaiming your quality of life. And that is a journey worth embarking on.

BOOK 6

Wall Pilates for Seniors

Introduction: The Importance of Exercise in Older Age

Aging is a natural, inevitable part of life. As the pages on the calendar turn, we notice subtle changes in our bodies. Perhaps we don't move as quickly as we used to, or we notice a slight stiffness in the joints that wasn't there before. While these changes are normal, they needn't be a sentence to inactivity. In fact, the opposite is true. As we age, maintaining an active lifestyle becomes not just beneficial, but critical, to our overall health and well-being.

Think of our bodies as a complex, beautifully designed machine. Like any machine, regular use and maintenance keep it running smoothly. Exercise is this necessary maintenance for our bodies, and its importance only amplifies as we age. It's a means to ensure that our "machine" continues to function optimally, allowing us to enjoy a quality of life that isn't hampered by preventable physical limitations.

When we speak of exercise, we don't just mean strenuous workouts that leave us breathless and fatigued. Exercise, particularly in older age, encompasses a wide range of physical activities designed to maintain or improve strength, flexibility, balance, and cardiovascular health. It's about encouraging regular movement, in any form that you enjoy and can safely perform.

Strength training is one such form of exercise. As we age, we naturally lose muscle mass, a process known as sarcopenia. This loss can lead to decreased strength and mobility, making daily tasks more difficult. Regular strength training can slow down this process, helping us maintain muscle mass and function. It's not about lifting heavy weights or becoming a bodybuilder. Simple, safe resistance exercises using bands, light weights, or even our own body weight can be effective.

Flexibility exercises are another key component. Over time, our joints can become stiffer and less flexible. Regular stretching can help to counteract this, improving our range of motion and making movement easier and more comfortable. This isn't just about reaching down to touch our toes. Gentle movements like those found in yoga or Pilates can be wonderful ways to improve flexibility.

Balance exercises play a crucial role in preventing falls, a common issue that can have serious consequences in older age. These exercises help to strengthen the core and improve stability, reducing the risk of falls. Simple activities like heel-to-toe walking or standing on one foot can be effective balance exercises.

Cardiovascular or aerobic exercises help to maintain heart health and improve endurance. Regular cardio exercise can help to keep our hearts strong and efficient, reducing the risk of heart disease. It's not about running marathons. Activities like brisk walking, swimming, or cycling can be great forms of cardio exercise.

But the benefits of exercise extend beyond the physical. Regular physical activity has been shown to have a positive impact on mental and emotional health. It can help to improve mood, reduce anxiety, and combat depression. It can also promote better sleep and improve cognitive function, helping to keep our minds sharp.

As we age, exercise becomes less about aesthetics and more about functionality. It's about maintaining the ability to perform everyday activities with ease, about preserving independence. It's about improving our quality of life, allowing us to enjoy our golden years to their fullest. But perhaps most importantly, it's about celebrating what our bodies can do, at any age. It's about appreciating the gift of movement, and using it to keep our "machines" running smoothly.

We're never too old to start exercising. Whether you're in your 60s, 70s, 80s, or beyond, there are exercises and activities that you can safely perform and enjoy. It's about finding what works for you, what you enjoy, and what you can maintain consistently. It's about making small changes that can have a big impact over time.

With age comes wisdom, and with wisdom comes the understanding that our health is our wealth. Exercise, a significant part of maintaining our health, becomes a valuable investment, not a chore. It becomes a joyful activity that we engage in, not only because we need to, but because we understand the multitude of benefits it brings.

The beauty of exercise lies in its adaptability. It can be tailored to suit our individual abilities, preferences, and health considerations. Whether it's a leisurely walk in the park, a yoga class, or a swim in the pool, every bit of movement counts. It's about embracing a mindset that values regular activity and understands its role in preserving health and promoting longevity.

Exercise, however, is not a magic bullet. It is most effective when combined with other healthy lifestyle choices. A balanced diet, adequate sleep, regular medical check-ups, and a positive outlook all play a role in our overall well-being as we age. They work synergistically with exercise to help us maintain our vitality and zest for life.

Moreover, it's important to approach exercise with a sense of balance. It's about understanding our bodies, respecting their limits, and not pushing ourselves to the point of injury. It's about distinguishing between the natural discomfort of a good workout and the warning signs of potential harm. Remember, the goal is to enhance our lives, not add undue stress.

In essence, regular exercise is a powerful tool that can help us navigate the journey of aging with grace, strength, and vitality. It's a celebration of our capabilities, a testament to our resilience, and a commitment to our well-being. As we age, exercise is not just about adding years to our life, but more importantly, adding life to our years.

When we move, we live, not just exist. We engage with the world around us, we enjoy our daily activities, and we make precious memories. We create a life that is vibrant, active, and filled with joy. That's the power of exercise. That's why it matters, especially as we age.

As we embark on this journey through the later years of our lives, let's do so with enthusiasm, determination, and a pair of well-used sneakers. Let's make every movement count. Let's celebrate our bodies, in all their aging glory, and give them the care and respect they deserve. Because in the grand scheme of life, staying active is not just about exercise. It's about living our best, most fulfilling lives, at every age.

Understanding the Aging Body

Aging is a natural, inevitable part of life, a journey that we all embark upon. It is a symphony of changes that unfolds over time, a constant evolution of our bodies. To fully appreciate this journey and navigate it with grace and wisdom, it is crucial to understand the transformations that our bodies undergo. With a deeper awareness of these changes, we can cultivate a lifestyle that supports our well-being and vitality at every age.

From the moment we are born, our bodies begin their journey of growth, development, and eventually, aging. It is a process as beautiful as the turning of the seasons, each bringing its own unique characteristics and challenges. The human body, in its wisdom and complexity, is a fascinating study of resilience and adaptation.

In our youth, our bodies are like blooming gardens, vibrant, energetic, and constantly growing. Our cells regenerate at a quick pace, our metabolism is high, and our physical and cognitive abilities are at their peak. Our skin is firm and elastic, our bones are dense, and our muscle mass is plentiful. We are, in essence, in the prime of our physical lives.

As we navigate our middle years, subtle changes begin to occur. Our metabolism slows down, leading to gradual weight gain. Our skin starts to lose its elasticity, giving way to fine lines and wrinkles. Our bone density begins to decrease, and muscle mass reduces. This is the body's natural response to the passage of time, a gentle reminder of the impermanence of youth.

However, the beauty of aging is not solely in its physical manifestations. It's in the richness of experience that comes with it, the wisdom gathered over decades, and the deep understanding of life's intricate tapestry. While our bodies may show signs of wear and tear, our spirits often grow stronger, grounded in the knowledge and insight that only time can provide.

Upon reaching our later years, the changes become more pronounced. Our bodies continue to slow down, and we may experience a decrease in stamina and flexibility. Our vision and hearing might become less sharp, and our cognitive abilities might not be as quick as they once were. We may notice changes in our sleep patterns, and our immune system might take a bit longer to respond to illnesses.

Yet, it's essential to remember that these changes are not indicative of decline, but rather a natural progression of life. They are not flaws to be hidden or problems to be fixed, but signs of a life lived, a testament to our journey. Aging is not a disease, but a biological reality that has its own beauty and rhythm.

And while the external changes are the most visible, the internal changes are equally significant. Our cardiovascular system, for instance, experiences changes such as a slower heart rate and less flexible arteries. Our respiratory system may not be as efficient, and our digestive system may slow down. Our kidneys and bladder may not function as they used to, and our hormonal balance shifts, particularly in women who go through menopause.

Understanding these changes is not about focusing on what we lose with age, but rather, appreciating what we gain. It's about acknowledging the changes and adapting our lifestyles to support our bodies in this new phase. It's about practicing self-care with intention, nourishing our bodies with balanced nutrition, staying active, getting regular health check-ups, and keeping our minds sharp.

Remember, each stage of life comes with its own beauty and wisdom. Each wrinkle, each gray hair, and each laugh line is a badge of honor, a symbol of the journey we've embarked on. They speak of the trials we've overcome, the joys we've experienced, the love we've given and received, and the wisdom we've accrued. And that is something to be celebrated, not feared.

Embracing the aging process with understanding and acceptance allows us to navigate our later years with grace and wisdom. It encourages us to focus on the richness of our experiences and the depth of our understanding, rather than the superficial signs of age. It teaches us to honor our bodies for their resilience and adaptability, rather than bemoaning the changes that come with time.

Moreover, understanding the aging process allows us to be proactive in maintaining our health. By recognizing the changes our bodies undergo, we can make informed decisions about our diet, exercise, and healthcare. We can take steps to strengthen our bones, protect our heart, maintain our brain health, and nourish our skin. We can approach aging not as a challenge to be overcome, but as a journey to be experienced fully and mindfully.

Our bodies are the vessels that carry us through life, and they deserve our care and respect at every age. By understanding the changes that come with aging, we can better appreciate the beauty of this journey and cultivate a sense of gratitude for every stage of life. We can redefine what it means to age and discover that it is a process not of decline, but of continuous growth and evolution.

In the end, aging is not just about the physical changes we undergo. It's about the life we live, the experiences we gather, the wisdom we accrue, and the person we become. It's about embracing the beauty of life in all its phases, and recognizing that every stage has its own unique gifts and challenges.

So, let's celebrate aging for what it truly is: a testament to our journey, a reflection of our resilience, and a tribute to the depth and breadth of our experiences. Let's approach it with understanding, acceptance, and grace, cherishing each moment for the gift that it is. After all, to age is to live, and to live is to age, and therein lies the beauty of our existence.

In the grand tapestry of life, aging is but a single thread, albeit a significant one. It weaves its way through our existence, subtly changing the pattern and color of our lives. But it is the cumulative effect of these threads that create the rich, complex tapestry that is a human life. It is the interplay of youth and age, growth and change, beginnings and endings, that give our lives depth and meaning.

As we age, we are not simply getting older; we are evolving, growing, and becoming. We are not losing our youth, but gaining wisdom, perspective, and depth. We are not declining, but unfolding, revealing new layers of understanding and experience with each passing year.

So, let us embark on this journey of understanding the aging body with open hearts and minds. Let us embrace the changes, honor the process, and celebrate the journey. For it is in this understanding that we find the true beauty of aging: not in the mirror's reflection, but in the depths of our own self-understanding, in the richness of our experiences, and in the profound appreciation for the gift of life itself.

Why Exercise is Crucial for Seniors

Exercise, my dear reader, is not merely the act of moving our bodies to keep fit; it is an expression of our vitality, our resilience, and our zest for life. It is the music that keeps our bodies dancing to the rhythm of health and well-being. As we age, the importance of maintaining this rhythm becomes increasingly crucial. This isn't just about adding years to our life but adding life to our years.

As we delve into the significance of exercise for seniors, let's not forget that our bodies are designed to move. Aging doesn't change this fundamental truth. Instead, it presents us with a beautiful opportunity to embrace movement in new, adaptive ways. By maintaining an active lifestyle, we not only support our physical health but also nourish our mental and emotional well-being. Exercise becomes less of a routine and more of a celebration of our body's capabilities.

The human body is a marvelous creation, a symphony of cells and systems working in harmony. Exercise, in this symphony, is the conductor's baton, guiding each section, each note, to play in perfect harmony. It keeps our muscles strong, our joints flexible, and our hearts robust. It helps control our weight, manage chronic health conditions, and reduce the risk of falls. It's not an overstatement to say that exercise is one of the most effective ways to stay healthy as we age.

Yet, exercise does more than just maintain our physical health. It has profound effects on our mental health as well. Regular physical activity can help reduce feelings of anxiety and depression, enhance mood, and promote better sleep. It is like a natural antidepressant, filling our minds with a sense of calm and our hearts with joy. The feel-good endorphins released during exercise can lift our spirits, helping us to face each new day with optimism and enthusiasm.

Beyond the physical and mental benefits, exercise also nurtures our social health. Whether it's a group fitness class, a walking club, or a dance class, participating in physical activities provides a sense of community. It allows us to connect with others, share experiences, and create lasting bonds. These social interactions can enhance our emotional well-being, reduce feelings of loneliness, and boost our sense of belonging. In this sense, exercise is not just a solitary endeavor, but a communal experience, a shared celebration of health and vitality.

As we age, our relationship with exercise naturally evolves. The high-impact activities of our youth may give way to gentler, low-impact exercises. But this doesn't mean we're slowing down. Far from it. We're simply adapting, finding new ways to stay active that honor our bodies' changing needs. Whether it's walking, swimming, yoga, or tai chi, there's a world of options out there for us to explore. The key is to find activities we enjoy, activities that make us feel good, not just physically, but mentally and emotionally as well.

While we're discussing the importance of exercise, let's not overlook the significance of balance and flexibility exercises for seniors. Improving balance and enhancing flexibility can help reduce the risk of falls, a common concern for older adults. These exercises can help us maintain our independence, allowing us to continue doing the activities we love safely and confidently.

One of the beautiful things about exercise is that it's never too late to start. Regardless of our age or fitness level, we can always take steps towards a more active lifestyle.

Every bit of movement counts. Even small changes can make a big difference. Starting with short, gentle exercises and gradually increasing intensity and duration as our fitness improves can have significant health benefits.

In the final analysis, exercise is more than a healthy habit; it's a powerful expression of our determination to live life to the fullest. It is a testament to our resilience, our refusal to let age define our capabilities. It is an act of self-care, a demonstration of our commitment to preserving our health and happiness. It is our way of telling the world, and ourselves, that we value our well-being, that we honor our bodies, that we cherish our lives.

Moreover, the benefits of exercise extend far beyond the individual. By staying active, we can inspire our loved ones, our friends, and our community to embrace a healthier lifestyle. We can become role models, showing that age is not a barrier to fitness, but rather a motivator, a reminder of the importance of taking care of our health.

In conclusion, exercise is not just crucial for seniors; it is a lifeline, a joy, a source of strength and vitality. It is a way of celebrating our bodies, honoring our health, and nurturing our spirits. It is a way of connecting with others, creating shared experiences, and building community. It is a way of saying 'yes' to life, of embracing each new day with energy, enthusiasm, and grace.

In the tapestry of life, exercise is a vibrant thread, weaving together the physical, mental, and social aspects of our health. It is an essential part of aging well, of living our best lives. So, let's lace up our shoes, unroll our yoga mats, dive into our swimming pools, and dance in our living rooms. Let's move, not because we have to, but because we want to, because we cherish our health, because we delight in the feeling of our bodies in motion. Let's exercise, not just to live longer, but to live better, to live fuller, to live happier.

As we journey through the golden years of life, let's remember that exercise is our companion, our ally, our friend. It is there to lift us up when we're down, to keep us strong when we're weak, to bring us joy when we're sad. It is there to remind us of our strength, our resilience, our capacity to adapt and thrive. It is there to celebrate our vitality, our zest for life, our unwavering determination to live each day with health, happiness, and grace.

So, dear reader, let us celebrate exercise, for it is not just a routine or a regimen, but a celebration of life. It is a testament to our resilience, a tribute to our vitality, a beacon of hope in our journey towards health and happiness. As we age, let us not see exercise as a chore, but as a gift, a privilege, an opportunity to nurture our bodies, nourish our minds, and nurture our souls. Let us embrace exercise, not just as a crucial aspect of aging, but as a vital part of living, a joyous expression of our determination to live life to the fullest. After all, isn't that what aging gracefully is all about?

CHAPTER 1

The Benefits of Pilates for Seniors

Pilates has emerged as a popular and effective form of exercise for people of all ages, but it holds particular appeal for seniors. Often touted for its focus on core strength, flexibility, balance, and mindful movement, it is a low-impact exercise that can be tailored to meet the individual needs and abilities of each participant. As seniors navigate the challenges of aging, Pilates can provide an array of benefits that contribute to a healthier, more active, and independent lifestyle.

The beauty of Pilates lies in its adaptability. Unlike some forms of exercise that can be demanding and strenuous, Pilates is kind to the body. It is a gentle yet challenging form of exercise that can be modified to suit any fitness level. This makes it an ideal choice for seniors who may have limitations due to age or health conditions. The movements in Pilates are controlled and deliberate, focusing on quality rather than quantity. This mindful approach reduces the risk of injury and makes the practice both safe and enjoyable for seniors.

Core strength is a critical aspect of our physical health that often declines as we age. The core muscles, which include the abdomen, lower back, hips, and pelvis, are essential for stability and balance. Pilates places a strong emphasis on strengthening these muscles, promoting better posture, and reducing the risk of falls. By focusing on core strength, seniors who practice Pilates can improve their balance and coordination, enhancing their ability to perform everyday tasks and maintain their independence.

Pilates also promotes flexibility, another key component of physical health that can decline with age. By incorporating stretching and lengthening exercises into each session, Pilates helps seniors maintain and even improve their flexibility. This can lead to better mobility, less stiffness, and a decreased risk of injury. Seniors who practice Pilates regularly often report feeling more agile and energetic, qualities that can significantly improve their quality of life.

One of the less tangible but equally important benefits of Pilates for seniors is its focus on mindful movement. Each exercise in Pilates requires concentration and awareness, creating a connection between the mind and the body. This focus on mindfulness can enhance mental clarity, reduce stress, and promote a sense of calm and well-being. For seniors, this mental aspect of Pilates can be just as beneficial as the physical benefits, contributing to better mental health and an increased sense of overall wellness.

As we age, maintaining strong bones becomes increasingly important to prevent conditions like osteoporosis. Pilates, being a weight-bearing exercise, can play a vital role in bone health. By putting mild resistance on the muscles and bones, it stimulates bone-building cells, helping to maintain bone density. It's a natural, medication-free way to help keep bones strong and healthy, adding one more reason for seniors to consider adding Pilates to their exercise routine.

Pilates is also an excellent choice for seniors because it can be practiced in various settings. Whether in a class with an experienced instructor, at home with a DVD, or even online, seniors can find a method that suits their lifestyle and comfort level. This versatility makes Pilates an accessible and convenient option for seniors, regardless of their schedule or mobility level.

Another benefit of Pilates for seniors is its ability to enhance body awareness. Pilates teaches practitioners to be mindful of their posture, alignment, and movement patterns. This heightened body awareness can lead to improved balance and coordination, helping to prevent falls and injuries. It can also contribute to better overall health, as seniors become more attuned to their bodies and more proactive in caring for their health.

In the realm of social interaction, Pilates classes provide an excellent opportunity for seniors to connect with others. Regular classes foster a sense of community and shared purpose, combatting feelings of isolation and loneliness that can sometimes come with age. These social connections can be a powerful force in promoting mental health and a sense of belonging, making Pilates not only a physical exercise but a social one as well.

Pilates also assists in the management of chronic diseases which are prevalent in seniors. Conditions such as arthritis, cardiovascular disease, and diabetes can all be better managed with regular physical activity, and Pilates, with its focus on gentle, low-impact movements, is an excellent choice. The exercises can help increase joint flexibility, improve circulation, and regulate blood sugar levels, making them beneficial for seniors living with these conditions.

Pain management is another area where Pilates shines. Back pain, in particular, is a common complaint among seniors, and the core strengthening and flexibility exercises in Pilates can often help alleviate this discomfort. By improving posture and alignment, Pilates can also help to reduce the risk of pain and injury in other parts of the body, making it a valuable tool for pain management and prevention.

As we age, it's natural for our respiratory function to decline somewhat. However, Pilates encourages deep, controlled breathing in conjunction with each movement. This focus on the breath can help to improve lung capacity and efficiency, making everyday activities such as climbing stairs or walking easier. It can also contribute to increased energy levels and a greater sense of vitality.

In conclusion, Pilates offers a host of benefits that can greatly enhance the quality of life for seniors. From improving strength, flexibility, and balance to promoting mental clarity and social interaction, Pilates provides a comprehensive approach to health and wellness. Its adaptability and low-impact nature make it a safe and effective exercise choice for seniors, regardless of their current fitness level or health status.

In summary, Pilates for seniors is not just about physical health; it's about overall wellness. It offers an approach to exercise that is holistic, mindful, and centered on the individual's needs. It recognizes that every senior is unique, with their own set of strengths, challenges, and goals. By offering a practice that can be tailored to meet these individual needs, Pilates empowers seniors to take charge of their health, stay active, and enjoy a better quality of life. The benefits of Pilates for seniors are many, and its potential impact on their health and well-being is profound. It is, without a doubt, a practice worth considering for any senior seeking a path to healthier aging.

Enhancing Mobility and Flexibility with Pilates

As the years pass by, we often start to feel a gradual loss of mobility and flexibility. Simple movements that we once took for granted can start to feel challenging, and we may find ourselves avoiding certain activities for fear of discomfort or injury. But what if there was a way to reclaim that lost freedom of movement and even enhance it? That's where Pilates comes into the picture.

Pilates is much more than just an exercise routine. It's a system of physical conditioning that places a significant emphasis on improving mobility and flexibility. Its creator, Joseph Pilates, was a strong believer in the power of controlled movements and balance to transform the body. He developed a series of exercises designed to strengthen and lengthen muscles, improve posture, and increase flexibility, all with the aim of enhancing physical vitality and well-being.

Flexibility, or the range of motion around a joint, is one of the key physical fitness components that Pilates helps to improve. When our muscles are long and flexible, they are able to perform their functions more effectively, and the risk of injury is reduced. Pilates exercises are designed to stretch and lengthen the muscles, promoting increased flexibility throughout the body.

Let's take the example of the Pilates roll-up. This exercise targets the spine, creating a C-curve as you roll down and up. Not only does it help to improve spinal flexibility, but it also promotes mobility in the hip joints, as the legs remain extended throughout the movement. Over time, practicing this exercise can lead to increased flexibility in the back and hips, making everyday movements like bending and reaching easier.

In Pilates, flexibility isn't just about the ability to stretch our muscles to their maximum length. It's about the harmony and balance between flexibility and strength. Too much flexibility without enough strength can lead to instability and injury. But when strength and flexibility are in balance, our bodies can move more efficiently and freely. Pilates exercises work towards creating this balance, building strength in the muscles while simultaneously increasing their flexibility.

Mobility is another crucial aspect that Pilates targets. While flexibility refers to the range of motion of our muscles, mobility refers to how freely our joints can move. A joint's mobility can be affected by several factors, including the flexibility of the muscles that surround it, the structure of the joint itself, and any existing injuries or conditions. Pilates exercises work on enhancing joint mobility by combining controlled movements with deep, focused breathing.

Take the example of Pilates leg circles. In this exercise, the hip joint's mobility is the main focus. As one leg is lifted and moved in circles, the hip joint is taken through its full range of motion. At the same time, the exercise also improves the flexibility of the muscles in the hip and leg, thereby enhancing overall mobility.

The beauty of Pilates is that it does not force the body into unnatural or straining positions. Instead, it gently guides the body through a range of movements that are natural and beneficial. This approach makes Pilates a safe and effective way to improve mobility and flexibility, even for those who may be starting from a place of limited mobility or flexibility due to age, injury, or a sedentary lifestyle.

Pilates is not about achieving the splits or touching your toes. It's about improving the way your body moves in everyday life. It's about being able to pick up a dropped object without straining your back, reaching for a high shelf without pain, or playing with your grandchildren without fear of injury. It's about enhancing your quality of life through improved mobility and flexibility.

The benefits of Pilates go beyond the physical. Enhanced mobility and flexibility can alsolead to mental and emotional benefits. The connection between mind and body is a central theme in Pilates. With improved mobility and flexibility, you might find that your mind becomes more agile and adaptable, mirroring the fluidity of your physical movements.

Enhancing mobility and flexibility through Pilates can also significantly impact your self-confidence. As you progress and observe changes in your body, you'll likely notice an improved sense of body awareness. This heightened self-awareness can lead to a better understanding of your body's capabilities, resulting in increased self-esteem and body confidence. The ability to move freely without pain or discomfort can make you feel more in control of your body and your life.

Moreover, with enhanced mobility and flexibility, you can experience a renewed sense of freedom. Imagine being able to participate in activities you once loved but had to give up due to physical limitations, or to discover new hobbies that you never thought you could do. With Pilates, you don't just improve your physical condition; you open up new possibilities for living a fuller, more active life.

Of course, like any exercise regimen, Pilates isn't a magic pill. It requires dedication, consistency, and patience. The improvements in mobility and flexibility won't happen overnight. But with regular practice, you will start to see changes. Little by little, you'll find yourself moving with more ease and grace, experiencing less discomfort, and enjoying a broader range of activities.

In conclusion, Pilates offers a unique approach to enhancing mobility and flexibility, blending strength training with stretching and controlled movements. It provides a safe, effective, and enjoyable way to improve your physical condition, leading to numerous benefits in your daily life and overall well-being. Whether you are already an active person or someone looking to start a fitness journey, Pilates can be a valuable tool to enhance your mobility and flexibility.

As you embark on your Pilates journey, remember that it's not about comparing yourself to others or striving for perfection. It's about listening to your body, respecting its limits, and celebrating its progress. It's about finding joy in movement and appreciating the wonderful things your body can do. As Joseph Pilates once said, "Change happens through movement, and movement heals." So, let's get moving!

Pilates for Strength and Balance in Seniors

As we age, we often face challenges that were once inconceivable during our younger years. The vitality and resilience that once characterized our every move seem to fade. However, it's essential to recognize that these changes do not signal an end, but rather, a transition into a stage of life that can be just as fulfilling and dynamic. Pilates, with its gentle, controlled movements, can be the very companion seniors need to gracefully embrace this new chapter.

Imagine a life where strength and balance are not merely remnants of the past but are integral elements of your daily routine. Pilates offers a way to make this a reality. For seniors, strength is not just about lifting heavy weights or running a marathon; it's about maintaining muscle tone and bone density. It's about being able to carry groceries, play with grandchildren, and enjoy a stroll in the park. Pilates helps in rebuilding strength by engaging the core muscles, the very foundation of our body.

Balance, on the other hand, is often an overlooked component of fitness, especially in seniors. With age, our balance tends to deteriorate, which increases the risk of falls. Through Pilates, seniors can enhance their balance by practicing exercises that make them more aware of their bodies and their alignment. This heightened awareness is not just physical; it permeates into a mental space. When you're balanced in your body, there's a sense of equilibrium that is also achieved in your mind.

Now, let's talk about the magical space where strength and balance converge - the core. The core is often thought of as just the abdominal muscles, but it is so much more. It's the center of your body and encompasses your abs, lower back, and pelvic muscles. Pilates places a significant emphasis on the core. For seniors, a strong core means better stability and less strain on the back and joints. It means a posture that exudes confidence and grace.

Pilates for seniors is not just an exercise; it's an experience that binds the body and mind. As you move through the Pilates poses and breathing exercises, there's a sense of being present in the moment. This mindfulness aspect of Pilates can be incredibly beneficial for seniors dealing with stress or feeling disconnected.

In addition, Pilates is adaptable. This is particularly important for seniors as they may have varying levels of mobility and health. The exercises in Pilates can be modified to accommodate these differences. Whether you're in the prime of your senior years or dealing with the aches and pains that come with age, Pilates has something to offer.

Let's not forget the social aspect. Joining a Pilates class can be a wonderful opportunity for seniors to socialize and build a community. It's a place where you can share your experiences, laugh, and encourage each other. This sense of belonging can have profound effects on mental health and overall happiness.

But what about those who may not be able to attend a class? The beauty of Pilates is that it can be practiced in the comfort of your home. With minimal equipment, you can create a sacred space for movement. The key is consistency. It's not about how much you do; it's about how often you do it. Regular practice, even if it's for a short period, can yield results.

At the end of the day, Pilates for seniors is about empowerment. It's about taking control of your health and realizing that age is not a barrier but a gateway to new possibilities. Through the strengthening and balancing practices of Pilates, seniors can find not just an exercise routine, but a lifestyle that embraces the beauty and wisdom of their years.

So, if you're a senior or have a loved one who is, take a step into the world of Pilates. Embrace the movements, breathe, and begin to see the transformation in strength and balance unfold. It's a journey that is not just physical but also deeply personal and spiritual. With each stretch, each breath, and each moment of stillness, you're not just moving; you're living.

Moreover, Pilates provides a safe haven for self-expression and self-discovery. As seniors engage in the subtle art of controlled movements, they often find hidden reservoirs of strength and grace within themselves. This discovery is not just about physical prowess but also about embracing an identity that transcends age and limitations. It's about realizing that the essence of who you are remains untouched by time.

The beauty of Pilates lies in its ability to be both gentle and challenging. The movements may appear simple, but as you delve deeper, you will find layers of complexity. This duality makes it an exciting and ever-evolving practice for seniors. There's always something new to learn, a new challenge to embrace.

One might wonder if starting Pilates later in life could be intimidating or difficult. However, it's important to remember that Pilates is not a competition. It's a personal journey. The only person you need to focus on is yourself. You define your limits and you set your pace. This sense of autonomy is particularly empowering for seniors as it reinstates a sense of control and independence.

For seniors with chronic conditions such as arthritis or osteoporosis, Pilates offers hope. The low-impact nature of the exercises makes it an ideal choice for those with joint issues or bone fragility. Not only does it help in alleviating pain but also plays a pivotal role in preventing further degeneration. It's like saying to your body, "I respect you and will take care of you."

Let's also touch upon the spirit. Pilates, with its roots in mindful movement, offers a conduit for spiritual well-being. It's not just about moving the body, but also about calming the mind. In a world that's often chaotic, Pilates provides the space for peace and tranquility. For seniors, this peace is not just a luxury, it's a necessity.

As we conclude this exploration into the realm of Pilates for seniors, let's take a moment to reflect on the possibilities it opens up. It's an invitation to a life that's vibrant, balanced, and fulfilled. It's a reminder that our bodies, even as they age, are incredible and deserving of care and love.

CHAPTER 2

Safety Considerations for Seniors Practicing Pilates

When we step into the world of Pilates as seniors, we're not just embarking on a journey of physical transformation, but also embracing a commitment to our overall well-being. With this commitment comes a responsibility: to ensure that we are moving in a way that is safe, respectful, and mindful of our bodies' unique needs and limitations. This chapter shines a light on the crucial aspect of safety considerations that every senior should bear in mind when practicing Pilates.

Pilates is a beautiful dance between strength and grace, but it's also a practice that demands attention to form, alignment, and technique. The first step towards ensuring safety is understanding that every exercise in Pilates is designed with a purpose. It's not about how many repetitions we can do or how quickly we can move, but about the quality of each movement. Every stretch, every lift, and every breath should be done with intention and mindfulness.

However, as we age, our bodies naturally go through changes. Muscles lose their elasticity, bones become less dense, and joints may not be as flexible as they once were. These changes, while a normal part of aging, necessitate adaptations in our Pilates practice to ensure we're exercising safely and effectively.

One of the most important adaptations is the careful selection of exercises. Not all Pilates exercises are suitable for all individuals. For example, seniors with osteoporosis should avoid exercises that require forward bending or twisting of the spine to prevent any potential injury. Similarly, those with balance issues should initially avoid exercises that challenge stability. Remember, Pilates is not a one-size-fits-all approach. It's a journey that should be tailored to your unique body and its needs.

Listening to your body is a skill that's often underrated, yet it's one of the most valuable tools we have for ensuring safety. Our bodies are incredibly intelligent. They know when something doesn't feel right and they communicate this to us through signals such as discomfort or pain. As we practice Pilates, we need to tune into these signals, respect them, and adjust our movements accordingly.

Working with a certified Pilates instructor, especially when starting out, can also greatly enhance safety. They can guide you through each exercise, ensuring you're maintaining proper form and alignment. They can also provide modifications to accommodate any physical limitations. Never hesitate to ask for help or clarification when you need it. Your safety and well-being are paramount.

Equally important is the setting in which we practice Pilates. Ideally, you should have a quiet, clutter-free space with a mat that provides adequate cushioning. Make sure the area is well-lit to prevent any accidents. If you're using any additional equipment like resistance bands or Pilates balls, ensure they are in good condition and used correctly.

Our bodies also require adequate hydration and nourishment to function optimally. Ensure you're well-hydrated before, during, and after your Pilates session. Similarly, nourish your body with wholesome, nutrient-rich foods to provide the energy needed for your workout and to aid in recovery afterwards.

Finally, it's important to remember that Pilates is a practice of patience and compassion. It's not about striving for perfection or pushing beyond your limits. It's about showing up for yourself, just as you are, and moving in a way that honors your body. When we approach Pilates with this mindset, we create a safe, nurturing environment for our bodies to grow stronger, more flexible, and more balanced.

In essence, safety in Pilates is about embracing an attitude of mindfulness, respect, and understanding towards our bodies. It's about acknowledging our limitations, yet also recognizing our potential. It's about moving in harmony with our bodies, not against them.

As seniors, we have the wisdom to understand that true strength is not abouthow fast or how far we can go; rather, it's about the resilience to keep moving, to keep trying, and to keep growing. When we bring this wisdom into our Pilates practice, we not only ensure our safety but also enhance the joy, fulfillment, and the profound sense of well-being that Pilates can bring into our lives.

Remember, our age does not define us, nor does it limit what we can achieve. However, it does give us a different perspective, a unique set of experiences, and, at times, a distinct set of challenges. As we embark on our Pilates journey, we should always be aware of these factors. We must respect our bodies, listen to their wisdom, and adapt our practice to meet their unique needs. And in doing so, we'll find that Pilates can be an enriching, empowering, and safe practice for us.

Pilates, at its heart, is a practice of self-discovery and self-care. It's a journey that asks us to show up, to be present, and to care for our bodies in the best way we can. When we approach it with a sense of curiosity, patience, and respect, we create a practice that not only strengthens our bodies but also nurtures our spirits. As seniors, we deserve a fitness practice that acknowledges our experience, respects our wisdom, and adapts to our unique needs. Pilates, when practiced with attention to safety, can be just that practice.

It is also worth mentioning that while the journey is ours to embark on, we are not alone in it. The Pilates community is a supportive and encouraging one. Reach out to fellow practitioners, share your experiences, and learn from theirs. We all have unique insights and wisdom to offer, and by sharing them, we can all grow together.

In conclusion, safety in Pilates is not merely about the absence of harm or injury. It's about creating a practice that enhances our overall well-being, respects our bodies, and nourishes our spirits. It's about being mindful, being present, and above all, being kind to ourselves. As we move through each stretch, each lift, and each breath, let us remember to do so with care, with respect, and with love for the incredible bodies that carry us through this life.

In the end, Pilates is much more than a series of exercises. It's an invitation to connect with our bodies, to explore our strengths, and to nurture our well-being. As seniors practicing Pilates, we have the opportunity to take this invitation and create a practice that is safe, fulfilling, and uniquely our own. With mindfulness, respect, and a focus on safety, we can enjoy the many benefits of Pilates while also honoring the wisdom and experience that comes with age. In this way, Pilates becomes not just a form of exercise, but a joyful celebration of movement, strength, and life itself.

Precautions for Seniors Starting Pilates

As seniors venture into the world of Pilates, it is vital to understand and take precautions to ensure a safe and injury-free experience. This journey into fitness can be both exhilarating and challenging, but with the right approach, it can also be incredibly rewarding.

Starting a Pilates program as a senior involves more than simply showing up for a class. It means taking the time to understand your body, recognizing its strengths, and acknowledging its limitations. It also means understanding how to adapt exercises to your unique needs. While Pilates is a wonderfully flexible form of exercise, it is not one-size-fits-all. It requires a thoughtful approach, especially when we are starting it later in life.

The first and foremost precaution when starting Pilates is to get a thorough health check-up. Before embarking on any new exercise regimen, it's crucial to have a clear understanding of your current health status. Consulting with your healthcare provider can help identify any potential risks or limitations that you may need to consider. Discuss your plans with them and ask for any specific advice or precautions you should take based on your health history.

Knowing your body's unique needs is essential in maintaining safety during Pilates. Every body is different, and what works for one person may not work for another. It's important to remember that Pilates is not a competition; it's a personal journey. If a certain move or posture doesn't feel right, it's okay to modify it or skip it altogether. The goal is to enhance well-being, not to push beyond comfort levels. In this regard, listening to your body is one of the most important precautions you can take.

When starting out, it's highly beneficial to work with a certified Pilates instructor who has experience with seniors. An instructor can guide you through the exercises, help you modify them as needed, and ensure you're doing them correctly to avoid injury. They can also monitor your progress and adjust your routine as your strength and flexibility improve. While it's tempting to dive into a new activity with gusto, it's essential to start slow and steady. Beginning with basic exercises and gradually moving to more complex ones allows your body to adjust to the new demands. It also helps to build strength and flexibility gradually, reducing the risk of injury.

Proper hydration and nutrition are also key precautions. Seniors are more prone to dehydration, and exercise increases this risk. Ensure you drink plenty of water before, during, and after your Pilates sessions. Equally, ensuring your body is well-nourished will provide the energy needed for your workouts and aid in recovery afterwards.

Rest is as important as the exercise itself. Pilates is gentle, but it still challenges the body. Allow yourself ample time to recover between sessions, especially when you're just starting. Over-exercising can lead to fatigue and increase the risk of injury.

Remember, it's not about how quickly you progress, but how consistently you practice. Consistency is key in Pilates, and a slow, steady approach is far safer and more effective than rushing through exercises or pushing yourself too hard.

Injuries often occur when we are not mindful of our movements. Hence, focusing on the quality of movement, rather than the quantity, is another vital precaution. Pilates exercises require careful attention to alignment, breath, and form. It's not about doing many repetitions, but about doing a few well-executed ones. This mindful approach not only improves the effectiveness of the exercise but also significantly reduces the risk of injury.

Lastly, always remember to warm up before starting your Pilates session and cool down afterwards. This practice prepares your body for the workout ahead and helps it to recover afterwards, reducing the risk of muscle strain or injury.

Pilates is an incredible journey of self-discovery, strength, and healing. But like any journey, it should be embarked upon with care and preparation. As a senior, taking these precautions will not only help you avoid injuries but also ensure that you reap the maximum benefits from your Pilates practice.

Embrace the journey into Pilates with an open heart, a mindful approach, and a respectful awareness of your body's unique needs and capabilities. It's about moving at your own pace, honoring your body's signals, and celebrating every step you take towards better health and fitness. This journey may challenge you, but it will also empower you. It will allow you to explore your physical strengths, improve your flexibility, enhance your balance, and contribute to your overall wellbeing.

While Pilates offers an array of benefits, especially for seniors, it's important not to forget the value of patience. Progress may be slow, but it is sure. Each small victory, whether it's being able to do an exercise you couldn't do before, noticing improved flexibility, or simply feeling better in your daily activities, is a testament to your progress.

Finally, remember that Pilates is not just a form of exercise; it's a lifestyle. It's about making healthier choices, taking care of your body, and fostering a sense of inner peace and balance. And this is perhaps the most important precaution of all: to view Pilates not as a chore or a duty, but as a gift to yourself. It's a time to focus on you, to listen to your body, and to nourish your health.

As you embark on this Pilates journey, remember to take each day as it comes. Celebrate your successes, learn from your challenges, and always, always listen to your body. By taking these precautions, you can make the most of your Pilates experience, enhancing not just your physical health, but your overall quality of life.

In conclusion, starting Pilates as a senior can be an exciting journey filled with new discoveries and achievements. By taking the necessary precautions, you can ensure a safe, enjoyable, and beneficial Pilates experience. It's never too late to start, and with the right approach, Pilates can be a wonderful addition to your life, offering benefits that extend far beyond the mat.

So, whether you are embarking on this journey for the first time or returning to it after a break, remember to approach it with care, patience, and a sense of adventure. After all, Pilates is not just about the destination; it's about the journey. And as with any journey, the key is to enjoy each step along the way. Happy practicing!

Injury Prevention in Pilates for Seniors

As we age, our bodies change, and so does our approach to physical activity. For seniors embracing Pilates, injury prevention is paramount. The beauty of this exercise form lies in its adaptability. Pilates can be gentle and restorative, but it also has the power to challenge and strengthen the body. Yet, the line between challenging oneself and pushing too far is thin. Straddling this line with grace and wisdom can make all the difference in a fulfilling Pilates practice.

Now, let's talk about the heart and soul of injury prevention in Pilates - the warm-up. Warming up is like whispering to your body that it's about to undertake a beautiful journey. It's the prologue to the story of your practice. By properly warming up, you're ensuring that the muscles and joints are ready for the movements they're about to perform. This is especially crucial for seniors, as our muscles lose elasticity over time. A good warm-up enhances blood flow and prepares the mind for a focused session. Consider the warm-up as setting the stage for your practice, where your body is the performer, and your breath is the music.

When it comes to preventing injuries, knowing your body is key. Seniors need to be mindful of their bodies' unique quirks and needs. Understanding and accepting the limitations of one's body is not a sign of defeat, but rather an emblem of wisdom. Be attentive to how your body responds to different movements. This attentiveness is your internal compass. It will guide you through your practice, helping you to navigate which movements to embrace and which to approach with caution.

One must also consider the spine. A treasure in Pilates, the spine is central to many movements. The flexibility of the spine decreases as we age. Seniors must, therefore, approach spinal movements with utmost care. Focus on movements that elongate the spine and improve posture. Engage the core muscles to support the back. Imagine your spine as a string of pearls, each movement adding luster to each pearl.

The breath is your guide. In Pilates, breath is not just breath; it is the rhythm that guides the dance of movements. For seniors, understanding the synchrony between breath and movement is essential. This synchrony is the magic potion that prevents injuries. When you move with your breath, your movements are more controlled. This control is what keeps the movements safe for the joints and muscles.

Hydration is another often overlooked aspect. Our bodies are akin to flowing rivers. When a river dries up, it loses its grace and fluidity. Similarly, a dehydrated body is more prone to injuries. Drink water before your practice to ensure that your muscles are hydrated. This is not just a physical act, but a symbolic one – a gesture of nourishment to the body that serves us so loyally.

There's also a delicate art to choosing the right movements. Pilates has a vast repertoire of exercises. However, not all exercises are suitable for everyone. Seniors should focus on movements that build strength, improve balance, and enhance flexibility without straining the joints. Avoid high-impact exercises and instead, embrace low-impact movements. Let your practice be a waltz – graceful, controlled, and smooth.

Lastly, let's talk about consistency. Consistency is the invisible thread that binds all these elements together. A sporadic approach to Pilates is like an untuned piano; the music is disjointed. Consistent practice tunes your body. The movements become more fluid, the breath more harmonious. As seniors, consistent practice is not about perfection; it's about gently pushing the boundaries of what's possible.

With age, comes wisdom. In Pilates, this wisdom is your shield. It protects you from injuries and guides you towards a practice that is fulfilling and nurturing. Let your Pilates sessions be a symphony, where each movement is a note, and your breath is the conductor. Embrace the warm-up as the overture that sets the tone, and let the conscious selection of exercises be the various melodies that compose your symphony. By paying attention to your body, engaging your spine, synchronizing your breath, hydrating, choosing the right movements, and being consistent, you are not just practicing Pilates; you are creating an art form.

As you stand on the mat or use the Pilates equipment, envision yourself as an artist. The mat and the equipment are your canvases, and your movements are the brushstrokes. Each brushstroke is important. Like a painter who knows that each stroke contributes to the final masterpiece, know that each movement contributes to your well-being.

In the golden years of life, Pilates is not just an exercise; it's a celebration. It's a celebration of what your body can achieve, of the elegance in your movements, and of the breath that brings life to your days. Let your practice be an ode to yourself. A tribute to the years that have passed and an embrace of the years yet to come.

So, dear practitioner, when you step on that mat, do it with grace. Do it with the knowledge that you are about to embark on a journey that is as much internal as it is external. You are about to engage not just your muscles but your soul. Let the core of your being be touched. Let the essence of who you are be celebrated. In this celebration, let there be joy, let there be vitality, and let there be a sense of eternal youth that transcends age.

Injury prevention is not just a series of steps; it's a philosophy. It's the philosophy of respecting your body, of cherishing it, and of understanding its infinite wisdom. It's about knowing that within you lies an ocean of potential, waiting to be embraced through the gentle waves of your movements.

Let your Pilates practice be the gentle breeze that invigorates your body, the warm sunlight that caresses your skin, and the soft earth that supports your steps. Let it be a reminder that every day is a gift and that within you lies a garden in bloom, no matter the seasons that have passed.

In the tapestry of life, let your Pilates thread be woven with care, love, and gratitude. For in the end, it is not just about movement; it is about the moments that take your breath away and the breaths that give life to your moments.

With each stretch, with each contraction, with each exhale, you are not just doing Pilates; you are living a poem that only your heart can understand.

Cherish it, for it is precious.

CHAPTER 3

Wall Pilates Exercises Tailored for Seniors

As we age, our bodies undergo transformations. The once spry, flexible, and agile bodies may now move a little slower, feel a little stiffer, and carry a few more aches. But, my dear reader, let this not dismay you. Instead, let it inspire you to embrace an exercise regimen that meets you where you are and encourages you to soar to heights you never thought possible. Among the myriad of exercise options available to us, Wall Pilates has emerged as a gem that is particularly beneficial for seniors. It's a practice that brings the wall into play as a unique prop that offers support, stability, and an added layer of challenge. But, what makes Wall Pilates so special for seniors? Let's delve into the intricacies of this wonderful discipline.

Pilates, by design, is a low-impact form of exercise that focuses on balance, core strength, flexibility, and body awareness. It is a discipline that encourages you to engage your mind and body in unison. But when you add a wall to the mix, the benefits increase manifold. The wall, in Wall Pilates, becomes an ally that promotes alignment, challenges stability, and enhances flexibility in a safe and controlled manner.

Imagine the wall as a silent guide, always present, always supportive. It doesn't judge or rush; instead, it patiently guides you through the movements. As you lean into the wall for a stretch or press against it for a resistance exercise, the wall stands firm, enabling you to explore your range of motion, to test your strength, and to deepen your stretches. As seniors, this provides an opportunity to exercise with a greater sense of safety and confidence.

One of the most beautiful aspects of Wall Pilates is its adaptability. It allows you to modify traditional Pilates exercises to suit your individual needs. For instance, if a floor-based exercise feels too challenging, you can perform a similar movement against the wall. The wall supports your body, reduces the strain on your joints, and makes the exercise more achievable. This adaptability makes Wall Pilates a highly inclusive practice, embracing individuals of all fitness levels and ages.

Let's consider a typical Wall Pilates session. It might begin with standing tall against the wall, your back pressed against the cool surface, as you take slow, mindful breaths. This simple act of standing erect and breathing deeply sets the tone for the session. It brings awareness to your posture, it calms your mind, and it prepares your body for the exercises to follow.

As you progress through the session, you might engage in exercises like Wall Push-Ups, Wall Squats, or Wall Leg Lifts. Each of these exercises targets specific muscle groups and challenges your body in different ways. Wall Push-Ups, for instance, strengthen your arms and back, while Wall Squats work your legs and core, and Wall Leg Lifts target your glutes and hips. The beauty of these exercises is that they can be performed at your own pace and intensity. You can choose how far to step away from the wall, how deep to squat, and how high to lift your leg. The power to customize each exercise lies in your hands.

But Wall Pilates is not just about strength; it's equally about flexibility. Exercises like the Wall Hamstring Stretch or the Wall Chest Opener encourage your muscles to lengthen, your joints to open, and your body to unwind. These exercises, performed with the support of the wall, allow you to stretch deeper and hold longer, thereby enhancing your flexibility and mobility.

As you near the end of your session, you might close with a series of Wall Roll Downs. This beautiful exercise encourages your spine to articulate, vertebra by vertebra, against the wall. It releases tension in your back, promotes spinal health, andleaves you feeling refreshed and invigorated. It's like a soft, gentle sigh from your spine, a thank you for the care and attention you've given it.

As seniors, investing in our health is one of the most critical and beneficial decisions we can make. With Wall Pilates, we gift ourselves the opportunity to age gracefully and healthily. This practice promotes not just physical well-being, but also mental and emotional wellness. It encourages mindfulness, it fosters a sense of inner calm, and it instills a spirit of resilience.

Remember, dear reader, age is but a number. It doesn't define us; it doesn't limit us. If anything, it empowers us. It empowers us with the wisdom of years and the courage of experience. So, let us embrace our age, let us embrace Wall Pilates, and let us embrace a healthier, happier, and more active lifestyle.

In practicing Wall Pilates, you're not just moving; you're dancing with the rhythm of life. The wall becomes your dance partner, leading you through a choreography of strength, balance, and flexibility. With every push, pull, stretch, and breathe, you're not just exercising your body; you're also nourishing your spirit. It's a dance that celebrates your presence, honors your journey, and fuels your ambition to keep moving, keep exploring, and keep growing.

So, as you embark on this beautiful journey of Wall Pilates, remember to be patient with yourself. Honor your body's rhythm, respect its limitations, and celebrate its capabilities. You're not in a race; you're on a journey. A journey of self-discovery, self-improvement, and self-love. A journey that reminds you that you're never too old to learn, to grow, and to shine.

And as you stand tall against the wall, pushing and pulling, stretching and strengthening, remember, you're not just exercising; you're expressing. You're expressing your strength, your resilience, your grace, and your tenacity. You're expressing your commitment to your well-being, your dedication to your health, and your love for your body. You're expressing your indomitable spirit that says, "Age is not a barrier; it's a milestone."

Wall Pilates is more than just an exercise regimen; it's a lifestyle. It's a lifestyle that encourages you to live actively, to live mindfully, and to live joyfully. It's a lifestyle that champions the belief that age is not a deterrent but a motivator. A motivator to live better, to live healthier, and to live happier.

In conclusion, embrace the wall, embrace Pilates, embrace your age. Life is a beautiful journey, and with Wall Pilates, you're ensuring that this journey is a healthy, active, and fulfilling one. So, step up to the wall, dear reader, and let's celebrate the beauty of movement, the joy of exercise, and the gift of health together. Let's celebrate the wonderful, inspiring, and powerful seniors that we are. Let's celebrate life, with Wall Pilates.

Lower Body Wall Pilates Exercises for Seniors

Here are some lower body Wall Pilates exercises specifically tailored for seniors:

- **Wall Sits:** Wall sits are a great way to improve leg strength and endurance. Stand with your back against the wall and slowly slide down until your thighs are parallel to the floor, just as if you were sitting on a chair. Keep your feet hip-width apart and your knees directly above your ankles. Press your back into the wall and engage your core. Hold this position for 10 to 30 seconds, then slowly slide back up. This exercise works the quadriceps, hamstrings, and glutes.

- **Wall Leg Lifts:** This exercise helps strengthen the glutes and hamstrings. Stand facing the wall at arm's length. Keeping your body straight, slowly lift one leg straight back without bending your knee or pointing your toes. Try not to lean forward. Lower your leg back down. Repeat this exercise 10 to 15 times, then switch to the other leg.

- **Wall Lunges:** Stand sideways near the wall with one hand on the wall for support. Step the leg closer to the wall back, placing your foot flat on the ground. Bend your front knee until it's at 90 degrees, while the back knee points towards the floor. Push back up and repeat. This exercise targets the quads, glutes, and hamstrings.

- **Wall Supported Calf Raises:** Stand facing the wall with your fingertips on it for balance. Slowly rise onto the balls of your feet, lifting your heels as high as you can. Lower your heels back down. This exercise targets the calf muscles.

- **Wall Squats:** Similar to the wall sit, but involves movement. Stand with your back against the wall and your feet hip-width apart. Begin to lower your body as if you're sitting down on a chair, then push through your heels to return to standing. This exercise works the quads, hamstrings, and glutes.

- **Wall Push-Offs:** This exercise is a gentler form of push-ups using a wall. Stand a little more than arm's length from the wall. Place your palms on the wall at shoulder height and shoulder-width apart. Breathe in as you lean your body towards the wall. Breathe out as you push your body away from the wall to return to the starting position. This exercise targets the arms, shoulders, and chest muscles.

- **Wall Angels:** Stand with your back against the wall. Extend your arms out to your sides with your palms facing out and press them into the wall. Slowly slide your arms up the wall while keeping your lower back and elbows in contact with the wall. Slide your arms back down. This exercise helps improve posture and works the shoulder muscles.

- **Pelvic Tilts:** Stand with your back against the wall. Bend your knees slightly. Flatten your back against the wall by tilting your pelvis, then return to the starting position. This exercise strengthens the abdominal and lower back muscles.

- **Wall Slides:** Stand with your back against the wall, feet shoulder-width apart. Slowly bend your knees and slide your back down the wall until your thighs are parallel to the ground. Slowly rise back up to the starting position. This exercise targets the legs and core muscles.

- **Heel-To-Toe Walk:** Stand with your back against a wall for support. Place one foot in front of the other so that the heel of one foot touches the toes of the other foot. Take a step, placing your heel in front of the toes of your other foot. Continue for 10-20 steps. This exercise improves balance and coordination.

Remember, it's important to go at your own pace and listen to your body. If any exercise causes pain, stop immediately. It's always recommended to consult with a healthcare provider before starting any new exercise regimen.

Upper Body Wall Pilates Exercises for Seniors

Here are some lower body Wall Pilates exercises specifically tailored for seniors:

- **Wall Chest Stretch:** Stand facing a wall with your right arm extended to the side at shoulder height, fingers pointing to the right. Place your palm and forearm on the wall. Gently turn your body to the left until you feel a stretch in the chest and front of the shoulder. Hold for 15-30 seconds, then switch to the other arm. This exercise stretches and opens the chest muscles, promoting better posture and breathing.

- **Wall Press:** Stand with your back against the wall. Place your arms at your sides with your elbows bent at 90 degrees, and the backs of your hands against the wall. Press your arms back into the wall and squeeze the shoulder blades together. Release, and repeat. This exercise targets the upper back and shoulders, helping to improve posture and reduce upper back pain.

- **Wall Snow Angels:** Stand with your back against the wall. Bring your arms up to the sides, elbows bent and the backs of your hands against the wall. Slowly raise your arms above your head, keeping them against the wall, as if making a snow angel. Lower them back down and repeat. This exercise is great for shoulder mobility and strengthening the upper back.

- **Wall Bicep Stretch:** Stand facing the wall. Place your palms on the wall above your head, fingers pointing downwards. Slowly lower your body until you feel a stretch in your biceps and chest. Hold for 15-30 seconds. This stretch is effective for releasing tension in the biceps and pectoral muscles.

- **Tricep Wall Push-Up:** Face the wall and place your hands on the wall, narrower than shoulder-width apart. Keep your elbows tucked in. Bend your elbows to bring your face closer to the wall, and then push back to the starting position. This exercise focuses on the triceps and can also engage the core muscles for stability.

- **Wall Y Raises:** Stand with your back against the wall and your feet hip-width apart. Extend your arms straight above your head in a Y position, with the backs of your hands touching the wall. While keeping your arms straight, slowly lower them down to your sides and then raise them back up. This exercise focuses on shoulder mobility and strengthening the upper back.

- **Wall Push-ups:** Face the wall and position your hands a little wider than your shoulders. Keep your feet grounded as you bend your elbows and bring your chest closer to the wall, then push back to the starting position. This exercise is a less strenuous version of a traditional push-up, working the chest, arms, and shoulders.

- **Wall Wrist Stretch:** Stand facing the wall. Place your palms against the wall with your fingers pointing towards the ceiling. Gently press into the wall to stretch the wrist and forearm. Switch the position of your hands so that your fingers point towards the floor for an additional stretch. This stretch helps increase flexibility and relieve tension in the wrists, which is beneficial for activities that require fine motor skills.

- **Arm Circles:** Stand with your back against the wall and extend your arms out to the sides, with the backs of your hands touching the wall. Make small circles with your arms, first in one direction, then in the other. This exercise helps improve shoulder mobility and strengthens the arms and upper back.

- **Wall Side Stretch:** Stand sideways to the wall, with your right hand touching the wall for support. Reach your left hand over your head and towards the wall, stretching the left side of your body. Hold the stretch, then switch sides. This exercise can help improve flexibility and mobility in the upper body, specifically targeting the oblique muscles.

As always, it's crucial to maintain good form during these exercises and to listen to your body's signals. If you feel any pain or discomfort, stop the exercise and consult with a healthcare professional if needed. Start with a small number of repetitions and gradually increase as your strength and mobility improve.

Core Strengthening Wall Pilates Exercises for Seniors

Core strength is essential for maintaining balance, posture, and overall functionality in daily life, especially for seniors. Here are some Wall Pilates exercises that focus on core strengthening, tailored for seniors:

- **Wall Plank:** Stand facing the wall, about an arm's length away. Place your hands on the wall at shoulder height. Slowly walk your feet back as you lean into the wall, keeping your body in a straight line from head to heels. Engage your core muscles to maintain this plank position for a few seconds before returning to the starting position. This exercise strengthens the entire core.

- **Wall Dead Bug:** Stand with your back against the wall and your arms by your sides. Engage your core and press your lower back into the wall. Lift your right arm overhead and your left knee towards your chest simultaneously. Lower them down and repeat with the opposite arm and leg. These mimics the traditional 'Dead Bug' exercise and focuses on the deep abdominal muscles.

- **Wall 100s:** Stand with your back against the wall and your feet about a foot away from it. Slide down until you are in a seated position. Extend your arms in front of you and start pumping them up and down while engaging your core. Take deep breaths in and out as you pump your arms. This exercise is a wall adaptation of the classic Pilates 100s, targeting the core.

- **Wall Leg Slides:** Stand with your back against the wall, feet hip-width apart. Engage your core and press your lower back into the wall. Slowly slide your right foot up the wall, keeping your knee bent. Lower it back down and repeat with the left leg. Keep your core engaged throughout the movement. This exercise strengthens the lower abdominal muscles.

- **Wall Side Plank:** Stand sideways to the wall and place your forearm against it. Keep your feet together and your body in a straight line. Engage your core as you press your forearm against the wall. Hold for a few seconds, then switch to the other side. This exercise strengthens the obliques and helps improve balance.

- **Modified Plank:** Stand facing the wall with your feet shoulder-width apart. Place your palms flat against the wall, slightly wider than your shoulders. Push against the wall as you would in a regular plank on the floor. Keep your body straight, engaging your core muscles. Hold for 10-15 seconds, rest, and repeat.

- **Wall Tendu:** Stand tall with your back against the wall. Extend one leg in front of you, keeping it straight and the toes pointed. Engage your core to maintain balance. Repeat this for 10-15 repetitions before switching to the other leg.

- **The Hundred:** This exercise focuses on the breath and the core. Stand back against the wall. Lift your arms to shoulder height, palms facing forward. Breathe in and on the exhale, press your hands towards the wall in a pulsing motion. Do this in sets of 10, five times, for a total of 50 pulses.

- **Wall Squats:** Stand with your back to the wall and feet shoulder-width apart. Lower your body until your thighs are parallel to the floor, as if you're sitting in a chair. Keep your core engaged and your back flat against the wall. Hold for a few seconds, then slowly return to a standing position.

- **Scapular Depression:** Stand with your back against the wall, arms at your sides. Without moving your arms, try to move your shoulder blades down towards your back pockets. This will engage your core and improve your posture.

- **Wall Mountain Climbers:** Face the wall and place your hands on it at shoulder height. Take a step back so that you are at a slight angle. Engage your core and lift your right knee towards your chest, then switch to the left. Keep alternating legs in a climbing motion. This low-impact version of mountain climbers is excellent for the core.

- **Wall Twist:** Stand sideways near the wall with your right shoulder facing it. Place your right hand on the wall at shoulder height. With your feet hip-width apart, engage your core and rotate your torso towards the wall, reaching your left hand towards your right. Return to the starting position and repeat on the other side. This exercise targets the obliques.

- **Wall Pelvic Tilts:** Stand with your back against the wall, feet hip-width apart. Engage your core and press your lower back into the wall. Tilt your pelvis up and back, flattening your lower back against the wall. Release and repeat. This exercise helps to strengthen the deep core muscles and improve lower back stability.

Remember that it's important for seniors to take it slowly and focus on form. It's always a good idea to consult with a healthcare professional before starting a new exercise routine, especially for individuals with existing health conditions. Engaging in these core-strengthening Wall Pilates exercises can be a wonderful way for seniors to enhance balance, mobility, and the joy of movement in daily life.

Suggested Weekly Exercise Plan Tailored for Seniors

Here's a suggested exercise plan for a week using the Wall Pilates exercises we've discussed. This plan is designed to gradually increase activity and is adaptable to individual needs and capabilities. Always remember to start each session with a warm-up and end with a cool-down period.

Day 1: Lower Body Focus

- Wall Squats: 2 sets of 10 repetitions
- Wall Supported Leg Lifts: 2 sets of 10 repetitions on each leg
- Wall Lunges: 2 sets of 10 repetitions on each leg
- Wall Supported Side Leg Lifts: 2 sets of 10 repetitions on each leg
- Wall Supported Hamstring Curls: 2 sets of 10 repetitions on each leg

Day 2: Rest and Recovery
Day 3: Upper Body Focus

- Wall Push-Ups: 2 sets of 10 repetitions
- Wall Angels: 2 sets of 10 repetitions

- Wall Chest Stretch: Hold for 30 seconds, repeat twice on each side
- Wall Supported Tricep Dips: 2 sets of 10 repetitions
- Wall Supported Bicep Curls: 2 sets of 10 repetitions

Day 4: Rest and Recovery
Day 5: Core Strengthening Focus

- Wall Supported Boat Pose: Hold for 30 seconds, rest, repeat twice
- Wall Toe Taps: 2 sets of 10 repetitions
- Wall Mountain Climbers: 2 sets of 10 repetitions
- Wall Twist: 2 sets of 10 repetitions on each side
- Wall Pelvic Tilts: 2 sets of 10 repetitions

Day 6: Full Body Focus

- Choose two exercises from each category (Lower Body, Upper Body, Core) and perform 2 sets of 10 repetitions for each.

Day 7: Rest and Recovery

Please note that these are just suggestions and can be adapted to suit individual needs and capabilities. It's essential to listen to your body and not push beyond your comfort level. If you feel any pain or discomfort, stop the exercise and consult with a healthcare professional. Remember, consistency is key when it comes to seeing results with exercise. Enjoy the journey and embrace the progress!

Don't forget to incorporate proper hydration and nutrition into your routine, as these are crucial for recovery and maintaining overall health. Pilates is not just about the physical movement; it's also about creating harmony between the mind and body. So, take this time to enjoy the movements, breathe deeply, and appreciate your body for all it does.

With time and consistent practice, you'll likely find that you feel stronger, more flexible, and perhaps even see improvements in your overall balance and coordination. Enjoy the process, and take it one day at a time. After all, every journey begins with a single step. And remember, age is just a number – it's never too late to start feeling stronger and healthier. Keep smiling and let the rejuvenating power of Pilates add a touch of grace to your golden years.

CHAPTER 4

Building a Routine: Sample Wall Pilates Workout for Seniors

Building a balanced and effective fitness routine is an essential part of maintaining good health, especially as we age. As we embark on this journey into the world of Wall Pilates for seniors, it is crucial to recognize that every person's body is unique, with its own strengths, limitations, and potential. Therefore, any workout plan should be seen as a starting point, an initial map that can and should be adjusted to fit your individual needs, capabilities, and goals.

Embarking on a Wall Pilates workout for seniors is a beautiful journey of exploration and self-discovery. It's about finding the delicate balance between effort and ease, between strength and flexibility, between exertion and relaxation. Let's dive into an example of how you might structure a Wall Pilates workout to maximize these benefits.

Every workout should start with a warm-up. The purpose of this is to prepare your body and your mind for the exercises ahead. The warm-up doesn't need to be complex or strenuous, but it should get your blood flowing and your muscles warm. For a Wall Pilates workout, this might involve some simple wall-supported movements like arm circles, side bends, and knee lifts, all performed with a focus on smooth, controlled movement and deep, even breathing. Remember, the warm-up is also a chance to check in with your body and get a sense of how you're feeling on this particular day. Listen to your body's signals and respect them. If something feels off, it's okay to adjust your plan or even take a rest day.

Once you're warmed up, you can move into the core of your workout. Wall Pilates workouts for seniors typically focus on exercises that enhance strength, balance, and flexibility. The beauty of Wall Pilates lies in its adaptability: the wall provides support and stability, allowing you to perform exercises at a pace and intensity that suits you.

For instance, wall squats can help strengthen the lower body, specifically the quadriceps, hamstrings, and glutes. To perform a wall squat, you would stand with your back against the wall, feet hip-width apart, and then slide your back down the wall until your thighs are parallel with the floor. Hold for a few seconds, then slowly push yourself back up. This move can be adjusted to your comfort level: you don't have to lower yourself all the way down. What's important is to keep the movement controlled and steady.

Wall push-ups are another fantastic exercise that can be integrated into your workout. They target the chest, shoulders, and triceps, strengthening your upper body. To perform a wall push-up, you would stand arm's length from the wall, place your palms against the wall at shoulder height, then bend your elbows and lower your body towards the wall before pushing yourself back to the starting position. Again, the focus should be on maintaining control and form over rushing through the repetitions.

Core strengthening is another key component of Wall Pilates. Exercises like wall-supported boat pose and wall mountain climbers target the muscles in your abdomen, back, and pelvis, enhancing stability and balance. These exercises can be modified to suit your capabilities, allowing you to challenge yourself safely and effectively.

The beauty of Wall Pilates, and indeed all forms of exercise, is that it's not a competition. It's a personal journey, a means of connecting with and caring for your body. So, be patient with yourself. Progress might be slow, but it will come. Celebrate each step you take on this path, each moment you choose to invest in your health and well-being.

After you've completed your series of exercises, it's time to cool down. This can involve some gentle stretches, deep breathing exercises, or perhaps a few moments of quiet relaxation. The cool-down period is just as important as the warm-up and the workout itself. It's a time to let your heart rate and breathing slow down gradually, to let your muscles relax and recover, and to mentally transition out of workout mode.

Stretching can be a wonderful way to end a Wall Pilates session. Using the wall for support, you can perform various stretches targeting the muscles you've worked during your workout. For instance, a chest stretch can be done by standing sideways to the wall, placing your palm on the wall, and then slowly turning your body away from the wall until you feel a gentle stretch across your chest. Similarly, a hamstring stretch can be performed by propping your heel up on the wall and gently leaning forward until you feel a stretch at the back of your leg.

Deep breathing exercises are also an essential part of the cool-down. These exercises can help you relax, release tension, and bring your focus back to your body and your breath. You might choose to do these exercises standing with your back against the wall or seated on a chair or exercise mat, whichever feels most comfortable for you. The key is to take slow, deep breaths, filling your lungs completely, and then exhaling fully, letting go of any residual tension or stress.

Finally, as you end your Wall Pilates workout, take a few moments to simply be. Stand or sit quietly, close your eyes if you like, and tune into the sensations in your body. Notice how your body feels after the workout. Does it feel warmer, stronger, more flexible? Do you feel more connected to your body, more present in the moment? These moments of quiet reflection can be a powerful way to deepen your connection with your body and reinforce the positive effects of your workout.

Crafting a Balanced Routine: Wall Pilates and More

Crafting a balanced routine is like creating a masterpiece. The beauty lies in the harmony of its elements, the interplay of colors, forms, and movements. In the context of fitness, this means combining different types of workouts to engage your whole body, enhance your overall well-being, and keep your routine interesting and enjoyable. Wall Pilates, with its focus on strength, flexibility, and balance, can be a key element of this harmonious ensemble.

So, how can you craft a balanced routine that incorporates Wall Pilates and other forms of exercise? Here's a closer look.

In the world of fitness, diversity is strength. Just as a balanced diet provides a variety of nutrients to nourish your body, a balanced workout routine engages different muscle groups, develops various physical skills, and meets multiple health needs. Therefore, a good starting point for crafting your routine is to think about the four main components of physical fitness: strength, endurance, flexibility, and balance.

Strength training, which includes Wall Pilates, is crucial for maintaining muscle mass, improving bone density, and boosting metabolism. It involves using resistance to challenge your muscles, helping them to grow stronger and more resilient. While traditional strength training often involves weights, machines, or resistance bands, Wall Pilates provides an effective and accessible alternative. Using the wall as a prop, you can perform a variety of exercises that challenge your body in new and unique ways, helping you to build strength without the need for specialized equipment.

Endurance or aerobic exercises, such as walking, swimming, or cycling, are designed to increase your heart rate and improve cardiovascular health. They also help to boost your energy levels, improve lung capacity, and support weight management. You might choose to incorporate these exercises into your routine on alternate days with your Wall Pilates workouts, or you might choose to combine them, perhaps by taking a brisk walk or cycling session before your Pilates workout to warm up your body and raise your heart rate.

Flexibility exercises are another important component of a balanced routine. These exercises, which include stretches and certain yoga poses, can help to lengthen and loosen your muscles, improve joint mobility, and enhance your range of motion. Many Wall Pilates exercises also promote flexibility, but you might choose to include additional flexibility exercises in your routine. For instance, you might finish your workout with a series of gentle stretches or a short yoga session to help your muscles relax and recover.

Balance exercises, finally, are crucial for maintaining stability, preventing falls, and promoting good posture. Again, Wall Pilates can be a great way to work on your balance, as many of the exercises require you to stabilize your body while performing controlled movements. Additional balance exercises, such as Tai Chi or standing yoga poses, can also be a valuable addition to your routine.

Now, while incorporating strength, endurance, flexibility, and balance exercises into your routine is important, it's also crucial to listen to your body and adjust your routine to suit your needs. If you're new to exercise or have been inactive for a while, it's wise to start slow, perhaps with gentle Wall Pilates exercises and short walks, and gradually increase the intensity and duration of your workouts as your fitness improves. If you have any health concerns or physical limitations, be sure to consult your doctor or a qualified fitness professional for guidance.

In addition, remember to give yourself permission to enjoy your workouts. Fitness is not just about improving your physical health, but also about nurturing your mental and emotional well-being. Choose activities that you enjoy, that make you feel good, and that fit comfortably into your lifestyle. Whether it's Wall Pilates, walking in the park, swimming in the sea, or dancing in your living room, the best exercise is the one that brings joy to your heart and a smile to your face.

In the grand scheme of things, physical activity is not just a means to an end, but an end in itself. It's an expression of your vitality, a celebration of your abilities, and a way to cultivate a positive and loving relationship with your body. As you engage in Wall Pilates, feel the strength in your muscles, the stretch in your limbs, and the balance in your movements. Notice how each breath fuels your body, how each beat of your heart echoes your life force. Relish in the sensation of being fully present, fully alive in your body.

In addition to your regular workouts, consider how you can incorporate more movement into your daily life. Maybe you could walk or cycle to work instead of driving, take the stairs instead of the elevator, or turn household chores into a mini workout. You might also look for opportunities to try new activities, such as hiking, dancing, or a team sport. The more varied and enjoyable your physical activities, the more likely you are to stay active and maintain a balanced routine.

Remember, too, the importance of rest and recovery in your fitness journey. Your body needs time to heal and adapt to the demands you place on it. Make sure you're getting enough sleep, and consider incorporating rest days into your routine. You might also try activities that promote relaxation and stress relief, such as meditation, deep breathing, or a gentle yoga sequence.

Lastly, always keep in mind that fitness is a personal journey, not a competition. What works for one person might not work for another, and that's okay. The most important thing is to find what works for you, what helps you feel strong, healthy, and happy in your own skin. Whether you're a seasoned athlete or a complete beginner, whether you're aiming to lose weight, build strength, improve your health, or simply enjoy some me-time, your fitness journey is a reflection of who you are and what you value.

In the final analysis, crafting a balanced routine is not just about the exercises you do, but the mindset you cultivate. It's about embracing the joy of movement, respecting your body's needs, and celebrating your progress. It's about finding balance not just in your workouts, but in your life. As you incorporate Wall Pilates into your routine, you're not just building strength, flexibility, and balance in your body, but also nurturing these qualities in your mind and your life. You're not just doing Pilates, you're living it.

So, step onto your mat, press your palms into the wall, and get ready to move, breathe, and flourish. Your balanced routine awaits, ready to carry you towards your fitness goals and beyond. And as you journey forward, remember to savor every step, every stretch, every breath along the way. Because in the dance of fitness, every movement is a step towards a healthier, happier, more balanced you.

Sample Wall Pilates Workout Plan for Seniors

Here's a sample Wall Pilates workout plan specifically designed for seniors. This plan aims to improve strength, flexibility, balance, and overall well-being. It's essential for seniors to perform exercises at a comfortable pace and to listen to their bodies to avoid any strain or injury.

Day	Exercise	Description	Repetitions	Duration
1	Wall Push-Ups	Stand facing the wall, place your hands on the wall at shoulder height. Bend elbows to bring your chest closer to the wall, then push back.	8-10	-
	Leg Lifts	Stand facing the wall. Place hands on the wall for support. Lift one leg back, keeping it straight. Alternate legs.	8-10 each leg	-
	Deep Breathing	Stand or sit comfortably. Inhale deeply through the nose, exhale slowly through the mouth.	-	5 mins
2	Rest Day	-	-	-
3	Wall Sits	Lean back against a wall, slide down until	-	20-30 secs

		knees are at about 90 degrees. Keep back flat against the wall.		
	Wall Angels	Stand with your back against the wall. Raise arms to the sides and slide them up and down against the wall, like a snow angel.	8-10	-
	Gentle Stretching	Perform gentle stretches focusing on the neck, shoulders, and back.	-	5 mins
4	**Rest Day**	-	-	-
5	**Wall Roll Downs**	Stand with your back to the wall. Slowly roll down, vertebra by vertebra, bending at the waist. Slowly roll back up.	8-10	-
	Side Leg Lifts	Stand sideways to the wall. Use the wall for support as you lift the outer leg to the side and lower it back down.	8-10 each leg	-
	Deep Breathing	Stand or sit comfortably. Inhale deeply through the nose, exhale slowly through the mouth.	-	5 mins
6	**Rest Day**	-	-	-

7					
Wall Chest Stretch		Place one arm against the wall with the elbow bent. Gently turn your body away from the wall to feel a stretch in the chest.	-		20-30 secs each side
Wall Supported Calf Raises		Stand facing the wall. Press palms into the wall for support. Rise up onto the balls of your feet, then lower back down.	8-10		-
Gentle Stretching		Perform gentle stretches focusing on the neck, shoulders, and back.	-		5 mins

This plan includes a mix of strength exercises, stretching, and relaxation techniques. It's important to remember that the key for seniors is to start slowly and gradually increase intensity and duration based on comfort levels. Also, consulting a healthcare provider before starting any new exercise program is always a good practice, especially for seniors.

Conclusion: Staying Motivated and Consistent in Your Practice

Embarking on a journey with Wall Pilates at the heart of your fitness regimen is a choice that speaks to a desire for strength, balance, and a harmonious connection between mind and body. But let's be real, the road to consistency is often paved with good intentions that somehow seem to slip through the cracks of daily life. Staying motivated and consistent in your practice is both an art and a science, and finding that sweet spot of dedication is truly a treasure worth seeking.

The first whispers of morning light beckon you to the mat, and some days, it feels like the stars align. The wall, your trusty companion in this practice, seems to be calling your name. On these days, each movement is a symphony, and you feel invincible. However, as the days pass, the novelty wears off, and the wall is just that, a wall. The symphony of movements now feels more like a tedious to-do list. This is the moment when the true test begins.

When the going gets tough, it's essential to dig deep and remember why you started. Was it to feel stronger? To age gracefully? To find a sliver of peace in the chaos? Whatever your reason, hold it close. Visualize the best version of yourself, standing tall, exuding confidence. Let this image be your North Star, guiding you through days clouded with excuses and procrastination. The magic lies in knowing that every time you choose to show up, you're one step closer to that person.

Being attentive to your emotional landscape is just as crucial as pushing through physical barriers. Create a space that you love. Surround yourself with colors, textures, and aromas that make your heart sing. The energy of your practice space can be a potent motivator. Let this space be your sanctuary, a place where you are free to explore the depths of your strength and the grace of your movements.

While it's important to have a space that resonates with you, it's also essential to stay adaptable. There will be days when life will throw you curveballs, and flexibility in your routine can be a saving grace. Being rigid in practice can sometimes be as limiting as not practicing at all. Celebrate the days when you can spend an hour at the wall, but also embrace the days when all you have is ten minutes. Remember, it's not about perfection; it's about connection.

In the symphony of life, variety adds spice. Change the tempo of your workouts. Add new Wall Pilates moves or perhaps fuse your practice with elements of yoga or dance. Keeping your routine fresh and exciting is like opening a new chapter in an enthralling book; you can't wait to dive in!

Having a buddy can also add a layer of accountability and fun. Engage a friend in your practice or join a community. Share your highs and lows. Be each other's cheerleaders. There is something profoundly enriching about being part of a tribe that shares your passion.

Yet, in the midst of all this, take a moment to acknowledge yourself. Celebrate your victories, no matter how small. Did you hold that pose for a second longer? Did you finally feel that muscle engage? Every drop makes an ocean, and every step you take in your practice is a testament to your commitment.

It is also important to listen to your body. Understand that there will be days when rest is more beneficial than exercise. It's okay to take a break. It's okay to breathe. Your Wall Pilates practice will be waiting for you when you're ready.

And when days turn into weeks, and weeks into months, you'll look back at the tapestry you've woven with each day of practice. You'll see not just a series of workouts, but a journey of self-discovery, of pushing boundaries, and of grace. This tapestry is uniquely yours, woven with threads of sweat, laughter, and maybe even a few tears. You'll see a stronger, more connected you. And as you stand there, perhaps leaning against the wall that has been your steadfast partner through this journey, know that every moment spent in practice was a brick in the foundation of your most authentic self.

As you continue to grow in your Wall Pilates journey, embrace the flow of life with open arms. Don't be too hard on yourself and remember that every day is a new beginning. Your practice is a living, breathing entity that evolves with you. Let it be a reflection of not just your physical strength but also your inner resilience and passion.

In this ever-changing world, your Wall Pilates practice can be an anchor. When the waters are calm, it can be a joyous celebration of movement. When the storms rage, it can be your safe harbor. Through the ebbs and flows, let the wall be a reminder of your strength and the boundless possibilities that lie within you.

Embrace the moments, the breaths, the triumphs, and the challenges. Let your practice be a dance - sometimes structured, sometimes freestyle, but always, always uniquely yours.

So, wake up each day and choose yourself. Choose the strength, the grace, and the sheer joy of moving. Let your Wall Pilates practice be a love letter to yourself, penned with each stretch, each breath, and each moment of stillness.

And somewhere along the way, without even realizing it, you will find that the wall has not just been a partner in your practice but a mirror reflecting the incredible, strong, and beautiful person you are. In every stretch, in every breath, remember - this is your journey, your tapestry, and every thread are woven with love, strength, and an indomitable spirit.

Let the rhythm of your heart guide the cadence of your movements. Your symphony is waiting. The maestro's baton is in your hands. The wall, your stage. It's time to create magic.

Strategies for Maintaining Motivation

Maintaining motivation is like tending to a delicate flame, with the slightest gust of wind having the potential to blow it out. But fear not! The following strategies can be your windbreakers, protecting and fueling your fire to keep your Wall Pilates journey ablaze.

Let's start with setting intentions. Imagine waking up and knowing that the day ahead is not just a series of mundane tasks but a tapestry of moments, each woven with purpose. Before you step onto your mat, take a deep breath and whisper to yourself why you are here. Is it strength? Grace? Or perhaps a sanctuary from the whirlwind of life? Let this intention be the anchor that holds you steady.

Now, as you immerse yourself in your practice, relish the power of progression. The beauty of Wall Pilates is that it is as fluid as the rivers - never stagnant, always moving. Some days, the currents will be gentle, while others will be tumultuous. Embrace them all. Celebrate each small victory, be it holding a pose a second longer or finding a depth in a stretch that seemed elusive before. These are the pearls of your practice. String them together and wear them as a badge of honor.

As you build your string of pearls, you'll find that the more you have, the more you'll want. This is where setting goals comes into play. But here's the secret - make them realistic and make them yours. Your goals should be like your favorite pair of shoes; the perfect fit. They should challenge you just enough to keep you on your toes but be attainable enough to not seem daunting.

Another endearing friend on your journey will be variety. Think of your Wall Pilates practice as a garden. Just as a garden flourishes with a diversity of flowers, so will your practice with an assortment of exercises. The wall is your canvas, and your body, the paintbrush. Don't just paint with broad strokes, but sometimes use the tip for finer details. Explore different movements and let your practice be a kaleidoscope of exercises that keep both your body and mind engaged.

Now, what's a journey without a companion? The camaraderie, the shared laughter, and even the shared groans of stretching muscles are the ingredients for a rich and fulfilling journey. Partner up with a friend or family member. Share your goals, your triumphs, and your challenges. Be each other's cheerleaders. On days when the flame of motivation flickers, you'll have each other to keep it alive.

In the symphony of Wall Pilates, let music be the maestro that guides your rhythm. The beats, the melodies, the crescendos - they speak a language that your soul understands. Create playlists that resonate with your heart. Let the music sweep you off your feet and into the embrace of your practice.

A word of caution though - in your quest for motivation, don't let your practice become a chore. It should be like the gentle ebb and flow of the ocean waves. Some days will be high tides and others, calmer waters. Listen to your body. Allow yourself the grace of rest when you need it. This is not a step back but rather, a gentle pause; a moment to breathe, to reflect and to savor the journey thus far.

Remember that Wall Pilates is not just a series of movements; it is poetry in motion. Each stretch, each breath is a verse. Don't just go through the motions, but feel them. Let them seep into your very core. On days when motivation wanes, close your eyes and remember the feeling of being in sync with your body. Chase that feeling.

Lastly, know that motivation is not a destination but a journey in itself. It's a windingpath with hills and valleys. There will be days when the sun shines bright and others when clouds loom. On those cloudy days, let the strategies mentioned be your silver lining. Your intentions, your progression, the goals you set, the variety in your practice, the companionship, the power of music, and the grace of rest, these are the threads that weave the fabric of your motivation.

As you travel this path, remember to embrace the art of patience. Just like how a seed doesn't turn into a blooming flower overnight, your Wall Pilates journey is one of gradual growth. Revel in the transformation, however slow it may seem. With every stretch, every push, every deep breath, you're becoming a better version of yourself.

It is also important to maintain a positive mindset. Visualize success and embrace positive affirmations. Tell yourself that you are strong, that you are capable, and that you are on this journey for all the beautiful rewards it holds. Each affirmation is like a gentle whisper to your soul, a reminder of your boundless potential.

In addition to your practice, nourish your body with a balanced diet and hydrate. A well-fed body is like a well-oiled machine, ready to take on any challenge with vigor. The food you consume is the fuel that powers your practice. Choose wisely and indulge in the richness of flavors that not only satiate your palate but also fortify your body.

Moreover, document your journey. Keep a journal where you can pen down your thoughts, experiences, and reflections. It's an incredibly powerful tool that allows you to express yourself and track your progress. On days when your spirits need lifting, leaf through the pages of your journal. It will serve as a reminder of how far you've come and the myriad of possibilities that lie ahead.

Lastly, practice gratitude. Be thankful for your body, for its strength, and for its resilience. Be thankful for the sanctuary that Wall Pilates offers. Gratitude has the power to open our hearts and minds to the beauty of the present. It reminds us that sometimes the simplest things can be the most profound.

In essence, maintaining motivation in Wall Pilates is about creating a symphony of strategies that harmonize with one another. It's about listening to the gentle whispers of your body, embracing the ebb and flow, and painting your canvas with broad and fine strokes alike. It's about recognizing that this journey is as much an inward pilgrimage as it is a physical endeavor.

So, step onto your mat with a heart full of intentions, a soul ready to embrace the beauty of progression, and a mind open to the endless possibilities. Let your Wall Pilates practice be the dance where your body and soul waltz in perfect harmony. And let the gentle flame of motivation illuminate your path, every stretch of the way.

The Importance of Consistency in Exercise

The journey of fitness is a map of perseverance, marked by the footprints of determination, the checkpoints of progress, and most significantly, the highway of consistency. Embarking on this journey, it's crucial to remember that while our initial enthusiasm might get us started, it is the steady rhythm of consistency that keeps us moving forward.

Consistency, in the context of exercise, is the reliable cadence of our actions. It's the echo of our commitment reverberating through our routines, the steady beat of practice that transforms our intentions into reality. It isn't merely about showing up on the mat or at the gym every day; it's about showing up for ourselves, day in and day out, in pursuit of our well-being.

Just as a river cuts through a rock, not through its power but its persistence, the transformative power of exercise is unlocked through consistency. It isn't the intensity of a single workout that brings about change, but the cumulative effect of numerous workouts strung together over time. It's this consistent practice that gently nudges our bodies towards greater strength, flexibility, and endurance.

When we engage in consistent physical activity, we're essentially communicating with our bodies. Each workout is a dialogue, a conversation where we push our boundaries, challenge our limits, and explore our capacities. Over time, our bodies respond to this dialogue, adapting and evolving in the process. Our muscles grow stronger, our endurance improves, and our flexibility increases. This is the beautiful symphony of adaptation, a melody made possible by the metronome of consistency.

Yet, the benefits of consistency in exercise extend beyond the physical realm, reaching into the deep trenches of our mental and emotional landscape. Just as our bodies thrive on the rhythm of routine, so do our minds. Regular exercise can serve as an anchor, a stabilizing force in the stormy seas of our daily lives. Amidst the whirlwind of responsibilities, deadlines, and stressors, our workout routine can be the steady pulse, the comforting routine that grounds us.

Moreover, consistency in exercise fosters discipline. It teaches us the art of commitment, of showing up for ourselves even when it's hard, even when we'd rather not. This discipline, once cultivated, seeps into other areas of our lives. It influences our work habits, our relationships, our approach towards challenges. Consistency in exercise, thus, is not just about building a stronger body; it's about crafting a stronger, more resilient self.

Consider also the relationship between consistency and motivation. They dance a delicate waltz, each influencing the other. In the beginning, motivation might lead. It fuels our initial actions, gets us started on our fitness journey. But as time wears on, as the novelty fades and the grind sets in, consistency takes the lead. It keeps us going, fueling our motivation in return. In this way, consistency isn't just a product of motivation; it's also a powerful source of it.

In our pursuit of consistency, it's important to approach it with a sense of compassion and flexibility. There will be days when our energy is low, when our spirits are dampened, when our routines are upended. On these days, let consistency be about doing what we can, however little that might be. It's better to do a shorter workout or a less intense one than to do nothing at all. Remember, consistency is not about perfection; it's about progress.

Navigating the journey of consistent exercise, we must also be mindful of the role of variety. While maintaining a routine is important, so is keeping things interesting and challenging. Incorporating different exercises, trying new workout styles, varying our intensity – these can all keep our fitness journey engaging and fun. Variety, in this sense, is the spice that keeps the dish of consistency from becoming bland.

Reflecting upon the importance of consistency in exercise, it seems evident that it is not just a tool, but a companion on our journey to better health. It is the quiet whisper in our ear, urging us to keep going, reminding us of our goals when our resolve wavers. It stands by us, steadfast and unwavering, through the highs of achievement and the lows of setbacks.

Consistency, however, is not a trait we're born with, but a skill we cultivate. It's a garden we tenderly nurture, watering it with our actions, weeding out distractions, and patiently waiting as it blooms. And as with any garden, the fruits of our labor are not apparent immediately but emerge over time. The strength we gain, the resilience we develop, the sense of accomplishment we experience – these are the blossoms of our consistency.

As we embark on the journey of exercise, let's remember to pack consistency in our fitness kit. Let it guide us through the days of sweat and struggle, leading us towards our goals. Let's appreciate it, not as a burden or a chore, but as a beacon, a lighthouse guiding us through the stormy seas towards the shore of our aspirations.

In the grand symphony of our fitness journey, let consistency be our rhythm, our steady drumbeat driving us forward. Let it resonate through our actions, echo in our routines, and reverberate in our progress. For it is through this rhythm of consistency that we dance the dance of transformation, twirling towards a healthier, stronger, and happier self.

The road to fitness is long, winding, and peppered with challenges. But, armed with the shield of consistency, we can navigate this road with confidence and grace. We can face the uphill climbs, endure the storms, and traverse the plateaus, knowing that each step we take, however small, is a step forward.

And as we journey on, let's remember to celebrate our consistency. Let's honor it, not just in the grand milestones we reach but in the everyday victories, the unseen progress, the silent transformations. For consistency, in its humble, unassuming way, is the true hero of our fitness journey. It is the golden thread weaving together the tapestry of our progress, the backbone of our transformation, and the heart of our journey towards better health.

In the end, consistency is not just about exercising regularly. It's about showing up for ourselves, honoring our commitment to our well-being, and embracing the journey with patience and perseverance. It's about understanding that fitness is not a destination but a journey, one that requires time, effort, and above all, consistency. So, let's lace up our shoes, roll out our mats, and with a spirit of determination and a heart full of resolve, let's embrace the powerful rhythm of consistency. Because in the symphony of health and fitness, consistency is the melody that sings the sweetest song of progress.

BOOK 7

The Workout Plan

Introduction: Crafting the Perfect Workout Plan

The tapestry of wellness and fitness is woven with a multitude of threads. These threads encompass a spectrum of elements from nutrition to sleep, from mental wellbeing to physical fitness. It's an intricate and interwoven pattern, where each thread impacts and influences the others. One such crucial thread, often considered the backbone of physical fitness, is a well-crafted workout plan. This chapter aims to guide you through the journey of creating a perfect workout plan, a plan tailored to your unique needs, aspirations, and circumstances.

Crafting a workout plan is akin to designing a blueprint. It's about laying a solid foundation upon which your fitness journey can flourish. It's the map that outlines your path to your fitness destination. More than a mere collection of exercises, a perfect workout plan embodies your fitness aspirations, reflects your lifestyle, and respects your limitations. It's a personalized fitness roadmap that leads you, step by step, towards your health and fitness goals.

Crafting this blueprint, however, is not a task to be taken lightly. It requires a deep understanding of oneself, a clear vision of one's goals, and an informed knowledge of fitness principles. It's a process that calls for introspection, planning, and research.

To begin with, it's crucial to understand your current fitness level. Assess your strength, flexibility, endurance, and overall health. This understanding acts as the starting point of your fitness journey, a baseline from which you chart your progress.

Next, identify your fitness goals. Whether it's losing weight, gaining muscle, improving flexibility, or boosting stamina, having clear and specific goals gives your workout plan a direction. It's the lighthouse that guides your fitness ship, ensuring you stay on course amidst the sea of workout trends and fitness fads.

However, it's not just about the destination, but also the journey. Your workout plan should not only lead you towards your fitness goals but also engage, inspire, and motivate you along the way. It should resonate with your interests, align with your lifestyle, and harmonize with your routine. Whether you're an early bird who loves the quiet serenity of dawn or a night owl who thrives in the solitude of late-night workouts, your workout plan should be a reflection of your preferences.

Moreover, it's essential to acknowledge and respect your limitations. Whether it's a physical condition, time constraints, or lack of access to certain resources, your workout plan should adapt to these realities. Instead of pushing you against these constraints, it should work around them, finding creative ways to help you stay active and fit.

An effective workout plan also embodies the principles of balance and diversity. From strength training and cardio to flexibility and balance exercises, it should incorporate a variety of workouts. This diversity not only ensures a holistic approach to fitness but also keeps the routine engaging and exciting.

Another key aspect of a perfect workout plan is progression. As your fitness level improves, your workout plan should evolve, introducing new challenges and pushing your limits. This dynamic nature of the plan not only fuels your progress but also keeps the workout journey engaging and motivating.

Crafting such a workout plan, however, is not a one-time task. It's a dynamic process that requires regular reviews and revisions. As your fitness level improves, as your lifestyle changes, as your goals evolve, your workout plan should adapt, reflecting these changes.

In essence, a perfect workout plan is more than a list of exercises. It's a living, breathing entity that grows with you, evolves with you, and journeys with you on your fitness path. It's your fitness companion, a trusted guide that navigates you through the maze of workouts, leading you towards your fitness goals.

Crafting this companion requires effort, knowledge, and introspection. It's about knowing yourself, understanding your needs, and align them to your aspirations. It's about weaving together the threads of your fitness level, your goals, your lifestyle, and your limitations into a personalized tapestry of fitness. It's about creating a plan that not only guides you towards your fitness goals but also respects your individuality, ignites your passion, and fuels your motivation.

Remember, fitness is not a destination, but a journey. And every journey needs a map. A map that not only leads to the destination but also makes the journey enjoyable, exciting, and fulfilling. The perfect workout plan is that map. It's the guide that not only charts your fitness path but also transforms the path into a journey of discovery, growth, and fulfillment.

In conclusion, the perfect workout plan is not a one-size-fits-all solution. It's a unique blend of science and art, a combination of knowledge and creativity, a fusion of planning and flexibility. It's a plan that's crafted with care, nurtured with passion, and pursued with dedication. It's a plan that's not just about working out, but about living well, being well, and feeling well.

The Importance of a Structured Workout Plan

Embarking on a journey of physical fitness, we often find ourselves standing at the edge of a vast ocean, contemplating the best way to cross. With so many possible routes, exercises, and techniques at our disposal, the starting point may seem overwhelming. The myriad of choices, while empowering, can also lead to confusion and even inertia. It's in moments like these that the importance of a structured workout plan shines brightly, illuminating the path forward.

A structured workout plan is like a roadmap guiding us through the landscape of fitness. It provides direction, clarity, and a sense of purpose. It breaks down our ultimate fitness goal into manageable steps, transforming a mountainous challenge into a series of achievable peaks. With each summit reached, our confidence grows, fueling our motivation and driving us forward.

This roadmap doesn't merely chart our path; it also ensures we navigate our journey safely. A well-structured workout plan takes into account our current fitness level, personal goals, and potential health constraints, creating a balanced and holistic approach to exercise. It emphasizes not just the quantity but the quality of our workouts, encouraging proper form and technique to prevent injuries. It encourages us to listen to our bodies, to understand the difference between beneficial discomfort and harmful pain, and to respect our limits while gently pushing them.

Moreover, a structured workout plan creates a sense of balance and harmony in our fitness journey. It ensures we work all our muscle groups evenly, avoiding imbalances that could lead to injury. It incorporates elements of strength training, cardiovascular exercise, and flexibility, promoting a comprehensive approach to fitness. This balance nurtures our body as a whole, fostering overall health and wellness.

Beyond the physical realm, a structured workout plan also cultivates mental strength and discipline. It instills in us a sense of routine and consistency, vital ingredients for progress. Each day, as we follow our plan, we reinforce the habit of exercise, making it a natural part of our daily lives. This consistency, in turn, fosters discipline, teaching us the value of commitment and the satisfaction of following through.

As we immerse ourselves in our workout plan, we learn to set and achieve short-term goals, building towards our long-term objectives. Each successful goal acts as a powerful affirmation of our capabilities, enhancing our self-efficacy and boosting our self-esteem. We learn to trust ourselves, to believe in our ability to take charge of our health, and to effect meaningful change in our lives.

A structured workout plan, however, is not set in stone. It is a living document, flexible and adaptable, evolving with our changing needs and progress. It encourages us to explore and experiment, to try new exercises, techniques, and routines, and to learn what works best for us. It invites us to be active participants in our fitness journey, to take ownership of our progress, and to embrace the joy of discovery and growth.

Indeed, the true beauty of a structured workout plan lies in its ability to transform exercise from a chore into a choice, from an obligation into an opportunity. It reframes our perspective, allowing us to see exercise not as a burden, but as a celebration of what our bodies can do. It encourages us to appreciate each workout, each movement, each bead of sweat as a testament to our strength, resilience, and commitment to our well-being.

Ultimately, a structured workout plan is not just a guide, but a companion on our fitness journey. It walks alongside us, providing direction when we feel lost, encouragement when we feel demotivated, and affirmation when we taste success. It reminds us that every step, every rep, every breath we take in the pursuit of fitness is a step towards a healthier, happier, and more fulfilled self.

In conclusion, the importance of a structured workout plan cannot be overstated. It isa tool, a teacher, and a beacon, guiding us on our path towards physical fitness and overall well-being. It provides structure, promoting consistency and discipline, and brings balance, ensuring we nurture our bodies holistically. It fosters safety, encouraging proper technique and mindful exercise. And above all, it empowers us, affirming our capabilities, boosting our confidence, and instilling in us a sense of ownership over our health.

However, creating a structured workout plan requires careful thought, consideration, and self-awareness. It demands a clear understanding of our fitness level, goals, and constraints. It necessitates a balanced approach to exercise, incorporating various elements of fitness. And it calls for flexibility and adaptability, allowing the plan to evolve as we progress on our fitness journey. The time and effort invested in crafting such a plan, however, are well worth the benefits it brings.

With a structured workout plan, we can navigate the vast ocean of fitness with confidence and clarity. We can transform the overwhelming into the manageable, the daunting into the doable. And most importantly, we can turn the solitary act of exercise into a shared journey of discovery, growth, and self-empowerment. As we follow our roadmap, we realize that the path to fitness is not just about reaching the destination, but about appreciating the journey and celebrating every step we take along the way.

So, let us embrace the importance of a structured workout plan. Let us harness its power to guide, protect, and inspire us. And let us remember, as we journey towards physical fitness and overall well-being, that our greatest strength lies not in our muscles, but in our minds, our hearts, and our unwavering commitment to our health.

CHAPTER 1

Incorporating Cardio, Strength Training, and Flexibility Exercises

In the tapestry of fitness, there are threads that stand out, holding the fabric together, giving it form and purpose. These threads are cardio, strength training, and flexibility exercises. Picture yourself as an artist, and your body as the canvas. With each brushstroke of cardio, strength training, and flexibility, you paint a vivid picture of health and wellness.

Imagine a day when the sun is shining, and the air is light. You put on your running shoes and step outside. As you run, the wind whispers secrets in your ears. This is the essence of cardiovascular exercise, or cardio as it is affectionately known. Cardio is the heartbeat of any fitness program. It invigorates the soul and animates the body. When you engage in cardio, you are pumping life through your veins. It is the rhythm of your feet on the pavement, the cadence of your breath as you climb a hill. Cardio exercises like running, swimming, and cycling elevate your heart rate and keep your circulatory system robust. It is the joy you feel as your heart sings and your lungs dance to the rhythm of movement.

But life is not just a dance; it's also a journey of strength and resilience. This is where strength training enters the picture. Imagine lifting weights. Feel the cool steel in your hands. With every lift, you're sculpting your muscles into a symphony of power. Strength training is the art of building muscle, of embracing resistance. It's not just about physical power; it's about fortitude. When you lift weights, or engage in bodyweight exercises like push-ups and squats, you're laying bricks of determination and perseverance. Your muscles grow, yes, but so does your spirit. With strength training, you build a fortress, not just of muscle but of character. You are a warrior, and the weight room is your battleground.

While cardio and strength training form the pillars of fitness, flexibility is the grace that binds them together. Picture yourself in a quiet room, the scent of lavender in the air. As you stretch, you feel the tension melt away from your muscles. This is the beauty of flexibility exercises. Flexibility is the gentle stream that nourishes the garden of your body. Through practices like yoga and Pilates, you cultivate a sense of calm and balance. Your muscles lengthen, your joints find relief. Flexibility is not just physical; it's a state of mind. It's the ability to bend like a willow in the wind, to adapt and flow. Flexibility teaches you the art of letting go, of finding peace in the present.

As you weave these threads together, you create a balanced fitness program that nurtures your body, mind, and spirit. Cardio, strength training, and flexibility are not just exercises; they are expressions of who you are. They are the chapters in the book of your life. So, lace up your running shoes, grip the weights with determination, and embrace the gentle art of stretching. Paint the canvas of your body with broad strokes of vigor, fine lines of strength, and gentle shades of flexibility.

Remember, fitness is a journey, not a destination. It's an ever-evolving story that you write with every heartbeat, every lift, every stretch. It's a love letter to yourself, a testament to your strength and grace. So, take the pen, and write your story with passion and purpose. Let cardio be the beat of your heart, strength training the might in your bones, and flexibility the harmony that guides your path. Together, they form the symphony of your life, a melody that only you can compose. A song that begins with a single step, a lift, a stretch, and builds into a crescendo of a life well-lived.

The Role of Cardio in a Balanced Workout Routine

As you embark on your fitness journey, the effervescent energy of cardio often acts as the rudder steering the ship. The heart, the drumbeat of our life, finds its rhythm through the joy of movement. Cardiovascular exercise is like a symphony for the heart, where each beat strengthens this muscular marvel and fortifies the essence of our well-being.

Now, let's paint a picture of a world where your heart is the sun, and the rays are the endless benefits of cardio that enrich your life. Imagine running through a meadow, the wind whispering secrets to the trees as your heartbeat syncs with the rhythm of life. This is where the magic begins, for cardio is not just exercise; it is an experience that connects you with the very core of your existence. The vigor, the sweat, the exhilaration; they are all testament to a life being lived to its fullest.

Cardiovascular exercise, often known as cardio, encompasses activities that increase your heart rate, pumping more oxygen to your muscles. Your lungs expand as if trying to capture the universe, and you become more alive than ever. From swimming the butterfly to dancing like no one's watching, cardio is the elixir that adds years to your life and life to your years.

Diving deeper, the role of cardio in a balanced workout routine can be likened to the foundation of a house. Without a sturdy foundation, the structure is incomplete. Cardiovascular fitness builds that base by improving heart health and increasing lung capacity. It's like a cascade of positivity that showers your body, from lowering stress levels to improving sleep patterns.

One might even call cardio the guardian of our mental sanctuary. Picture your worries as shadows lurking in your mind. As you sprint, it's as if beams of sunlight pierce through the darkness, casting the shadows away. The endorphins, fondly known as the happy hormones, come out to play. These are the moments when you realize that cardio is more than physical; it's therapy.

Now let's not forget how cardio can be the hand that guides you through the journey of weight loss. It's a natural partner in shedding those extra pounds. What's more, it boosts your metabolism, so your body becomes a calorie-burning furnace even when you're not working out. It's like your body is thanking you by working extra hard to achieve the goals you set.

For the adventurer in you, cardio is also the key that unlocks new doors. You'll find that as your endurance increases, so does your ability to explore. Whether it's hiking up a mountain or playing tag with your kids, every step will remind you of the gifts cardio has bestowed upon you.

We must also pay homage to the heart, the star of the show. With every beat, it tells a tale. Cardio ensures the tale is one of strength and longevity. A healthy heart means reduced risk of heart disease, stroke, and high blood pressure. It's like giving your heart the armor it needs to keep beating strongly.

As we reach the crescendo of this ode to cardio, let us not forget that while it plays a pivotal role, it is but a single instrument in the orchestra of a balanced fitness regimen. Alongside strength training and flexibility exercises, cardio creates a harmony that resonates through every fiber of our being.

In the tapestry of life, cardio is the thread that adds vibrancy and strength. It's the poetry in motion and the rhythm to which the heart dances. It is not just an exercise but a celebration of the life that courses through our veins. So, let us lace up our shoes, let our heartbeats be our guide, and step into the boundless possibilities that await. Through fields, through waves, through the very air we breathe, let's embrace the essence of movement. Let's revel in the sheer joy of feeling our heart race as we chase the horizon.

In the interplay of muscles and joints, the heart takes the center stage with cardio as its most captivating performance. But, like every great artist, the heart too needs a supporting cast. And this is where strength training and flexibility come into the picture. While cardio keeps the heart robust, strength training builds the sinews that keep it cradled. The flexibility ensures that the symphony of movement is smooth and uninhibited.

Life is an intricate dance, and cardio teaches us the steps. It beckons us to a world where our breaths whisper the stories of our vigor, where our sweat is the nectar of our toil. It's important, however, to remember that cardio doesn't demand grandiosity. It's in the little things - taking the stairs, chasing after your dog, or even grooving while you cook. Each heartbeat, a note in the opus of your life.

In the end, what does it mean to have a heart if not to feel it pound in our chest with fervor? It's the rhythm that proves we are alive, the cadence by which we measure our days. Cardiovascular exercise is the opportunity to dance to the beat of our own heart, to not just exist but to live.

In every swift run, in every splash in the pool, we are given the chance to carve ourselves into something stronger, something more resilient. The role of cardio in a balanced workout routine is that of a trusted friend that holds our hand through the tempest, steadies us, and helps us find our footing.

As you move, think of each breath as a thank you note to your body for its wondrous ability. Envision your heart, resilient and strong, as it carries the weight of your dreams, hopes, and every adventure yet to be had. Cardio is more than a physical endeavor; it's an ode to the very essence of life, a tribute to the heart that loves without measure.

So, run with abandon, swim with gusto, dance like the world is your stage. Let the beat of your heart be the sound that guides you through the quiet nights and the stormy days. For in this symphony of life, your heart is the maestro, and with cardio, you ensure that the music never fades.

Let this be your anthem, your rallying cry as you brave the world. With a heart fortified by the joys of movement, there is no summit too high, no ocean too deep. In the concert of life, let your heart sing its loudest through the beauty of cardio. It's not just an exercise; it's the very poetry of existence.

As the sun sets on our journey through the wonders of cardio, take a moment to feel your heartbeat. That, my friend, is the rhythm of a life well-lived. In embracing cardio, you embrace the boundless, the untamed, the very vigor that makes life worth living. Through the beats of your heart, the world will listen to your song.

Strength Training Essentials

In the vast tableau of human existence, strength shines as an elemental force, a testament to our primal roots and our indomitable will. As we wade through the currents of life, strength is our bedrock, a resolute companion that never leaves our side. And in the realm of physical fitness, strength training is the master sculptor that chisels us into embodiments of power and resilience.

In the journey of self-transformation, every push, every pull, every lift in strength training is a potent verse in the ballad of our becoming. Each rep is an affirmation of our will, a testament to our spirit that refuses to bow down. It's not merely about building muscle or enhancing performance. It's about the remarkable narrative of human resilience, of the extraordinary feats we are capable of when our bodies and minds work in harmony.

Imagine the simple act of lifting a weight. It's not just a piece of metal that you're hoisting. It's the weight of your dreams, of your ambitions, of every battle you've fought and every mountain you wish to conquer. The weight is heavy, not because of its physical mass, but because of the stories it carries, the narratives of strength and endurance that you etch into its very core with every lift.

And when the weight descends, it doesn't signal an end. Instead, it heralds a new beginning, a fresh opportunity to rise stronger. The descent is a time of reflection, a quiet interlude where you gather your resolve, stoke the embers of your determination, and prepare to soar once again. Strength training, in essence, is a dance of ascents and descents, a rhythmic interplay of effort and rest, challenge and recovery.

The beauty of strength training lies in its universality. It doesn't discriminate; it doesn't favor. It stands as an open invitation to anyone daring enough to embrace the pursuit of power. From the novice taking their first tentative steps into the world of fitness to the seasoned athlete, strength training is an arena where everyone can carve their own path, write their own tale of triumph.

But what does it mean to be strong? Is it merely about lifting heavier weights or executing more reps? These are merely measures, yardsticks that quantify our progress. True strength, however, transcends these physical dimensions. It's about the capacity to endure, the courage to persist, the fortitude to rise each time we fall. It's about the fire that burns in our hearts and fuels our will to overcome, to thrive amidst adversity.

Strength training is a celebration of this indomitable spirit. Each workout is a ritual, a sacred space where we honor our potential, challenge our limits, and nurture our resilience. It's not just about the sweat that trickles down our forehead or the burn that ignites our muscles. It's about the smiles that bloom through the fatigue, the satisfaction that swells in our hearts, the exhilaration of knowing that we are capable of so much more than we ever imagined.

As you embark on your strength training journey, remember that it's not a destination but a voyage. It's not a race against others, but a dance with yourself. It's a journey of self-discovery, a quest to unveil the strength that lies dormant within you. So, lift with conviction, pull with purpose, push with passion. Let the symphony of your strength resound in every corner of your being, in every fiber of your existence.

When you look in the mirror, let it reflect not just the physique you're sculpting, but the strength you're cultivating, the resilience you're nurturing, the power you're unleashing. Let it mirror the transformation that is unfolding within you, the metamorphosis that is turning you intoa force to be reckoned with.

In this journey, be patient. Strength training is not about instant gratification. It's a slow burn, a gradual unfurling of your potential. It's about nurturing your body, respecting its rhythm, and allowing it the time to adapt, to grow, to strengthen. It's about honoring the process, embracing the journey, and finding joy in every step of the way.

Remember, strength is not merely a physical attribute; it's a state of being, a mindset, a way of life. It's about standing tall amidst the storms, about navigating the turbulent waters with grace and grit. It's about being resilient in the face of adversity, about finding the courage to rise each time you fall. It's about facing your fears, conquering your doubts, and daring to reach for the stars.

So, lift. Lift with all your might. But more importantly, lift with all your heart. Let every rep be a statement, a declaration of your courage, your resilience, your indomitable spirit. Let every set be a testament to your determination, your grit, your relentless pursuit of strength.

Strength training is not just a workout; it's a lifestyle, a philosophy, a testament to the human spirit's indomitable strength. It's about discovering your power, unleashing your potential, and becoming the best version of yourself. It's about pushing your boundaries, challenging your limits, and rewriting the narrative of what you're capable of.

As you embark on this journey, remember, strength is not a destination; it's a journey. It's not about reaching a certain level of physical prowess; it's about the ongoing pursuit of growth, the relentless quest for improvement, the unending journey of self-discovery.

So, go forth. Embrace the challenge. Welcome the struggle. Revel in the effort. Celebrate every victory, however small, and learn from every setback, however big. Because in the end, it's not about the weights you lift; it's about the strength you gain, the resilience you build, the character you develop. It's about the person you become in the process.

In the realm of strength training, every day is a new opportunity, a new challenge, a new adventure. So, harness your potential, embrace your strength, and carve your own path. Because the journey to strength is not a straight line; it's a winding path, a rollercoaster ride, a thrilling adventure.

Strength training is not just about the body; it's about the mind, the spirit, the soul. It's about fostering resilience, cultivating grit, nurturing determination. It's about the transformation that happens within, the metamorphosis that unfolds, the power that is unleashed.

So, embrace strength training. Embrace the effort, the challenge, the struggle. Embrace the journey, the process, the transformation. Embrace the strength within you, the power within you, the potential within you. Because strength is not just about lifting weights; it's about lifting yourself, lifting your spirit, lifting your life. It's about rising, thriving, and shining in the face of adversity. It's about becoming the best version of yourself, one rep at a time.

In the end, strength training is not just a workout; it's a way of life. It's a philosophy, a mindset, a journey. It's about discovering your strength, unleashing your potential, and rewriting the narrative of what you're capable of. It's about becoming stronger, better, more resilient. It's about embracing the journey, honoring the process, and celebrating the person you're becoming.

Flexibility Exercises for a Complete Workout

Flexibility is the unsung hero of fitness. It is the quiet, subtle force that underpins our every move, our every step, our every twist and turn. It is the foundation of our physicality, the canvas on which we paint our athletic endeavors. And like any fine art, flexibility requires practice, patience, and a deep understanding of the form.

Flexibility exercises, often overlooked in the pursuit of strength or stamina, hold the key to a complete and balanced workout. They help to ensure that our bodies remain supple and agile, ready to respond to the demands we place upon them. They lubricate our joints, lengthen our muscles, and promote a greater range of motion. They help us to move with ease, to flow with grace, to bend without breaking.

When we think of flexibility exercises, we often imagine yogis contorting their bodies into impossible shapes. But flexibility is not just for the super bendy or the ultra-athletic. It is for everyone, at every age, at every stage of fitness. You don't need to be able to touch your toes or do the splits to enjoy the benefits of flexibility exercises. You just need to start where you are and stretch a little further each day.

A complete workout should always include a dose of flexibility exercises. They can be as simple as a gentle forward fold to stretch the hamstrings, a delicate twist to loosen the spine, or a mild hip opener to release tension in the lower body. They can be incorporated into the warm-up, to prepare the body for the workout ahead, or in the cool down, to help the muscles recover and relax. They can be done on a mat, with a strap, or even against a wall.

But flexibility exercises are not just physical; they are also mental. They require focus and concentration, as we tune into our bodies and listen to their subtle signals. They invite us to slow down, to breathe deeply, to inhabit the present moment. They teach us patience, as we hold the stretch and wait for the body to yield. They cultivate a sense of inner calm, as we quiet the mind and focus on the sensation of the stretch.

As we practice these exercises, we begin to notice a shift. Our bodies become more pliable; our movements more fluid. We feel less stiff, less tight, less bound by tension. We move with greater ease, with less effort, with more freedom. We find that we can reach a little further, bend a little deeper, twist a little more. And this newfound flexibility spills over into other areas of our fitness, enhancing our strength, improving our balance, boosting our endurance.

Flexibility exercises also provide a pathway to self-discovery. As we explore the edges of our flexibility, we learn about our limitations and our potential. We come face to face with our resistance, our fear, our discomfort. And in this encounter, we have the opportunity to grow, to push past our boundaries, to expand our comfort zone. We learn to breathe into the discomfort, to stay present in the challenge, to find ease in the effort.

So, embrace flexibility exercises as an integral part of your workout. Respect them for the value they bring, for the balance they provide, for the growth they encourage. Practice them with patience, with awareness, with kindness towards your body. And as you do, you will find that your flexibility is not just about how far you can stretch, but about how deeply you can connect with your body, how fully you can inhabit your movements, and how gracefully you can navigate the ever-changing landscape of your fitness journey.

CHAPTER 2

Sample Weekly Workout Plans with Wall Pilates

Sample Plan 1: Beginner's Workout Plan with Wall Pilates

Embrace the energizing feel of the crisp morning air as you roll out your mat and prepare to embark on a journey towards a stronger and more flexible body. Wall Pilates, a delightful twist on traditional Pilates, beckons you to unlock the doors to fitness with the humble support of a wall. Here, in this beginner's workout plan with Wall Pilates, let's explore a week of invigorating exercises that balance, tone, and awaken your body.

Monday: Setting the Stage

Ah, Monday! The beginning of the week is the perfect time to set the tone for the days ahead. Let's start by engaging our lower body with the foundational Wall Pilates exercise, Glute Bridges. Lay your mat next to a sturdy wall and press your feet against it. Feel the support of the wall as you lift your hips, igniting the fire within your glutes. The wall is not just a prop; it's your partner in this dance of strength.

Tuesday: Embracing the Core

As Tuesday greets you with its embrace, it's time to focus on the core. Wall Push-Ups is the exercise of the day. Place your hands on the wall and step back. Now, with a gentle smile on your face, lower yourself toward the wall, feeling your arms and back working in harmony. Rise back up and feel the joy of movement. This isn't just an exercise; it's a celebration of the power within you.

Wednesday: Celebrating Midweek with Poise

Wednesday, the day when the world is brimming with possibilities. Engage in Wall Sits today. As you lean against the wall, slide down until your knees form a right angle. Hold. Feel your quads, glutes, and hamstrings singing in unison. They are the unsung heroes, supporting you in every step you take.

Thursday: Sailing Through the Wind

Thursday breezes in with a whisper of grace. Today, we take on the Wall 100s. This core exercise requires you to lie on your back, with your feet just touching the wall. As you pump your arms, envision yourself as a graceful bird, wings fluttering, soaring high. Your body is light, and your spirit is free.

Friday: Cycling into the Weekend

Friday is here, and the scent of the weekend is in the air. Let's add some fun with Wall Bicycle Crunches. Place your feet on the wall and crunch, bringing opposite elbow to the knee. Feel like a child again, riding an imaginary bicycle with the wind in your hair.

Saturday: Embracing the Freedom

The weekend is finally here! Bask in the freedom as you engage in Wall Lunges. Stand sideways to the wall and lunge, feeling your legs and core come alive. Each lunge is a step forward in your journey, a journey where each day brings new strength and grace.

Sunday: A Gentle Farewell

Sunday, a day of rest, but let's bid farewell to the week with one last dance - the Leg Circles. Stand tall, with your feet pressed lightly against the wall. As you draw circles with your toes, imagine you are sketching your dreams, your aspirations. The week ends, but your journey continues.

As the week winds down, take a moment to reflect on the symphony of movements you've created. Your body is an instrument, and through Wall Pilates, you've played the first notes of a beautiful melody that will only grow richer with time. The wall has been your partner, your support, and your guide. Cherish this bond, for it is a part of the tapestry of your fitness journey. Embrace the tenderness of your muscles, the cadence in your breath, and the harmony in your movements. This is just the beginning, and as each day dawns, remember to greet it with the joy of movement and the promise of a dance that never ends. The wall, your constant companion, awaits your return with open arms, ready to support you as you take on new challenges and reach new heights.

Sample Plan 2: Intermediate Workout Plan with Wall Pilates

Here's an intermediate Wall Pilates workout plan spread over one week:

Day 1: Balance and Core Stability

- Single Leg Stance with Wall Support (3 sets of 30 seconds each leg)
- Wall Plank Hold (3 sets of 30 seconds)

Day 2: Grace and Flexibility

- Wall Arabesque (3 sets of 8 reps on each leg)
- Wall Straddle Stretch (hold for 1 minute)

Day 3: Upper Body Strength

- Wall Push-Ups (4 sets of 12 reps)
- Wall Shoulder Press (3 sets of 10 reps)

Day 4: Lower Body and Core

- Wall Lunges (3 sets of 12 reps each leg)
- Wall Sit with Leg Lifts (3 sets of 10 lifts each leg)

Day 5: Cardio and Core

- Wall Mountain Climbers (3 sets of 20 reps)
- Wall 100s (complete 100 arm pumps)

Day 6: Flexibility and Relaxation

- Wall Roll Down (3 sets of 5 roll-downs)
- Wall Leg Swings (3 sets of 10 swings each leg)

Day 7: Full Body and Celebration

- Wall Jumping Jacks (3 sets of 20 reps)
- Wall Side Kicks (3 sets of 8 reps per side)

Remember to maintain a steady breathing pattern throughout the exercises and focus on engaging the correct muscle groups. This intermediate plan incorporates a blend of strength, flexibility, and cardiovascular exercises to ensure a well-rounded routine. Always listen to your body and adjust the intensity or modify the exercises as needed. Enjoy the journey and embrace the progression!

Sample Plan 3: Advanced Workout Plan with Wall Pilates

Let's now explore a week-long Advanced Wall Pilates workout plan:

Day 1: Embrace the Challenge

Your first day invites you into the world of advanced wall Pilates with the Wall Handstand Hold. Start with 3 sets of 10-15 seconds and gradually increase your hold time as you gain confidence. Follow it up with the Wall Push-Up with Single Leg Lift, completing 3 sets of 10 reps for each leg. These exercises will challenge your balance, core stability, and upper body strength, setting the tone for your advanced workout plan.

Day 2: Flexibility and Strength

On the second day, meet the Wall Split Stretch. Position yourself in a lunge with your back foot elevated on the wall behind you. Gradually straighten your front leg into a split position, holding for 30 seconds and performing three times on each side. Finish the day with Wall Plank with Knee Tucks, doing 3 sets of 10 reps each side to strengthen your core and test your stability.

Day 3: Cardio Blast

The third day introduces a cardiovascular focus with the Wall Burpee. Perform 3 sets of 10 reps, combining a wall push-up with a jump towards the wall and back. Follow this with High Knee Runs with Wall Support for 3 sets of 30 seconds. This day will get your heart pumping, improving your cardiovascular fitness and endurance.

Day 4: Balance and Grace

Day four is all about balance and grace. Start with the Wall Supported Single Leg Squat, performing 3 sets of 8 reps on each leg. Then, proceed to the Wall Arabesque with Pulse, where you'll perform an arabesque with your foot on the wall and pulse the elevated leg for 3 sets of 12 pulses. These exercises will test your balance, strength, and coordination.

Day 5: Power and Endurance

On the fifth day, challenge your power and endurance with the Wall Jump Squats for 3 sets of 15 reps and Wall Plank to Pike for 3 sets of 10 reps. These powerful exercises will challenge your lower body strength and core stability, pushing your endurance to new levels.

Day 6: Relax and Restore

Your sixth day is for relaxation and restoration. Here you'll perform a Wall Downward Dog Stretch, holding for 1 minute, and a Wall Chest Stretch, also held for 1 minute. Despite being an advanced workout plan, it's crucial to have a day dedicated to flexibility and restorative exercises, providing your body with the necessary recovery time.

Day 7: Celebrate Your Progress

On the final day, celebrate your progress with a full-body workout. Perform the Wall Handstand Push-Up for 3 sets of 5 reps and the Wall Mountain Climber with Twist for

3 sets of 15 reps each side. These exercises will round off your advanced workout plan by challenging your strength, stability, and cardiovascular fitness.

As always, remember that each day is a step forward in your fitness journey. Listen to your body and modify the exercises as needed. Each day of this advanced plan offers a unique challenge, helping you to push your boundaries, improve your fitness, and embrace the joy of movement with wall Pilates. Congratulations on choosing the advanced path! Here's to your strength, courage, and tenacity. Enjoy the journey.

CHAPTER 3

Adjusting Your Workout Plan Based on Goals and Progress

Life is a journey of constant growth, change, and adaptation, and your fitness routine should be no exception. The key to a successful fitness journey is the understanding that as you evolve, so too should your workout plan. Your goals and progress act as markers on this journey, guiding the path you tread and the turns you make.

Imagine your goals as the destination on your fitness journey. Initially, you might have set out with a goal to improve your strength or enhance your flexibility. However, as you delve deeper into the world of wall Pilates, you might find new areas to explore. Perhaps you discover a passion for improving your balance or a desire to challenge your cardiovascular fitness. These new interests act as signposts, indicating when it's time to adjust your workout plan.

Adjusting your workout plan might feel daunting, but it's essential for continuous growth. If you've been focusing on strength and find your flexibility needs attention, start incorporating more stretching exercises into your routine. If balance becomes a newfound passion, consider exercises that challenge your stability. Remember, adjustment doesn't mean a complete overhaul of your routine. You can make small changes, gradually shifting your focus while still maintaining a holistic approach to fitness.

In the same vein, progress is a powerful motivator and a critical indicator of when to adjust your routine. As you become more proficient in your exercises, you'll find certain moves becoming easier. It's a delightful realization: the once-challenging exercise is now a breeze. But it also signals that it's time to up the ante. Consider increasing your repetitions, adding more challenging exercises, or even repeating the routine. The beauty of wall Pilates lies in its versatility and scalability, allowing you to continually progress and evolve your workout plan.

Tracking Your Progress: Tools and Techniques

While the journey is of the utmost importance, knowing how far you've come can provide a powerful boost to your motivation and a sense of accomplishment. Tracking your progress is like leaving breadcrumbs on your path; it allows you to look back and marvel at how far you've come.

Keeping a workout journal is an excellent method for tracking your progress. It's a tangible record of your journey, filled with your victories, challenges, and observations. Write down the exercises you did, the number of repetitions, and how you felt during the workout. Make a note of the improvements you observe and the areas you wish to work on. Over time, flipping through the pages of your workout journal will reveal your progress, your growth, and the transformation of your abilities.

In today's digital age, technology offers a myriad of tools to track your progress. Fitness apps can log your workouts, monitor your heart rate, and even provide guided routines for you to follow. They offer the convenience of having your fitness data at your fingertips, allowing you to observe trends, set goals, and track your improvements.

Lastly, remember that progress is not just about numbers. It's about how you feel, how your body moves, and how your relationship with fitness evolves. Notice how your posture improves, how your movements become more fluid, or how you can hold a pose longer than before. Realize when you're better able to handle stress, when you have more energy, or when you feel a greater sense of inner peace. These are all signs of progress, as meaningful and significant as any number.

As you continue your journey with wall Pilates, keep in mind that your workout plan is a living, breathing entity, meant to grow and change as you do. And as you traverse this path, leave markers, take note of the scenery, and celebrate how far you've come. This is your journey, unique and beautiful in its rhythm and pace. Embrace it, enjoy it, and most importantly, keep evolving with it.

In fitness, as in life, it's not just about reaching the destination but about enjoying the journey. Every day is a new opportunity to learn, grow, and transform. As you progress, your strengths will come to the fore, and your weaknesses will turn into opportunities for improvement. And in the process, you'll discover that the greatest accomplishment is not in attaining a goal but in the journey towards it.

Your workout plan is not set in stone. It's a dynamic, adaptable blueprint that changes as you do. The strength of a fitness routine lies in its ability to grow with you, reflecting your changing needs, goals, and capabilities. Adjustments are not a sign of failure but an indication of growth. They show that you're listening to your body, honoring your progress, and courageously stepping into new challenges.

Similarly, tracking your progress is more than just noting down numbers. It's about celebrating victories, learning from challenges, and acknowledging your growth. It's about seeing how far you've come and looking forward to where you're going. It's about recognizing that every step you take, every bead of sweat you shed, every moment you push beyond your limits brings you one step closer to your goals.

And while technology and tools can provide valuable data and insights, never underestimate the power of introspection. The ability to listen to your body, to tune into its signals, and to honor its needs is the most powerful tracking tool you could ever have. It's what allows you to align your workout plan with your needs, ensures you're moving in the right direction, and motivates you to keep going, even when the going gets tough.

As you embark on this journey of wall Pilates, remember that the path to fitness is a marathon, not a sprint. It's a journey of discovery, growth, and transformation. And with every step you take, every adjustment you make, and every milestone you reach, you're not just moving closer to your fitness goals - you're also becoming a stronger, healthier, and more resilient version of yourself. So, embrace the journey, celebrate your progress, and above all, enjoy the ride. Because the true joy of fitness lies not just in the destination, but in the journey itself.

Tracking Apps for Your Wall Pilates Progresses

Tracking progress is an essential part of any fitness journey, including wall Pilates. Here are some tools and apps that can help you:

- **Fitness Trackers:** Gadgets like Fitbit, Apple Watch, or Garmin wearables can monitor your heart rate, steps, calories burned, and even sleep quality. These can give you an overall picture of your health and wellness and provide insights into how your body responds to your workouts.

Pilates Specific Apps:

- **Pilates Anytime:** This app offers access to thousands of Pilates videos, including wall Pilates. It can help you track which workouts you've completed and explore new ones as you progress.

- **Pilatesology:** Offers classical Pilates classes. Like Pilates Anytime, it can track which workouts you've completed and offers a variety of levels and focuses.

General Fitness Apps:

- **MyFitnessPal:** This app is primarily for tracking nutrition but also allows you to log your workouts. It can be useful for seeing the overall picture of your fitness and nutrition.

- **Strava:** While known for running and cycling, Strava can also be used to record your Pilates workouts. You can note down how you felt, what exercises you did, and track your progress over time.

- **Fitbod:** This app creates personalized workout plans based on your fitness level, goals, and available equipment. It also tracks your workouts and adjusts your plan as you progress.

Note Taking Apps:

Evernote or Google Keep: These can be used to keep a workout journal, where you note down what exercises you did, how you felt during and after each workout, and any other thoughts or observations you have. This can be a great tool for tracking progress and reflecting on your journey.

Video Recording:

Using your phone or camera to record your workouts can be an excellent way to track your progress. By comparing videos over time, you can see improvements in your form, strength, and flexibility.

Spreadsheets:

Using Google Sheets or Excel, you can create a custom workout log. This allows you to track which exercises you did, how many reps, how you felt, and any other metrics that are important to you.

Remember, the best tool or app for you will depend on your personal preferences, goals, and the metrics you want to track. It's a good idea to try out a few different options to see which one you like best and which one best helps you track your progress in wall Pilates.

Adjusting Your Workout Plan: When and How

There's a rhythm to every fitness journey, a dance between the body and the mind, unfolding as we strive toward our goals. Your workout plan is the choreography of this dance. However, it's not set in stone. As you grow stronger, as your body changes and your objectives evolve, so too should your workout plan.

Adapting your workout plan is crucial, but when is the right time for it? Well, the answer lies in listening to your body and understanding its signals. If you find that your workout is no longer challenging, or if the last few reps of your routine don't leave you feeling that burn, it might be a sign that your body is ready to take on more. Alternatively, if you've been pushing too hard and you're constantly feeling fatigued, or if you've sustained an injury, it might be time to take it down a notch.

However, the need for change doesn't always stem from the physical. Sometimes it's the mental side of things that call for a shift in strategy. If you find yourself dreading your workouts, it could be a sign that you're stuck in a rut. When the spark fades, and your routine becomes a chore, it's time to rekindle that passion and excitement by trying something new.

So, how do we go about adjusting our workout plan? It starts with setting clear, attainable goals. Whether you're aiming to increase your strength, boost your flexibility, or simply want to feel better in your body, having a clear vision of what you want to achieve is crucial. This vision will guide the changes you make and keep you motivated along the way.

Once you have your goal in sight, consider the steps you need to take to reach it. Maybe you need to incorporate more strength training exercises into your routine, or perhaps it's time to introduce some new Pilates moves that target different muscles. It could even be as simple as increasing the intensity of your current exercises, either by adding more reps or by using a resistance band.

Remember, change is a process, not a one-time event. It's okay to adjust your plan gradually. In fact, it's preferable. Small, consistent changes are easier to manage and are more likely to stick in the long run.

Adapting your workout plan also involves a certain level of trial and error. Not every change will be a perfect fit, and that's okay. The key is to stay open and flexible, to learn from each experience and use it as a stepping stone towards finding what works best for you.

Your workout plan is not just a roadmap to your goals; it's a reflection of who you are and what you need. It's a personal journey of growth, discovery, and change. By listening to your body, setting clear goals, and making consistent, thoughtful changes, you can ensure that this journey continues to challenge, motivate, and inspire you every step of the way.

Conclusion: Maintaining Your Workout Plan Long-Term

The sweet embrace of a new dawn, with the sun peering through your curtains and a fresh day ahead, is the perfect time to think about maintaining your workout plan long-term. It's a day to recommit to the promises you made to yourself. As the rustle of leaves dances through the air, you remember the first day you decided to embark on this fitness journey. Your heart was aflame with determination, and you knew that this time, it would be different. But how do you turn that spark into an everlasting fire?

Well, first and foremost, let's talk about your "why". Your reason for working out is the compass that guides you through the stormy days when motivation is as elusive as a butterfly in the wind. Is it the desire to chase after your kids without gasping for breath, or the yearning to look in the mirror and fall in love with the person you see? Embrace your "why". Hold it close to your heart, as it is the heartbeat of your commitment.

But, as we all know, love alone cannot sustain a relationship. Your relationship with your workout plan is no exception. You need to spice things up! Break the monotony by exploring new fitness classes or taking your workout to the beautiful embrace of Mother Nature. Allow the colors of your experiences to paint your fitness canvas.

And what about when life throws curveballs your way? When your job demands late nights, or family obligations eat up your time? It's during these moments that flexibility becomes your best ally. Be kind to yourself. Understand that sometimes a 15-minute workout is just as valuable as an hour. Sometimes the best workout is taking a moment to breathe deeply and embrace the world around you.

Now, let's not forget your tribe – the people who support, encourage, and inspire you. Surround yourself with those who fan the flames of your passion. Share your goals with them, work out with them, and let their energy ignite your own.

Wall Pilates BIBLE

As the months turn into years, you'll find that your workout plan becomes more than just a schedule; it becomes a part of who you are. It's woven into the very fabric of your being. It becomes less about maintaining and more about living.

And on those days when the sun doesn't seem to shine as brightly, when your muscles ache and your spirit wanes, take a moment to look back on how far you've come. Let the person you were when you started this journey wrap you in a hug and whisper, "Thank you."

In a world that is ever-changing, your commitment to maintaining your workout plan long-term is a testament to the unchanging power of will, love, and determination. You are painting the masterpiece that is your life, and every drop of sweat is a stroke of paint on that canvas. Your legacy.

Apps that Can Keep Motivation High during Your Wall Pilates Journey

Keeping your motivation high for Wall Pilates can be easier with the help of some amazing apps and tools. Here are a few:

- **MyFitnessPal:** This app is not only for tracking nutrition but also for logging in your workouts. You can keep track of your Wall Pilates sessions and see how they contribute to your fitness goals.

- **Fitbit:** If you have a Fitbit wearable, you can use it to track your exercise and set goals. The Fitbit app allows you to join community groups, including those focused on Pilates, where you can find support and motivation.

- **Peloton:** Known for cycling, Peloton also offers a variety of workouts including Pilates. The app has a community feature to keep you motivated.

- **Daily Burn:** This app provides a wide range of workouts including Pilates. It's perfect if you like to mix up your workout routines.

- **YouTube:** While not specifically a fitness app, YouTube is an incredible resource for free Pilates workouts, including Wall Pilates. You can follow along with different trainers and find videos that really motivate you.

- **Pilates Anytime:** This is a subscription-based service with over 3,000 Pilates videos including tutorials and workouts.

267

- **Google Calendar:** Sometimes, the best motivation is simply scheduling your workouts. By scheduling your Wall Pilates sessions as appointments in Google Calendar, you make a commitment to yourself.

- **Instagram:** Follow Pilates instructors or hashtags like #WallPilates and #PilatesCommunity. This can provide you with a daily dose of inspiration and motivation.

- **Headspace:** Incorporating mindfulness and meditation into your routine with Headspace can enhance your focus and commitment to your Wall Pilates practice.

- **Endomondo:** This fitness app allows you to track fitness activities, set goals, and even join challenges which can be really motivating.

- **Pact**: This app lets you earn cash for staying active, paid by members who don't stick to their workouts. Make a weekly pact to exercise more or eat healthier, and set what you'll pay other Pact members if you don't reach it.

- **Trello or Asana:** These are primarily project management tools, but can be very effective in planning and tracking your fitness goals and workouts.

Remember, while apps and tools can be very helpful, your inner motivation and commitment are key. Surround yourself with positivity and never forget why you started your fitness journey in the first place. Happy exercising!

The Importance of Long-Term Commitment

As the sun sets on a long day, you tie your shoelaces, set your favorite playlist, and head out for a run. The cool breeze against your face and the rhythmic pattern of your heartbeat sync perfectly with the music in your ears. You feel alive, invigorated. Today, you made a commitment to yourself and your fitness journey, and you're following through. This commitment is not just for today, tomorrow, or the next week. This is a long-term commitment, a promise to yourself that will shape your future.

The importance of long-term commitment in a fitness journey is as vast as the ocean. This commitment is the ship that steers you towards your destination amidst the raging storms and calm days alike. It's the backbone of your determination, the fuel to your willpower, and the key to unlocking the best version of yourself.

Think of your body as a garden. Just like how a seed doesn't sprout into a blooming flower overnight, your body needs time to adapt, evolve, and transform. Fitness is not a race, but a journey of continuous growth. Long-term commitment gives your body the time it needs to gradually adjust to the new routines, thereby reducing the risk of injuries and ensuring consistent progress.

Long-term commitment in fitness is synonymous with self-love and self-care. It's about appreciating your body for all it does for you and reciprocating that love through regular exercise and healthy habits. The relationship between you and your body is lifelong, and by committing to your fitness long-term, you're nourishing that relationship.

Imagine standing on top of a mountain, the world stretching out beneath your feet, the wind whispering tales of triumph in your ears. The journey to the top wasn't easy. There were times when you stumbled, when you fell, when you wanted to give up. But you didn't. You kept going, one step at a time. That's what long-term commitment looks like. It's about picking yourself up every time you fall, about keeping your eyes on the goal even when the path gets tough.

In our fast-paced world, we often want instant results. But fitness isn't instant coffee. It doesn't offer quick, temporary results. It offers a lifetime of health, vitality, and happiness. And for that, it requires a long-term commitment. Committing to your fitness long-term means embracing the process, celebrating the small victories, and persevering through the challenges.

Life is unpredictable. There will be days when the skies are clear, and sticking to your fitness routine will feel as effortless as breathing. But there will also be days when the storm clouds gather, and every step towards your fitness goals will feel like a battle. On these days, remember why you started. Remember the promise you made to yourself. Let that be your guiding light.

In the grand scheme of things, long-term commitment to fitness transcends beyond the physical realm. It molds your character, shapes your mindset, and nurtures your spirit. It teaches you discipline, resilience, and self-belief. It shows you that you are capable of achieving whatever you set your mind to.

As you journey through your fitness path with a long-term commitment, remember to be patient with yourself. Transformation takes time. There will be plateaus, there will be progress, and through it all, there will be you, evolving, growing, and transforming. Fitness is a lifelong journey, and a long-term commitment ensures you make the most of this journey. So, keep going. Keep growing. Keep committing to your fitness, and watch as you unfold into the best version of yourself.

Strategies for Long-Term Workout Plan Maintenance

The beauty of movement is that it can be a dance with the world around us, a celebration of what our bodies are capable of, and a testament to our inherent willpower. Keeping this dance alive, keeping the celebration going, keeping that willpower ignited, is the essence of long-term workout plan maintenance.

The journey to fitness is not a sprint; it's a marathon that calls for endurance, patience, and commitment. It's not about achieving quick results and then retreating back into old habits. It's about cultivating a lifestyle that embraces activity, health, and well-being as integral parts of your daily routine.

So, what does it take to maintain a long-term workout plan? There's no one-size-fits-all answer, but there are strategies that can help you navigate this path, make it enjoyable, and more importantly, make it sustainable.

Understanding the why behind your fitness journey is the first crucial step. This understanding can provide you with the motivation that fuels your commitment. Are you working out to be healthier, to feel more confident, or perhaps to manage stress? Your why can be as personal and unique as you are. When the going gets tough, reminding yourself of this can be the spark that reignites your motivation.

Building a routine that you genuinely enjoy is another pivotal strategy. Exercise should not feel like punishment. It should be something you look forward to, a time you set aside for yourself. Whether it's yoga in the early morning quiet, a brisk walk during lunchtime, or an intense session at the gym in the evening, find a routine that resonates with you. Appreciate the sweat, the elevated heart rate, the soothing stretches, and the powerful feeling of being in sync with your body.

Listening to your body is essential. It's a relationship, a give and take. Some days, your body might be ready to take on a challenging workout, and on others, it might need a gentler approach. Respecting your body's signals can prevent injuries and burnout. This is not a sign of weakness; it's a sign of wisdom.

Long-term commitment to a workout plan also involves setting realistic and measurable goals. These can act as milestones on your fitness journey. But remember, the focus should not solely be on the end goal. Each day you show up, each workout you complete, is a victory in itself. Celebrate these small wins; they are stepping stones to your bigger goals.

Finding a supportive community can also make a significant difference. Whether it's a local running club, an online fitness group, or a trusted workout buddy, having others to share your journey with can boost your motivation and provide a sense of accountability.

Finally, remember that the path to fitness is not a straight line. There will be ups and downs, progress and plateaus, victories and challenges. But every step taken is a step forward. Embrace the journey with kindness and patience towards yourself.

Remember, fitness is not a destination; it's a way of life. It's about making choices each day that respect your body and promote your well-being. And the beauty of it is that it's never too late to start or to keep going. With each sunrise comes a new opportunity to move, to celebrate your body, and to commit to the dance of fitness.

So, lace up those workout shoes, unroll that yoga mat, fill that water bottle, and step into the rhythm of your fitness journey. It's a dance that lasts a lifetime, a celebration of you.

DEAR READER, I HOPE YOU ENJOYED MY BOOK. PLEASE FIND A LINK WHERE YOU CAN FIND ALL VIDEOS RELATED TO THE MAIN EXERCISES THAT HAVE BEEN DESCRIBED IN THIS BOOK.

ENJOY YOUR TRAINING!

Made in the USA
Las Vegas, NV
23 October 2023

79560350R00155